Sweet Sanctuary

**Center Point
Large Print**

**This Large Print Book carries the
Seal of Approval of N.A.V.H.**

Sweet Sanctuary

Sheila Walsh

and

Cindy Martinusen-Coloma

CENTER POINT LARGE PRINT
THORNDIKE, MAINE

This Center Point Large Print edition is published
in the year 2011 by arrangement with
Thomas Nelson Publishers

Publisher's note: This novel is a work of fiction. Names,
characters, places, and incidents are either products of the
author's imagination or used fictitiously. All characters are
fictional, and any similarity to people, living or dead,
is purely coincidental.

ISBN: 978-1-61173-221-4

Library of Congress Cataloging-in-Publication Data

Walsh, Sheila, 1956–
Sweet sanctuary / Sheila Walsh & Cindy Martinusen-Coloma.
p. cm.
ISBN 978-1-61173-221-4 (library binding : alk. paper)
1. Mothers and sons—Fiction. 2. Large type books.
    I. Martinusen-Coloma, Cindy, 1970– II. Title.
PS3623.A36615S94 2011b
813′.6—dc22

                                        2011030016

This book is dedicated with love to my son, Christian. In all the craziness of life, it is a sweet sanctuary to be your mom.
—SHEILA WALSH

To Gail Rose McCormick,
I've admired you for years, but my respect and appreciation only continue to grow.
I love you, Mom.
—CINDY MARTINUSEN-COLOMA

1

The morning was already off to a difficult start when Wren found the flyer tucked inside her ten-year-old son's backpack. Sandwich making and mental planning for her meeting with the library director came to a halt.

Where had the paper come from? Charlie's music teacher must have given it to him. She couldn't think of any other possibilities.

If not for the location given on the paper, Wren would have dismissed it completely. But the touch of cold in the late summer morning, winter's gentle whisper, spoke to the deepest part of her mothering instinct. Wren felt a chill down her back, and she carried the flyer as she closed the kitchen window, reading the words for the third time.

> Summer Music in Malta
> "Play with the masters
> where the masters played."
> June 15–August 1st
> Applications due November 1st

Charlie's father lived on the Mediterranean island of Malta, or he had the last she'd heard any news about him. Charlie didn't know this. He only knew his dad lived in Europe somewhere, and that they hadn't heard from him since Charlie was a toddler. The absent father was their norm and thus seemed no absence at all.

Wren wanted to wake Charlie and ask him about the flyer, but instead she took a deep breath to calm herself. Anything that hinted of her ex-husband sent her into a momentary panic. He'd abandoned them to pursue his dreams in Europe, and after ten years, Wren had become warily comfortable that he wouldn't return.

She'd been packing Charlie's lunch and putting a quote for the day into his backpack when she'd found the paper. The quote she'd written was taken from *Peter Pan*: "All the world is made of faith, and trust, and pixie dust."

The words took on new meaning now, and seemed more for her than for Charlie. She wrote "Love, Mom" with a heart at the bottom and slid the card into the zippered compartment. She kept the flyer on the counter to ask him about it and made coffee.

On mornings like this, Wren wished for Anne Shirley from her favorite childhood series *Anne of Green Gables*, or Jane Austen or another of her friends from literature, to discuss life over coffee—or perhaps tea would be more appropriate. Their blend of sense and sensibility and bosom friendship would surely bring clarity to the worries that kept disrupting Wren's sleep. Even Scarlett O'Hara could offer brittle but sound Southern advice. Wren hadn't been sleeping well, as if unwanted change tapped at her subconscious and this flyer was the catalyst.

The women would sympathize with her past mistakes—falling in love and marrying spontaneously without reason or logic, which now meant raising a son without that all-essential male influence. She hoped they'd encourage her in the life Wren lived now—safe and controlled, organized and meaningful.

"Mom," a voice sounded at the edge of Wren's thoughts.

Jane, what would you tell me to do with my life? And how much therapy will Charlie need when he grows up?

Wren imagined Scarlett taking her by the shoulders and declaring, "Fiddle-dee-dee—if I can fight the Union and save my plantation, then you can keep it together!"

"Mom. Mom. Mom."

Wren turned from where she'd been staring into the open refrigerator. "I didn't hear you."

"What book were you living in?" Charlie, still wearing his pajamas, rubbed his eyes with his head tilted to one side.

"It's Women in Literature month at the library." She smiled, trying to brush away the lingering pessimism. Charlie nodded as if this were the most normal thing in the world.

"Do your book characters know if there's any milk for my cereal?"

That's what she had been doing in the refrigerator. Wren reached in for the gallon of milk, holding it up to see if any was left. Charlie was notorious for leaving empty milk or juice cartons in the refrigerator.

"Didn't we just buy this milk?" Wren asked as Charlie opened the pantry to search for his cereal. She considered asking him about the music flyer, but decided to wait until he was a little more awake.

"I've been drinking three glasses a day so I'll grow taller. I'm the shortest kid in fifth grade."

"I remember your grandpa said he grew so much one summer that his classmates didn't recognize him when he went back to school."

"That would be so cool. I wish that would happen to me."

"Here, I think we have enough for your cereal." Wren set the milk on the tile countertop next to his cereal bowl as Charlie hopped onto the barstool with a box of Cheerios in his hand.

Wren returned to search the refrigerator, hoping to find a hidden coffee creamer tucked behind the leftover lasagna, some take-out cartons, the yogurt, and orange juice. She always bought more than one creamer to avoid being caught without any.

The day will not be ruined because you don't have cream for your coffee, she told herself.

"Mom, is everything okay?" Charlie asked as if he were an adult stuck inside a ten-year-old body.

Wren glanced at him as she closed the refrigerator without finding creamer. Perhaps this was the moment to ask him about the flyer. He watched her with that morning sleepy look she found adorable, and Wren decided to wait until he'd had a few more minutes to wake up.

"Everything is great. Not too much sugar this time. Cheerios don't need sugar."

"Oh yes they do."

"Sugar stunts your growth."

"Funny. Now don't be avoiding my questions. Are you running from the law or something?"

Wren raised an eyebrow and tucked a loose strand of her brunette hair behind her ear. "I do need to pay a parking ticket."

Charlie poured his cereal, then flooded the bowl with the last of the milk. He dropped in two spoonfuls of sugar and nearly a third but stopped at Wren's warning expression.

"Maybe you're a double agent, and the gig is up."

"Double agent? Since I speak only English and a little *Français*, I wouldn't make a good double agent."

"Or so she says," Charlie said, giving her a scrutinizing look before stuffing a spoonful of cereal into his mouth.

11

"You can interrogate me further in one minute. I need to see if the dryer got the wrinkles out of my blouse. Less than ten minutes till takeoff—we're running a little late already."

"Don't spies know how to iron?"

"Not this spy," Wren said and opened the back door.

"I knew it," Wren heard Charlie say as she stepped onto the cold stone walkway in her bare feet, making her wish for her slippers. She shivered in the morning chill and spotted a single gold leaf resting on the green back lawn. In the distance came the faint rhythm of the waves on the rocks below the property.

Wren tiptoed across the damp lawn and picked up the leaf. Summer was making its final exit, and before long the harsh Maine winter would bind them inside or keep them wrapped up whenever they opened the door, shoveling snow from the walkway and scraping their car windows every morning.

Sometimes Wren almost missed the Chicago winters when at least the roads were cleared and the electricity didn't regularly shut off. Wren and Charlie had survived one winter in the caretaker's house on the property of her family's old vacation home, but she'd planned for them to move on before facing another one. Now they'd need to stock up on firewood and prepare the house and themselves for winter's fury. More than that, the longer they remained on this property, the longer she felt they were cheating fate.

This land could become a trap, holding them captive and stealing their future as it had stolen so much of her family's life since childhood. Wren wasn't willing for it to take Charlie's dreams and future as well.

When he was three months old, after his father left them, Wren had held Charlie up to watch their first sunrise, just the two of them. She'd promised that she'd take care of him, give him the greatest life possible, and do everything she could to provide him with the very best.

Wren had a plan, and if the pieces came together today, she'd be much closer to fulfilling her promise to her son. Today might be one of those turning-point days. The outcome of her meeting with the library director would mean either proceeding forward, or else—Wren wasn't quite sure and didn't want to consider it. The morning interruption with the flyer and its reminder of her ex-husband was a mere distraction, she decided. She needed to press forward and keep ominous thoughts far away.

Wren tucked the leaf into her robe pocket and hurried into the laundry area in the woodshed beside the house. As she opened the dryer, the heat warmed her face. But it was too much heat. She looked at the knob; it was pointed at *hot*.

"No, no, not this shirt."

Wren returned to the house, holding the shrunken vintage blouse before her. Charlie nearly spit out a mouthful of Cheerios, trying to hide his laughter.

"Poor Mom. Another shirt eaten by the dryer monster."

"I need to learn how to iron," Wren muttered to herself as she sped down the hall to finish getting ready. This had been one of her favorite blouses. She quickly tossed clothing from her closet until she found a poor substitute in a plain blue dress shirt. She buttoned it up, smoothing it over her black cigar pants.

"Charlie, are you ready?" Wren called when she heard him using his drumsticks on various objects around his bedroom.

"I'm ready, Mom," Charlie called back, and she heard final taps on the elaborate chimes he'd created from various metal and glass objects from around the house, including a metal sculpture she'd made in college, some tin roofing from the shed, and several of their drinking glasses. He burst into her bedroom and whistled when he saw the clothing piled on her bed.

"I know why this is happening," Charlie said in a sing-song voice.

"Why what is happening?" Wren tucked one last bobby pin into her hastily twisted French bun and took a last look in the mirror at her light makeup.

"All of our bad mornings this week."

"You can tell me in the car. I have an important meeting with Dr. James right after I take you to school. We can't be late." Wren should have been preparing for that meeting.

Charlie followed her down the hall. "Does the word *important* come from the word *import?* Maybe it comes from people importing ants. Get it? Import-ant?"

"How do you know a word like import?"

"Franklin's dad is in the import business. So what import-ant meeting do you have?"

Wren noticed the tag on the back of Charlie's shirt. "If you get your shirt turned right side out and get those teeth cleaned before they turn green, then I'll tell you about my meeting tonight over tacos."

"Deal." He stuck out his hand, and Wren shook it quickly.

"Now go. Teeth."

Charlie turned back down the hall, and Wren dashed to the kitchen where she gathered up her bag—checking to be sure the book she was reading was tucked inside for her lunch hour—along with Charlie's lunchbox and a cup of cream-less coffee.

"Charlie, let's go," she called.

Wren saw the flyer as she heard his quick foot-steps coming toward the kitchen. Late or not, she had to ask. "I found this paper in your backpack."

Charlie rushed into the room, ending in an

abrupt skid as he saw what she was holding. His face displayed his telltale guilty expression.

Before either could speak, the doorbell rang.

"Who's that?" Charlie asked, turning toward the door.

"Let me get it," Wren said, setting everything down on the counter. Who could it be? They were too far out for many visitors, especially for a Wednesday morning. Before Wren could reach the door, it creaked opened and a face peered inside.

"Oh, lovely, you're home! I was afraid you'd already gone for the day."

Grandma Ruth bustled into the entryway.

"Nana!" Charlie yelled, rushing past Wren and diving into Ruth's arms. "Look, Mom, Nana's here."

Wren stared at her grandmother, unable to process the sudden arrival.

"Are you staying with us?" Charlie asked.

"That I am Charles, that I am."

Through the front window, Wren saw a taxi turn around in the driveway.

"Grandma." Wren embraced her petite grandmother. "What a surprise."

"Not so much of a surprise. God sent me." Ruth produced a sweet Betty White smile.

"Really? I knew it!" Charlie said. "Woohoo! I knew God was listening."

What is going on? Wren tried to muster a sincere smile. "Did you try calling? I didn't know you were coming."

"Of course you didn't."

"Oh." Wren could think of nothing else to say. She wondered if this had something to do with Charlie's suspicious behavior or the flyer about Malta.

Charlie picked up one of Ruth's suitcases outside the open door and carried it awkwardly into the living room. "Nana already said it was God who sent her. Because I prayed, remember I prayed, Mom? That's why all these things are happening."

Charlie and Wren had been praying more regularly at bedtime. While she struggled to bring God into her daily life and the little worries of the day, Charlie's faith seemed to encompass him wholly. But Charlie's recent prayer had shaken her considerably.

"Yes, I remember, but I'm sorry, Grandma, we're late." She looked at Ruth. "I could . . . take the day off?"

"Oh no, no, no, darling. I'll be just fine. It was a bit of a journey, as you can imagine. I took the train up and then the taxi—it's been a long night and morning. I'll enjoy resting up. Maybe I'll start dinner?"

Wren raised an eyebrow. Ruth was notorious for her lack of cooking skill.

"It's Taco Wednesday—you can come with us," Charlie said.

Wren carried in Ruth's second suitcase, surprised at how heavy it was, then she grabbed

17

Charlie's violin case beside the door. "I'm really sorry to leave with you just arriving. Are you sure you'll be okay?"

"I take care of myself every day, don't worry. If I need something, I have your cell phone and you have mine."

"Okay, and please take my bedroom, though it's quite messy right now. I couldn't find anything to wear this morning. How about . . . how about I come home for lunch?"

Ruth folded her hands and smiled. "That would be lovely. I'll make tea."

"Charlie, I have your violin case, you go get in the car . . . right now," Wren said, emphasizing *now* as her growing tension leaked into her tone. She smiled at Charlie's quizzical expression. "We need to go, little man."

"Let me get my backpack." He raced back toward the kitchen.

"Sorry again to run, but love you, Grandma." Wren kissed her grandmother's cheek and caught the scent of White Shoulders perfume.

"See you at lunch," Ruth said. "I have a surprise to tell you both."

"A surprise? You know I'm not big on surprises," Wren said with a frown. She had rarely seen anything good come from a surprise.

"Then a little teaser. You're going to throw me a party!"

"Bye, Nana," Charlie called as he raced

18

through the middle of them, ran down the drive, and jumped up toward the overhanging wisteria vine that grew over the front walkway.

"Yes! Nana's here," Charlie shouted as he opened the car.

"A party?" Wren asked, trying not to grimace.

"Well, not just you, but you, your sister, and brother."

"What?" Wren hadn't seen her siblings in years and only rarely spoke to them. They'd gone their separate ways and for good reasons, all stemming from their childhood here on this very land.

Ruth patted Wren's arm. "I'll tell you more at lunch. Stop worrying, dear. Now off to work."

As Wren scurried to the car, she wondered what her grandmother was up to. And how in one morning had Wren and Charlie's well-protected life started to seem so fragile and frayed?

2

"Did Nana say we're having a party?" Charlie asked when Wren slid behind the wheel of her faded Subaru.

"Something like that."

"Cool!"

Wren turned on the engine; the clock made her groan.

"Uh-oh. Mrs. Bailey might make me write sentences," Charlie said with an exaggerated sigh.

"And I'm going to be late for my importing-ants meeting."

Charlie laughed and slapped his knee. "Good one, Mom."

Wren glanced over at the wide smile that revealed two slight dimples in his cheeks. She could never resist his joy-filled laugh—something about it broke her heart and mended her at the same time. Maybe she shouldn't be worrying about everything, finding fear in things like music flyers and anything that made her think of her ex. Regardless of how the morning had begun, she needed to refocus for her meeting with Dr. James. She had to set aside her concerns and questions for now.

Ten minutes later they pulled in front of the school and Wren walked in with Charlie, apologizing to the front desk secretary for their tardiness again.

Wren bent down to look Charlie in the eye. She wanted to wrap him in her arms and give him a thousand kisses like when he was smaller, but they'd made a deal at the beginning of fifth grade that all kisses were reserved for inside the car.

"Have a great day, okay?" she said.

Charlie set down his violin case and surprised her with a solid hug, right there in the school office.

"It's okay, Mom. Everything is going to be okay."

Wren watched Charlie race down the hall with his backpack bouncing and his body bent toward his music case. Moments like this, when she paused to take him in, her heart physically ached with love. She'd made a promise to Charlie while holding him in her arms. Wren would do everything she could to keep that promise.

Most every light turned red on Wren's five-mile route from Charlie's school to the Cottage Cove Public Library. The drive seemed staged to test her patience.

Wren tapped the steering wheel, muttering her frustrations under her breath with a loud, "Oh please!" when the car in front of her didn't move as the light turned green. She hadn't been this late to work, ever, and especially not when she had a meeting with the library director. Today would determine whether her hours were increased and hopefully she'd also get a go-ahead for a special paid side project. Her thoughts kept drifting . . . what if she didn't get it? What would they do?

Finally she pulled into the tree-lined parking lot adjacent to Library Park and the two-story brick building; and today of all days, someone had parked in her usual spot. The guy even had the gall to be sitting in his SUV talking on the phone.

After opening the hatchback of her car, Wren

plopped her purse and satchel inside a box of books she'd found at an estate sale. They were a nearly complete set of first edition *Railway Children* books by Edith Nesbit—another of Wren's favorite authors. They'd be a nice addition to the library's rare and collectable book section.

"Let me help you," said a voice from behind, and Wren nearly tossed the entire box into the air.

"You scared me to half to death," she gasped, turning toward the man.

"Sorry. Why don't I make it up to you by carrying your books?" It was the cell phone talker / parking spot stealer Paul Callahan—the very man her coworker Sue thought would be perfect for her. Wren avoided him whenever she could.

"I can manage, thank you," Wren said, but she nearly dropped the box when she tried reaching up to close the hatchback. Paul leaned over, a little too close for comfort, and pulled the hatch down.

"Thanks," Wren said grudgingly.

"And the box?" Paul took it from her arms before she could reply.

"I'm perfectly capable—"

"Of course you are," Paul said with a slight smile.

"I'm kind of late too." Wren clicked the car lock on her keychain and glanced around the parking lot, searching for some distraction to get her away from Paul.

"I think I can keep up," Paul said, matching

22

Wren's pace. Her shoes clacked on the pavement, but she couldn't walk fast and make them be quiet.

"Autumn's in the air—my favorite season. Can you smell it?" Paul turned toward the brick entrance of the library. He was tall and irritatingly handsome, and she couldn't smell autumn, all she could smell was Paul's fresh and woodsy scent.

"Still smells like summer to me." No way she'd admit her love of autumn to Paul—then they'd have something in common.

"How's Charlie?"

Wren frowned. Just like a charmer to ask the single mom about her child.

"He's fine."

I've got to stay away from this man. Wren's history of falling for the wrong guy was a sorry tale and she was determined to rectify it. Giving up on dating altogether seemed the easiest way.

Paul was talking about the outdoor films in Library Park that Wren had spearheaded, and how much he enjoyed them. She'd seen him there with his sister and her three children.

"It was really great to have that this summer," he was saying, but Wren was only vaguely responding. She knew only bits and pieces about Paul. He owned a fishing boat company as well as a café along the boardwalk. He was usually seen at community events, often with a woman at his side, though she didn't know if he was dating any of them; she tried not to pay attention to such details. Why was he at the library right now anyway? Didn't he have his businesses to run? He continued to talk about his sister and the film night.

". . . it gave Emma and the kids something to look forward to every Friday night. It's been a rough time for them with the divorce and all, and those movies helped more than you realize. Great choices too. *Goonies* is one of my all-time favorites."

Wren should accept his words as a compliment. She shouldn't assume that just because women flocked to him, he was a womanizer. And she shouldn't be paranoid thinking there must be some- thing hidden and wrong with him. Despite what she should and shouldn't do, every time Wren was around Paul, her fortress gate clamped shut.

Someday, as an older woman after Charlie was married and settled down, then maybe Wren would meet a distinguished Englishman who liked to travel the villages of Scotland, Wales, and Ireland. They'd have a cottage over there, and one near Charlie and her grandbabies. They'd sit above the sea, drinking tea as he read Thoreau or Dickens aloud to her.

Paul opened one of the double glass doors, holding it with one arm and the box in the other.

"Thank you. Have a nice day," Wren said in an overly polite tone, taking the box before he could respond.

"You too, Wren." Paul sounded either confused or humored, she couldn't decide which.

Wren set the box of books down on a chair in front of Dr. James' office. She took a folder from her bag and whispered a simple prayer—something she realized she should have done earlier that morning. "Please help this go well, God," then she tapped before opening the door.

"Good morning, Wren," the older man said, rising from his chair.

"I'm very sorry to be late."

"Not to worry. I was reading my morning blogs. It's sad that even an old codger like me has traded in the morning paper for web news."

Wren smiled but didn't respond since she would pick the newspaper over Internet news any day.

"Please have a seat. Have you had coffee yet?"

"I'm fine, thank you." Wren bit her lip and immediately wished she'd said yes to the coffee. Her own black brew had remained barely touched in the car. And it would have given her a few more moments to collect herself—she was anxious about what Dr. James would tell her. If she didn't get the increase in her hours, she'd have to start looking for a different job or a second one, or else forget the plans to move to Boston for Charlie to attend music school next year. The added hours would pay for the move, and the special project would cover the registration and part of the tuition for Charlie's new school.

Wren took a breath to clear her mind of rambling and prepared to begin her presentation, but Dr. James spoke first.

"Wren, I've been going over your request. It's thorough and most reasonable. But I'm very sorry, there's no way I can increase your hours. Secondly, at this time, we're putting a hold on the literacy project, so I can't offer you that position either."

Wren stared at Dr. James and then down at her hands. Just like that, in a few short sentences, everything crumbled like a carefully constructed sand castle at the mercy of the waves.

Dr. James sat at his large oak desk and pulled off his glasses as he spoke. The lines around his eyes looked deeper than she remembered.

"This is the unfortunate reality of the library right now."

Wren shifted in her seat, trying to keep her shaking fingers still. She cleared her throat. "When I was hired, it was under the agreement that I would work from three-quarters to full-time within six to nine months. It's been over a year now. Do you see this changing in the near future?"

"I know that was our arrangement. That was certainly the expectation, and I'm very sorry. This is by no means a reflection on your work. In fact, without you, the library would be in much worse condition than it is. Your work with the community and in establishing our summer film nights in the park has been essential to our stability in the past quarter."

Wren pinched the bridge of her nose as a headache built in her forehead. The move . . . the music school . . . it was all going up in smoke. Now what would they do?

"What happened to the literacy program?"

"It's our funding. We're facing some extreme budget cuts. This is something the board hasn't announced yet, so please keep this between us for now. We'll make the formal announcement on Monday. Today I'm going to inform the entire library staff that we're facing some pretty severe budget cuts. Most people will lose hours so that we don't have to lay people off. I promise that I won't cut your hours, at least not at this point. In my twenty-nine years in Cottage Cove, we've never faced the real possibility of shutting our doors."

"You mean, the library might close?"

"Again, this is unofficial, and we don't want to spread any panic. But the board is discussing some options like moving to a smaller facility, cutting the days of operation, or trying to work in conjunction with the college or with the library system in Bangor in some capacity. I haven't liked any of the ideas so far."

Wren couldn't imagine the library moved somewhere else. It was built on historic land and was a central part of Cottage Cove. The idea of the library closing completely or being part of some other larger library system was even worse.

"Is there anything I can do?" she asked, a sense of dread cloaking her shoulders and weighing her down.

"If I can think of something, I'll let you know. Your work has been amazing, and I'd like to see you on our board at some point in time. That is, once we make it through this rough patch. I believe in positive thinking." Dr. James smiled and sighed contently.

"Well, thank you," Wren said, but she couldn't muster much sincerity behind the words. She and Charlie had already been in Cottage Cove longer than she expected. The rent at the caretaker's house was minimal, supposedly enough for her to save money. She'd saved very little with her hours not full-time, and there were few other jobs available in the small coastal town that fit her qualifications. It was a catch-22; she couldn't leave Cottage Cove without making more money, but she couldn't make more money without leaving Cottage Cove. And only months earlier Wren's mother had talked about selling the property. Change was inevitable, but now she had no idea what road to take.

Wren and Dr. James made small talk before saying good-bye. She opened the door, turned, and nearly ran into Paul Callahan.

"Oh, you again," she said, feeling her brave

28

face falling to pieces. Was he stalking her?

"Are you all right?" he asked with dark eyebrows lowered in concern.

"That seems to be the question of the day. Sorry." Wren could feel the tears building and wished she could escape Paul's concerned expression.

"We keep bumping into each other," Paul said with a lighter tone to his voice as if to cheer her up.

"I do work here."

"We could run into each other at coffee after you get off work, if you'd like to talk?"

Wren realized she was shaking her head before he even finished talking.

"Another time perhaps," Paul said with a smile that appeared unfazed by her rejection. Wren wanted to tell him to stop smiling at her. His smile created a kind of loop-dee-doo in her stomach.

"I need to get to work."

"How did Dr. James seem to you?"

"Fine, why?" Wren wondered if he was fishing for information about the upcoming budget cuts. But why would he care?

"Just checking. By the way, if you ever need someone to talk to, I'm around."

The sincerity in his voice halted any sarcastic response she could think of as Paul knocked on Dr. James' door.

"There he is," Dr. James said with a voice full of enthusiasm. "You've been perusing the books, I see."

"I don't take enough time to read lately." Paul walked inside and passed a few books to Dr. James.

"Thoreau? I saw you as a Hemingway man."

"I'm trying to widen my horizons."

Wren walked away with her head pulsing into a pound. She dropped her purse at her cubicle and with a simple wave to the other library staff she passed, she went out to be alone with the books and gather her thoughts.

In the map section, where shelves of atlases stood tall and thick, Wren leaned against a wooden column and took a deep breath. The library patrons often deserted the map section, and Wren was glad that was the case at the moment. The scent of old books and papers calmed her nerves as she turned a globe with her index finger. The countries and oceans of the world spun beneath her hand, and Wren wondered about all those places and the billions of people and creatures in each one. Her own problems shrunk considerably as she thought of people in other countries who suffered famine and poverty or extreme government rule. *Be grateful for what you have,* she reminded herself, but no real peace came even as she went through her gratitude list.

- Charlie. A nice home. I can pay our bills. My snow tires are in good condition, and the car is still running even after 100,000 miles . . .

Wren had five more minutes to gather herself before she needed to prepare for the children's story time. The hush of the library was solace to her. The thousands of books neatly lined up were doorways into hundreds of places, lives, experiences, and events. Books only gave, and Wren possessed complete control over their offerings. If she didn't like a book, she could put it aside, or if she wanted a break, she closed the pages. It was the perfect relationship.

- Books—I'm always grateful for those. A job I love . . .

Budget cuts. She closed her eyes. *Why didn't I have a backup plan? What about the upcoming appointment at the music school in Boston? Why is Grandma Ruth here and why does she want a party with all of us together?*

Wren shook her head at how quickly gratitude succumbed to worry.

All her plans seemed to be unraveling, and Grandma's arrival in the midst of it felt like another tug at the thread. Something played at the edges of her mind . . . Charlie's prayer.

It had been a simple one after their nightly reading. Before the "amen," Charlie added, "God, please make my mom happy again."

That was it. But the pain struck her deep in the heart. Her son was asking God to fix her?

"Why don't you think I'm happy? I have you, and our life here . . . I'm very, very happy."

"You don't sing around the house like you used to," Charlie had said. "I'll ask God for you to sing again."

"When did I sing before?"

"You always would sing when you did things around the house."

Wren hadn't realized she did that.

"Since we moved here, you seem sadder and sadder."

Wren had tried to deny it, but the truth of her son's words was like a shade being ripped from a window. She hadn't known it until he spoke it. What was wrong with her? Her job was perfect for her. All she needed was to make a little more money, and then she could provide her son with what he deserved—a chance at his dreams, something she'd never had.

"God is going to fix everything," he'd said with confidence.

"Of course He is," Wren had said, kissing Charlie on top of his head. God had given her so much already. Charlie was her gift. Sometimes it amazed her to think that there were other mothers who loved their children as much as she loved Charlie. Their life together was full and rich. But he detected a sadness that she hadn't known was there.

Now among the books and maps of the library, Wren heard Charlie's prayer in her head again and felt a shiver down her spine. Sometimes it seemed God tore everything apart before mending it the way He wanted. Wren was certainly not ready for that, and yet it felt as if He'd already begun.

3

Children's story time ended with the little two- to four-year-olds giving Wren good-bye hugs and waves as they went to check out their books. Wren was cleaning up the stage area when she felt a tug on her sleeve.

"Miss Evans, I weally love the stories," said four-year-old Ben. His grandma stood watching with a smile on her face.

"Which one is your favorite, Ben?" Today's reading had been a day of bears with Corduroy, Goldilocks, and a little Winnie the Pooh.

He looked up toward the ceiling as if thinking deeply. "Ummm, I think the Pooh Bear."

"I weally love Pooh Bear too," Wren said with a wide grin.

"Thank you! See you next week." Ben hopped off with several waves back toward her, and despite the intense morning, Wren laughed and realized just how much her mood had lifted in the past hour. The children's round faces and eyes that grew big at the stories she read were one of the highlights of her week.

"Hey, did you hear anything?" Wren's intern Jasmine asked as they finished straightening up.

"About what?"

"There's a rumor of budget cuts. I guess nearly everyone has been called in to meet with Dr. James at various times this afternoon."

Wren smiled. Jasmine was often distracted by bits of gossip, while the rest of the library duties seemed to bore her. Wren had more than once had to ask her to leave her phone in her purse. She didn't see Jasmine pursuing a future in library studies after the semester was over.

"You don't have anything to worry about. The intern program is funded through the college."

"I know, but I was just wondering."

"I'll let you know when I can talk about it." Wren hid her grin at the pout that appeared on Jasmine's face.

Wren was glad to leave for lunch instead of facing more questions from her friends and coworkers. As she picked up her keys and bag from her cubicle, a head peered over the partition.

"I saw Paul Callahan here this morning," Sue

said with a sly smile that crinkled her deep laugh lines deeper.

"You and your matchmaking," Wren said, turning to leave.

"Somebody needs to take care of that love life of yours, since you sure won't. But I need to find someone new for you—I hear Paul's already dating someone."

"Oh," Wren said, and it surprised her to feel irritated by the news. Why did he ask her to coffee and offer to "be there" for her? He was exactly as she expected after all.

"Does that bother you?" Sue said, studying her face.

"No—why would it?"

Sue sighed dramatically. "Are you going out for lunch?"

"My grandmother showed up this morning with two very large suitcases, so I'm running home to see what's going on."

Sue's mouth dropped, and she hurried around the cubicle. "What? Sweet Grandma Ruth?"

"Yes, sweet Grandma Ruth."

"She didn't give you a jingle first?"

"No, and that's not like her at all."

"I thought she was happy in her retirement community." Sue sat on the edge of Wren's desk. Wren had told Sue more than she realized in the year they'd worked cubicle to cubicle. Sue certainly paid attention.

"I think she *is* happy there. But she mentioned me throwing her a party."

"*You* throwing *her* a party?"

"Yes, but oh—I hope everything is all right with her." Wren didn't mention Ruth's declaration that God had sent her. What if her grandmother was sick?

"Hmm, this is strange. Maybe she ran away from the retirement community." Sue tapped her chin.

"Well, I'm off to find out."

"Good luck. Can't wait to hear all about it. Finally, some drama in Wren's life!"

"Great," Wren said with a wave good-bye.

Wren drove the winding coastal route toward the family property the original owners had named Fern House. She was determined not to think about her morning meeting with Dr. James. The conversation kept creeping into her thoughts, so she tried to take in the beauty of a late summer day. The sea was as blue as the sky above it, rolling with frothy white edges toward the rocky Maine shoreline. Fishing boats dotted the horizon, and Wren wondered if any of the boats belonged to Paul Callahan.

Days like today reminded her of childhood summers at the vacation home before that one fateful year. They'd spend afternoons down at the beach, or go out on hikes into the dense woods; often family would come up for week-ends, or they'd all be stuffed around the property for the annual family reunion.

As Wren steered down the long driveway, the two-story main house came into view. It had been closed up for several years now. Since Mom had married Harvey, she no longer came out in the summer as she'd done for years after Dad's death.

Wren and Charlie had explored the main house when they'd first moved into the caretaker's cottage, and once in a while Charlie asked to see it again. She couldn't blame him—it would be fascinating for any kid. But Wren found the house strangely lifeless and inhabited by the ghosts of vacations past. The furniture, pictures, and summer treasures they'd found on the beach were all still there. Even their old rubber boots and fishing poles were nestled in the mudroom with the frayed wicker picnic basket and faded beach chairs. It felt too familiar, yet dead as well, and memories filled the rooms and porches as if waiting to awaken whenever someone ventured inside the door.

The caretaker's cottage was across the driveway from the main house and closer to the property edge where it dipped down toward the sea.

Wren pulled her car into the small parking space near the front door. She reached for her purse on the passenger seat and noticed the cell phone tucked into the crease. It was the inexpensive prepaid phone she'd bought Charlie to keep inside his backpack for emergency use. They'd discussed what defined an "emergency," and why he couldn't use up the limited minutes on anything but a true problem.

Wren flipped the phone over, and she saw that the power was on. She touched a button to see if he'd used it, and instead of a phone number, she saw a name on the call log.

Dad.

Wren stared at the name and for a brief moment thought of her own dad, but of course, her dad was dead—could this be Charlie's father? Derek had cut off contact after she received the divorce papers and his final good-bye. Charlie had been a baby, and Derek hadn't asked to speak with his son. Instead, he'd talked about his fresh start in Europe, how he'd send money to help with Charlie, and how very sorry he was that he couldn't be a better husband and father. Wren had heard from Derek's cousin that he was living with a Czech woman. Later, the cousin checked in on her and said Derek had moved to Malta and married a woman from the island.

Now, after all these years, somehow Derek and Charlie had made contact? They'd talked on the phone—the evidence was before her eyes. Charlie had programmed Derek into his contact list. And Wren had known nothing about it.

Her emotions raged, ping-ponging back and forth between Charlie and Derek. She looked at the call log again. They'd only spoken once, and for less than five minutes. But why hadn't Charlie told her about it?

Wren stared at the phone and, on impulse, hit the Send button and heard it ringing. A voice spoke. A voice she hadn't heard in nearly a decade and yet instantly recognized.

"Hey there! Hello? Charlie? Is that you, buddy?"

Wren hung up the phone and dropped it to her lap. A moment later the phone rang, and Wren tossed it back over to the passenger seat until it finally went silent. She stared out the windows toward the cottage. Everything appeared different now. The little house didn't feel so safe and secluded as it had just one day before.

Wren thought of her grandmother waiting inside. She needed to pull herself together until she could talk to Charlie. Then she'd call Derek.

Dropping her head against the steering wheel, Wren closed her eyes and wondered where God was during moments like this. Sometimes He seemed so very far away.

"Grandma?" Wren called out as she walked through the front door five minutes later. The teapot steamed on the stove.

"Grandma?" she called again and searched the small two-bedroom house. Her bed was now made and clothes hung up in her closet, which made Wren grimace at the thought of Ruth cleaning up after her.

Peering out the screened-in back porch, Wren noticed the open gate at the back of the yard. Charlie had strict instructions never to open the gate, and Wren had rigged up a bolt above the tall lock to keep him from using it. Why would her grandmother open it?

When she reached the gate, Wren could see through the trees and flowering bushes to her grandmother sitting under the faded gray gazebo. It took great effort to force her feet to walk forward. One step, another step . . . this shouldn't be a big deal. The past was the past. She had enough problems in the present.

"I haven't been in this garden even once since we've lived here," Wren said as she reached Ruth. Her grandmother had brought out a pot of tea and two cups. A yellow tablecloth covered the old wrought iron table and fluttered in a light sea breeze.

"It's a shame to have all this hidden," Ruth said. "Have some tea with me. You can see the ocean from here."

Wren glanced back at the house, then pulled out a chair across from Ruth, brushing a few leaves from the seat. The beauty of the hidden garden couldn't be denied. Her parents had been married here, and it had been the scene of their family reunion—the one that changed everything. Now it was hidden behind a high fence and tended by the gardeners her mother hired to care for the property every spring. The fence had been built after her father's death, secluding the garden from the rest of the property. Fence or no fence, there was something here that was hard to let go of; Wren thought it was probably true for each one of them in her family, no matter how far they went, even if they didn't fully recognize it.

Wren could see the old sea trail down to the ocean where the waves wrapped around the dark gray rocks. Perhaps the gardeners ate their lunch here every week. Wren hoped someone could enjoy it.

Ruth filled Wren's cup with tea, and for a moment, the quiet between them and the sound of the sea, the shimmer of birch leaves in the breeze, and the scent of late summer flowers brought Wren a touch of peace. Then she set the teacup down as she realized that this was how it had happened before; they'd been lulled into forgetting the dangers around them. And suddenly, the dangers were pressing in on all sides.

"Grandma, please don't show Charlie how to open the gate. It's too close to the path down to the water."

"All right, sweetie, but this is where I'd like to have my birthday party."

"Your birthday party. Yes, we need to talk about that." Wren studied Ruth's contented expression. How could her grandmother keep making this idea worse? A party in the back garden—was she serious?

"I've kept my age secret for most of my life, but now I'm ready to admit that I'm turning ninety in three weeks. And for my birthday, I'd like a party. It might just be my last one, you know."

"Why, is something wrong?"

Ruth laughed and poured herself more tea. "Oh no, no, no. My doctor says I'm as healthy as a ninety-year-old woman can possibly be. But still, nearly every one of my friends has taken off for the sweet by-and-by, and I'd better stop pretending that my time isn't upon me as well."

Ninety? Ruth always maintained that a lady never revealed her age, but Wren had guessed much younger.

"I can't believe you're coming clean about this." Wren's mind ran through Ruth's request, and it was admittedly hard to deny a woman of nine decades a party. But perhaps they could come up with a few other options.

"It's necessary that I do so."

"Why is that?" Wren took a sip of tea. A Black-capped Chickadee hopped in and out of some bushes. This little bird had been one of the first that Wren and Charlie had cataloged in their birding book when they first arrived in Maine.

"Because I'm using my age as leverage, sweetie. I have more requests."

"More?" Wren bit her lip.

"First, I want all of my grandchildren and great grandchildren to come to my party—no excuses."

"All of them?" Wren said as it settled in what Ruth was saying. Her sister, brother, her cousin Jonathan—they hadn't been together since her father's funeral. There were only two great grandchildren—Charlie and her sister Barb's son. It had been three years since her short visit with her sister, brother-in-law, and nephew. The time between Wren's phone calls and visits with her siblings was like a rock skipping over water that left few ripples in their normal lives. None of them wanted more ripples, and a party like this was like an avalanche of rocks.

Ruth continued, "It's not a lot of time to be together—just a few days, and I'm not asking you to do much of the work. I'll hire a caterer, and we'll bring this party together as simply as possible."

Wren pressed the palms of her hands against her eyes. "I don't know that everyone can get up here in three weeks. I haven't talked to Barb in months . . . Jack, well, I'm not even sure where he's living now. And Jonathan was retiring from the army last I heard."

"Jonathan's out of the country. But I think your brother and sister will be able to attend."

"You've talked to them?" Wren wanted to drop her face into her hands and beg Ruth to do something, anything else other than this. They could all go on a cruise, or a trip to Hawaii, or have a nice, short dinner together in some neutral city. But her grandmother had a look of resolve on her sweet face, and how could Wren deny an almost ninety-year-old woman her birthday wish?

"You're sure about this? You know we haven't all been here, on this property, since . . . that summer."

Ruth nodded with her lips together in a sweet smile. "I do know that. And it's time to have some peace in this family."

Getting them all together was going to be anything but peaceful, although Wren didn't know how to tell her grandmother that.

"And the other thing." Ruth smiled and took a long sip of tea.

"More?" Wren sighed, staring far out toward the horizon. It couldn't get any worse.

"I want you to sing at my party."

Wren turned sharply toward Ruth, whose expression gave no hint of retracting her words.

"No. That's one thing I won't do."

"Let's talk about it later, okay?" Ruth said and poured more tea.

There was nothing to talk about, but Wren let it be for now. Singing in public again was one thing that no one could make her do—not Charlie, not her grandmother, not even God. Wren instantly retracted that last thought, fearing a lightning bolt from the blue sky. *Father, I know you won't ask me to do something like that. Right?*

Later that afternoon Wren was packing up her

things after work and rehearsing how to talk to Charlie about his father without saying something she might regret when she noticed a voice message on her phone. Wren dropped into her office chair as she heard the sarcastic voice on the message.

"So, little sister, I just had a call from Grandma Ruth. She asked me to attend her ninetieth birthday party, which is apparently at your house, or should I say, the family's house, and Mr. No-show-to-his-nephew's-eighth-grade-graduation Jack will be attending with his wife—his wife? Did you know our brother got married? Did you know Grandma is turning ninety? *What* is going on, Wren? Why don't you ever let me know what's happening in this family? Call me back ASAP."

Wren leaned forward in her chair. "Ready or not, the storm is coming."

4

Wren was waiting in the pickup line at Charlie's school when she saw his cell phone on the passenger seat and slipped it into the glove box. She didn't want to sound angry or upset when she asked about Derek, yet keeping her emotions under control was proving a problem even as she sat there. She thought over different ways to bring it up, feeling tears building one moment and her heart beating in anger the next.

She inched forward behind the long line of other parents as a school bus pulled out, emitting a dark burst of diesel smoke behind it. She covered her face and rolled up the windows, coughing at the black cloud.

Then she saw Charlie. As he shuffled from the school with his head bent, every other worry—her job, siblings, Grandma, the party, even Derek—was replaced with a singular concern: something was wrong with her son.

His usual wide smile and bright eyes appeared muted, and his back was hunkered down as if he carried a weight much heavier than his over-stuffed backpack and violin case.

Wren reached across the seat and pushed open the passenger side door as Charlie reached the car.

"What happened?" she asked before he closed the door. Her words, meant to soothe, instead seemed to crack his resolve, and he blinked his eyes in the rapid way that meant he was trying to stop the tears. Wren searched the pickup line, the teachers directing traffic and kids, and the school itself for any sign of turmoil, then looked back to her son.

"Charlie?"

"Nothing," Charlie muttered.

"Something. Are you all right?"

He nodded, still blinking and staring forward.

"Should we go talk to your teacher?"

Charlie shook his head and clenched his jaw.

Wren put the car into drive, hoping he'd be more open once they left the school grounds.

"It's Taco Wednesday."

"Uh-huh."

"Remember Nana's here."

"Fun," he said with little enthusiasm.

"Tell me what's up, or I'll have to resort to something drastic."

"It's nothing, Mom."

Wren considered him for a moment. Sometimes Charlie did need time before he was ready to talk, but this seemed serious enough for her to risk pressing him a little further.

"If you don't tell me, I'll run around your school wearing a pink wig."

"Mom, stop."

"If you don't tell me, I'll bite off your thumbs."

She saw a twitch of a smile, and Charlie tucked his hands under his legs.

"I'll . . . I'll . . ." She wasn't coming up with anything else that might make him laugh.

"Okay," Charlie said with an exaggerated sigh. "Sometimes it's hard being Franklin's friend."

Wren considered that a moment, relieved it wasn't something critical—already her thoughts had bounced from school bullying to scary janitors in the bathroom. "I'm sure it is. Did something happen that made it hard today?"

He nodded with his eyes still on the road ahead.

Wren waited as she turned onto the highway, hoping he'd continue. Sometimes it took until bedtime or the next morning for Charlie to tell her what was bothering him.

"Franklin had to go to the principal's office today for pushing Jesse P. down."

"Oh no. Why did he do that?"

"Jesse P. was teasing him about SpongeBob SquarePants."

"Well, that wasn't nice of Jesse P. Was he teasing Franklin for liking SpongeBob?"

Charlie sighed and rested his face onto his hands. "He said that SpongeBob was stupid, and he wished a fisherman would catch him and eat him."

"That's a terrible thing to say. Though I don't think SpongeBob would taste very good."

"Mom, SpongeBob is kind of for little kids."

"What? I love SpongeBob. Does that mean I'm a little kid?"

"Mom, you know what I mean. It's okay for you to like him 'cuz you're a grown-up, but Franklin wears SpongeBob shirts and shorts that are too small for him."

"Oh," Wren said, thinking about the gulf of maturity in Charlie's classroom. She'd seen one of his classmates wearing a "Vampires Bite" T-shirt, and then there was Franklin, whose mother had to convince him to leave his super-man cape at home.

"It's just that Franklin got so mad. He yelled in class and pushed Jesse P. down, and I think he would have punched him except Mrs. Bailey stopped him. He might get suspended."

"Oh no." She wondered how Franklin's mom, Missy, was dealing with this. She'd call her tonight after Taco Wednesday—Missy would surely need an ear by then. And poor Franklin would take this hard. He was the most sensitive and kind boy—Charlie was uncommonly sweet, but Franklin was different. There was an innocence about him that the other kids had outgrown by now. It was becoming obvious that he wasn't maturing at the usual rate, which made him more endearing.

Missy frequently shared her challenges in raising a boy with sensory-integration disorder. It was sometimes misdiagnosed as a form of autism and had similar characteristics, yet there was even less known about it. Various sounds could set him off, an airplane overhead distracted him in class, and he often spoke and acted in ways that were socially inappropriate. Wren feared Franklin would experience the cruelty of other children as his disorder became more apparent at school. She shuddered to think of the boy crushed by criticism and teasing.

But what should she say to Charlie about it?

Charlie continued, "He doesn't have any other friends at school except me. But I don't want to play with him all the time. I don't have very many friends because I'm always with Franklin, and no one wants to play with us."

Wren didn't know what to say. This was one of those times in motherhood that stumped her.

"And then, then after Franklin left . . ."

Wren waited again with her eyes on the forested highway. They only had ten minutes left on the drive home. Wren wondered if she should pull over and give him more time to talk.

"Felix said that I'm autistic too."

Wren looked over at Charlie as he stared out the opposite window. "Oh, sweetie."

"I told him that Franklin isn't autistic, and that I'm not either. He kept calling me 'autistic, autistic, Charlie is autistic.' "

Wren's anger stirred, rising from her stomach through her chest. She wondered where the teacher had been, and who exactly was this Felix kid. "What did you say?" It took effort to keep her voice calm.

"I told him he was stupid because he didn't know who was autistic and who wasn't. Then Mrs. Bailey made me and Felix stay in during recess—both of us."

"She did?" Wren gripped the steering wheel. She'd e-mail Mrs. Bailey about this tonight, and she had a strong urge to take that little Felix by

the ears and give him a few of her own words—
bully was the nicer among them.

"I don't want people thinking I'm like Franklin."

"They don't, Charlie. He just said that because"
—*he's a nasty little boy*—"he wasn't being very nice. Maybe he's unhappy or gets teased about things too."

"He gets teased by kids 'cuz he wears the same clothes almost every day. But it still made me mad."

"I'm sure it did, but it's also hard because Franklin has talents and unique things that no one else has. It's just that he's different from other kids."

"I just want to be normal and have normal friends. And sometimes I really want to play other things than just spaceman like what Franklin wants. Like I really would like to play dodge ball."

"Have you talked to Franklin about it?"

"No, he'll just think I don't want to be his friend anymore."

"Could you tell him that sometimes you want to play dodge ball and other things, not just spaceman?"

"I tried, and he got mad at me."

"Well, maybe you can play with him on one recess and then other times you do what you want."

"Maybe." His tone said he didn't really like the plan.

"I know this is really tough. But I'm proud of you for trying so hard with Franklin and for not just dropping him. You've been a good friend to him."

"He doesn't think so."

"Maybe we can talk together with his mom."

"Maybe," he said again in a dejected tone.

"Charlie."

"What?" He looked up with his large brown eyes.

"You are a very wonderful person."

"Why?" A small smile twitched at the corner of his mouth.

"Because a lot of people wouldn't care the way you do. I know it's easier to just ignore him and make new friends. But you're trying, and that says a lot for someone your age. Most people would run away from a situation like this."

As she said the line about running away, a tinge of guilt touched her.

Wasn't that what she did and continued to do whenever the situation became too hard? She ran. She'd moved from Chicago because she feared Derek might find them one day. She'd run from her siblings after the huge argument at the funeral. She'd done everything possible to keep from remembering the family reunion and its aftermath. Now the habit of running when things got tough kept her searching for a way out of

Ruth's party. Wren had even thought about being conveniently sick with some disease that forced her to another region of the U.S. during the autumn months—anything to avoid seeing her brother and sister again.

"Let's pick up Nana and go for tacos. Then we can get an ice-cream cone on the boardwalk."

Charlie shifted in his seat. "Can I have two scoops?"

"Maybe, but let's see if you want two scoops after eating at Macho Taco."

"Ice cream is made of milk. It might help me grow."

Wren laughed and reached across to mess Charlie's hair. "You'll grow when you're supposed to grow, mister. There's no hurry, in my opinion."

"You'll always want me small. But I'm nearly a teenager."

"Don't give me gray hairs yet—I have three years."

They bantered back and forth about Charlie growing up and Wren being unhappy about it. But his mood had lifted for now. Wren kept glancing from the road to take in the way he laughed with his chin lifted and how he scrunched his eyebrows while trying to think of a funny joke.

"When we get home, why don't you wait in the car, and I'll get Nana. My stomach is growling for some grub."

"Yeah, I could eat an elephant."

"Is that all? I could eat a whale."

"That's nothing. I could eat the moon."

"Hmm, that's hard to beat. I concede, you win." Wren exited the highway, going toward the coastline and Fern House, as Charlie drummed his victory beat on the dashboard.

"We need music," Charlie said, reaching for the iPod. For a moment, Wren thought of the cell phone in the glove compartment. She wanted to ask him about it—and about the flyer too, since she believed they were certainly connected. But Wren didn't want to lose this moment.

"Andrea, please," she said.

"Andrea Bocelli? Noooooo," Charlie said dramatically, with both hands on his forehead.

"You used to love Andrea Bocelli. I remember when—"

"I know, you remember when I could sing all of his songs in Italian."

"Well, it was your own kind of Italian. I don't think someone from Italy would understand you, but it was adorable."

"I was like four."

"Okay, but I wouldn't mind a break from Chopin, and no Skillet right now. I need something more relaxing."

"I'll surprise you."

A moment later the sweeping operatic introduction of *"Con te Partiro"* rose through the speakers. Wren smiled; he'd picked Andrea Bocelli for her after all.

Charlie held a serious expression and sat up straight with his hands in the air as he played an invisible violin for the intro. She laughed as he dramatically sang along in his best mimic of Italian. Wren joined in and the music filled her with something of joy and hope. This was one of those perfect moments she savored with her son. How she wished to collect them into a jar to take out and relive throughout the rest of her life. She'd have jars and jars of memories lined up through the corridors of her mind.

They pulled up to the cottage and, for a moment at least, the weight of the world fell behind them like the notes of the song.

5

Wren headed toward the front door while Charlie waited in the car, looking through their iPod for more music. The smell of smoke plumed out the door.

"Grandma, where are you?" Wren raced toward the kitchen where a haze drifted in the air.

"Welcome home, huh? I can't seem to turn myself into a cook." Ruth stood in the kitchen with the oven door open and the fan humming loudly. She beat at the air with an oven mitt. The dining room windows were wide open, and apron-clad Ruth pointed toward a charred something in a casserole dish on the counter.

"That's the only thing that burned?" Wren swiped at the smoke lingering in the kitchen.

"Yes. Just the Super Smokey Tuna Casserole."

Wren laughed, relieved that Ruth and the house were safe. She consoled her grandmother over the casserole burned beyond recognition, but she felt grateful too—neither she nor Charlie were fans of tuna casserole, and right now, it would take a CSI investigator to identify the remains.

"Tonight is Taco Wednesday anyway. It's our weekly tradition. Charlie's in the car waiting for us."

"Yes, yes. I just thought I'd treat you both to one of my mother's recipes," Ruth said.

"Thanks, Grandma. That was nice of you."

"I'll get my sweater and purse," Ruth said.

Twenty minutes later Charlie pulled open the door for Wren and Ruth at their favorite Mexican restaurant, his feet sliding from the effort. They were greeted by bright Mexican decor and the sound of mariachi singers strolling around the restaurant playing a festive song.

"Hey, Mom, it's Ramon."

Wren glanced up to see the owner walking around the register counter with his usual ear-to-ear smile that seemed to emanate through his entire being. She'd never known anyone so full of cheer, except maybe Santa Claus.

"Ah, Senora and young Senor, it is very good to see you for your Taco Wednesday. You brought your sister with you tonight?" Ramon winked at Wren and reached out to shake her hand with both of his hands.

"This is my grandmother, Ruth."

"Grandmother? What? You are *tres bonita*, Senora."

Ruth laughed and swatted at him before Ramon shook her hands with his as well. "You're going to make an old woman blush."

"Let me escort you to your table." Ramon offered Ruth his arm, and they walked to the vinyl red booth near a bubbling indoor fountain.

The chips were warm and the salsa fresh with just the right bite to it. Everything seemed to taste especially good tonight. Ruth's presence and the return of Charlie's smile made everything better. Ruth was a great storyteller, regaling them with tales from her childhood during the Depression era. Wren settled back against the booth, crunching chips and watching the interaction between her grandmother and son.

"You didn't have a TV or a telephone?" Charlie asked in amazement as if he were hearing about someone who lived during the age of the dinosaurs.

"We didn't even have a car. My father hitched

up the horse and buggy so we could go to church every Sunday. It wasn't till I was about your age when my father bought our first car."

"Wow. I'm going to tell my teacher about you." Charlie scooped some salsa onto his chip.

"You can call me Nana Encyclopedia for all the wars and presidents I've been through. When I was born, women couldn't even vote."

Charlie's face shone with awe. "I hope I live to be as old as you."

Wren choked on her chip, but Ruth laughed good-naturedly.

"I hope you do too." Ruth leaned across the table toward Charlie. "I'll tell you something about your mother that I bet you don't know."

"Try me," Charlie said.

"Did you know that your mom used to be one of my favorite singers?"

Wren bit her tongue as she took a bite of her chip.

"My mom?" Charlie said, glancing up at Wren.

Wren tasted blood but tried to cover her agony and smiled. "I stopped all that a long time ago, except when I don't realize it, from what some-one tells me." Wren winked at Charlie.

"How come you stopped?" he asked.

Wren glanced at Ruth, who waited for the answer as if she didn't already know why Wren had stopped singing.

"It just wasn't what I'm supposed to do with my life, I guess."

"But you could still sing, like at church or places like that," Charlie said with his forehead squeezed together as it was when he was thinking very hard. Wren knew with Charlie's love of music, he probably couldn't fathom someone stopping, even if they weren't called to music as a career. Music seemed to flow through her son's veins, and she remembered a time when she'd known something similar. But for her, singing had come to a quick end, freezing up cold and dissipating into nothing. She still found her greatest pleasure in listening, but that was as far as it went. She would protect Charlie from a similar end to his gift—that had always been her goal, from the first time she realized how much he loved it.

Charlie slurped the last bit of drink through his straw. "We should do a song together sometime. I'll play the violin and you can sing."

Ruth smiled, appearing utterly satisfied. Wren felt a shudder of fear and anger. *Calm down,* she told herself. But it was as if every wall of her fortress was being invaded in one day. Her earlier peace dissolved and the panic threatened to overwhelm her.

She'd never told Charlie about her deep love of singing. Long ago she'd put away all the photographs, performance programs, and sheet music. Wren didn't want the questions, she didn't want to be pressured about it, she didn't want to relive the past, and she most certainly wasn't going to start singing again.

"We'll talk about it another time, okay?"

But Charlie didn't want to talk about it another time. "Mom, why?"

"You can perform together at the party," Ruth said.

Wren wanted to walk out of the restaurant then and there, but the singing mariachis moved toward their table as if divinely orchestrated to do so.

"Later," she mouthed to Charlie, trying to hide how upset she felt. She forced a smile at the three mariachis as they strummed away on their ukuleles.

Evening had fallen by the time they parked near the waterfront. Wren wanted to go home and put this day to bed, but Charlie had brought up the promised ice cream. The street lamps shone against the deepening blue of the sky. The hills to the west held the last of a pink sunset above them. The cool sea air rose up from the water, making Wren wish for a warmer jacket although the freshness soothed her tight emotions.

They walked toward the waterfront, passing quaint boutiques, a flower shop, a candy store, a candle and soap store, and a museum that had displays of early colonists and explorers of Maine.

"Good evening, Wren and Charlie," said a

woman's voice, and a woman appeared outside the Old Mill Bakery. The scent of brownies wafted out behind her.

"Margaret, hello. How are you?"

"I'm doing well, and you two?"

"This is my grandmother, Ruth. Grandma, this is Margaret, the owner of the best bake shop in the northeast."

"No, in the whole world," Charlie added with a rub of his stomach. Margaret brushed the top of Charlie's head as they made introductions.

"I have some mini cupcakes that need a home tonight." Margaret bent toward Charlie. "Would you mind taking them off my hands? Otherwise Mr. Brown is going to be tempted to break his new diet."

"I think we better help Mr. Brown out," Charlie said with a pursed smile and nod of his head.

"Very kind of you—come inside." Margaret led the way into the shop. Her display cases shone behind clean glass and trays packed with perfect rows of baked delicacies—cookies, cupcakes, desserts, and cakes. On a table behind the counter were piles of fresh-baked bread.

"This place is heaven," Ruth said, looking around. "Too bad I'm stuffed."

Margaret disappeared into the back room and returned with a bakery box. "Have you been reading our new book, Wren?"

"We're in book club together at the library,"

Wren explained to Ruth. "Not yet. I'm reading too many books right now."

Charlie stood on his tiptoes to get a better view of the miniature cupcakes Margaret was carefully placing in the box. "She really is. You should see all the books by her bed."

"Your mom's work in the library is probably like me owning this place. I definitely eat too many baked goods." Margaret patted her round middle with a laugh.

"Yes, and I tell myself no new books, but then someone at the library recommends something or I come across a little gem . . . I'm hopeless with the allure of a good story."

"Well, I have a guy I'm hoping may allure you as well."

"Oh no," Wren said, shaking her head.

Ruth raised her head from where she was peering into the display case. "She needs a guy."

Wren glanced at Charlie, who watched the women. "I *have* a guy. This one little man is all I need."

Ruth and Margaret glanced at each other as if they didn't believe her. But at least no one said anything further about Wren's dating life, or lack thereof.

"This would be a great place to get the desserts for the party," Ruth said as she found a booklet of decorated cakes, cookies, and cupcakes.

"A party?" Margaret asked.

"Wren and my other grandchildren are throwing me a ninetieth birthday party."

"That's lovely. I'll give a good discount to my favorite librarian and the best boy in the world . . . and of course to you, Ruth."

"We can't pass up that offer."

The trio continued down toward the pier. Wren wished for some time alone, to think and sift through the events of the day. Her job situation was a problem, but what really bothered her was not knowing what was happening with Derek. Finding the phone, seeing that name "Dad," hearing Derek's voice, it churned her stomach every time her mind went over it. If Ruth wasn't here, Wren would have certainly addressed the issue and probably not in the best manner. For that, she was grateful. Perhaps God had designed it this way, but Wren was having a hard time seeing His hand in her life right now.

While Charlie ran into a small arcade to spend several dollars of his allowance, Wren and Ruth stood outside and looked out toward the boats in the marina with their lights dotting the darkening harbor. Wren considered telling Ruth about Derek, but why worry her grandmother?

"The days are getting shorter," Wren said as a flock of gulls cried and flew overhead; some landed on the posts of the dock where rows of moored fishing and sailing boats rocked gently on the waves.

"Yes. I'd forgotten what a lovely town this is," Ruth said with a sigh.

"It's a wonderful place to live, especially this time of year when there's a short reprieve between the summer tourists and the foliage hounds."

"Oh yes, the autumn frenzy."

"It'll be here before long."

"We'll have to remind your brother and sister of the traffic when they head up for the party."

"You know, Grandma, we might want a few alternatives for the location. The weather gets pretty unpredictable this time of year. And I doubt Barb and Jack will want to stay on the property." Wren knew her siblings were quite particular about their accommodations; it was five-star or nothing for Barb, and Jack was usually along the same lines unless he was off on some eco-tour in the Himalayas or the outback of Australia. Now that he was married—something she still hadn't processed—Jack might have changed, but it would still be awkward with them all at Fern House.

Ruth's plan had all the makings of a major family disaster, just like the one they'd had at their father's funeral. Ruth would be devastated if that happened, and that was reason enough for Wren to try and thwart her good intentions.

"You don't want to see your brother and sister for very long, do you?"

The pointed question stopped Wren's thoughts

short. "It's not that. It's just . . . well, I'd love to see them if I felt the potential for something cataclysmic wasn't there. I don't want your celebration ruined. I mean, Dad didn't know that his funeral was ruined, but this is your special birthday, and we don't want this memory to be of another falling out."

"I have great faith in the three of you."

Wren glanced at Ruth to see if she was serious, and the look on her face said just that. Where she found this great faith in them, Wren didn't know, and she hated to disappoint her grandmother.

Wren decided she'd do all she could to be the peacemaker. She wouldn't bring up the "incident" from childhood, or the funeral disaster, or anything else unpleasant. They should be able to make it through a few days together, right? Barb was the wild card. She'd never been one to tame her tongue, and Wren expected that hadn't changed in the past few years. Wren, as the middle sibling, had often tried to make peace, which in turn made Jack and Barb believe she wasn't loyal to either of them. It had been a lose-lose situation in the past, and Wren didn't know what would make it different now.

"You worry too much," Ruth said, patting Wren's back.

"Grandma—"

"How has your worry helped you?"

Charlie dashed out of the arcade then,

exclaiming how he'd finally reached 100,000 on his favorite game.

At the ice-cream shop, Charlie asked for two scoops of chocolate chunk chip. Wren passed, knowing she'd be the one to finish Charlie's. Ruth ordered a mini cone with strawberry cheesecake ice cream.

As they walked back outside and up the narrow street lined with quaint shops and cafés, Ruth pointed across the boardwalk toward Paul's restaurant. The sign said Callahan's Café and Catering.

"That restaurant does catering. Do they have good food?"

Charlie followed Ruth across the street and Wren trailed behind, hoping Paul wasn't inside and able to see her coming toward the café. "Yes, they're pretty good. I forgot they do catering."

"Let's go in and see if they have a price sheet and menu."

"How about later? They probably have it all online."

"But we're already here."

Wren glanced at Charlie, who was busy licking his ice cream as it tilted to one side.

"I'll wait with Charlie. I'm sure he can't take his ice cream inside. I can hold yours if you want to run in."

Ruth gave her a quizzical look, then handed over her ice cream. A few minutes later she returned with some papers in her hand.

"What a cute little place," Ruth said as she walked across the boardwalk toward them. "And the price is what I was budgeting."

"Do they have the kind of food you want at your party?"

"I hadn't fully decided, but this sounds great. They have an array of appetizers like salmon bites, a giant baked brie, artichoke, oysters, a hot lobster dip. It all sounded so good. The nice guy there, I can't remember his name, he said we could come in and do a tasting. He said to tell you and Charlie hello."

Wren glanced back toward the window, but she couldn't see Paul inside. Part of her nearly laughed out loud at the irony of this birthday party. Just when she thought it couldn't get more stressful, now Paul Callahan might be catering the event.

This just gets better and better.

The living room clock ticked through the night as if to mock Wren's every second of sleeplessness. The couch felt stiff under her back, and no amount of shifting helped her find comfort. The faint stench of burned casserole hung in the air, but no one else stirred in the house.

One of the novels she was reading sat on the end table, but Wren knew she wouldn't be able to get into the story with this pervading restlessness attached to the night.

Wren and Charlie had lived in relative peace for the past years with only the usual daily challenges to overcome. Now, in one day, everything was crumbling in on them. Without more money at work, it would be impossible to carry out the plans she'd so carefully made for Charlie. And how had he gotten in touch with Derek? Just the thought of her ex-husband, and how he could ruin everything she'd created, gave her chills. On top of all this she was supposed to throw a party and deal with her estranged siblings?

In the ten years since Charlie's birth, she'd become more goal oriented, working hard to build a secure life for them, while yearning for something deeper for both her and Charlie. She'd tentatively explored faith and spirituality, never quite feeling like she'd gotten it figured out.

During one of her more desperate times when Charlie was sick and they were alone in Chicago, Wren had knelt by his toddler bed and begged God to help her. She supposed it was the first real unveiling of her faith. She didn't have one stunning moment when God descended and filled her life with His presence. He'd come into her life slowly and deliberately. He didn't intrude, or push, or fill her life with false flattery. Over time it seemed God was just there in the little things, and she noticed them more and more until she could no longer deny Him. She felt His hand reaching toward her, and she took it in a final, true commitment to Christ.

But the tension between life being what you make it and having faith in a higher power was something she found difficult to balance despite her time in prayer, devotion, and Bible studies.

Since coming to Maine, they'd attended church regularly, and Wren joined a women's Bible study for a while, where she met Franklin's mom, Missy, who quickly became her friend and accountability partner to discuss Christianity and pray together.

But Wren consistently found herself trying to solve her own problems. Sometimes it seemed she only sought God when things were challenging, while at the same time she wondered if the events of today were really God punishing her for her continued failures as a mother, a person, and a Christian. Her faith had a solid foundation, but it seemed whatever she built on that foundation was made of rotting wood and rusted nails. Did she allow God to live and breathe in the daily routine, in her every decision? Why wasn't she able to hand Him her many fears and worries? As Ruth had pointed out, Wren knew her worries never produced anything of value.

Yet her worries gave her some misguided sense of control. If she could worry about it, then she could prepare for it. Today was the perfect example of how her fears did nothing to prepare her for the real challenges of life. Everything she'd worried about had blown up in her face.

Wren turned to face the back of the couch, then to her left side, and finally sat up. She bent her head toward her knees and prayed into the darkness.

Father, everything I've worked so hard to build is falling apart. I need your help. I'm afraid. Afraid about the future, afraid about Derek, afraid and hurt that Charlie is hiding things from me, afraid of seeing my family and rehashing the past, afraid, afraid, afraid . . .

The fears mounted like a dark presence growing from behind the couch and threatening to consume her. She squeezed her eyes shut, unable to move. The prayer froze in her thoughts until she whispered aloud, "Help me. Rid me of this fear. Be my safety, be real to me, be a shelter and refuge from this world."

Wren heard the sound of the clock and sighed at the peace calming the room.

"I want to know you more—I'm not always faithful in seeking you—but truly I do want to know you more. I want to know what you want for us. And I long for something that's missing —maybe the happiness Charlie asked you to bring me. I really don't know what I want or need. But I'm trying to trust that you do. Help me, please."

6

A dream lingered as Wren woke way too early and with a sore neck. There was barely enough light sifting through the windows to recognize morning's approach. She rubbed her neck as she sat up on the couch. From down the hall in her own very comfortable bed came the sound of her grandmother's snoring. After one night on this couch, Wren would never ask a guest to sleep here again.

The dream. She had been with someone, having morning coffee. He had made it, and she'd awoken to the scent. Then he—a man she couldn't see—brought her a cup, and they sat together on a loveseat with their feet entwined on the coffee table and Wren leaning against his shoulder. They discussed something, she couldn't remember what, but it was nothing astounding. It was just enjoyable, like the normal day-to-day happenings that so many couples discussed over coffee.

A cold chill ran through her shoulders and down her spine. The dream left her empty; she hadn't known such a feeling of loneliness in a while. Wren had adapted to life as the sole adult, welcomed it even, as the easier route. Being with someone wasn't all morning coffee and entwined feet. It was hard work, sacrifice, and then of course, he might leave you for a life of his own.

But there was that ache to talk to someone, to make decisions as a team, to share the bills, to have someone to pick up milk on the way home. Someone who would look at Charlie the way she did and would enjoy time with him, laughing at his jokes and marveling at how quickly he outgrew his shoes. A man to share the bed, who would kiss her, touch her, make love with her, and let her rest her head on his shoulder in the morning.

Her prayer last night had brought her peace. Why hadn't she dreamt about God being present with her, nearly in human form? Why this dissatisfied morning, like an itch she couldn't reach?

Wren stood up, tossing a throw pillow back onto the couch. She walked to the kitchen to make her own coffee. Stupid dream.

The clock on the stove said 4:55, but Wren knew there was no going back to sleep now. She started the coffeemaker and looked through the refrigerator. She and Charlie usually ate different breakfasts. He went for the cereal, though Wren sought ways to get some protein and fruit in him in the morning. She needed to lose five more pounds of the fifteen that had crept on in recent years—probably from coffee creamer and mochas with whipped cream. Her breakfast was usually yogurt and granola with blueberries, eggs with salsa, or a granola bar depending on how much time they had.

Since she was awake, Wren decided to make French toast as a treat for all of them. As she pulled out the eggs, Wren wondered when she should talk to Charlie about Derek. Before bed he'd acted as if he was getting sick, though Wren knew it had everything to do with the situation with Franklin. She'd meant to call Missy about it, but it was late by the time Charlie was tucked into bed with their reading and short prayer.

She heard her cell phone ringing in the living room. Who would be calling this early? Before she reached her phone, she guessed who it was.

"Only my sister would call at five a.m."

"Well, sorry, I need to get to work."

Wren closed her eyes and sighed, but reminded herself of the pact she'd made with herself to keep the peace as much as possible. This was such a Barb move, to care nothing about waking Wren up or inconveniencing her because her life wasn't as important as Barb's.

"You didn't call me back." Her sister's irritation rang through the line.

"I couldn't last night—we were busy and it was late by the time we got home."

"You could have found five minutes."

Wren bit her tongue and said nothing.

"So Grandma is there?"

"Yes. She arrived yesterday morning." Wren

73

sat on the bar stool and gazed at the coffeemaker, willing it to hurry. This conversation needed coffee.

"And how long have you known about all of this?" Barb sounded more annoyed than usual.

"All this, as in Grandma's birthday plans?"

"Uh, yes. What other plans would I be talking about?"

"Since yesterday morning." Wren fought the sarcasm from coming through in her tone.

"Oh."

"Barb, I'm as surprised as you are. I didn't even know about Jack getting married until I listened to your message. Grandma didn't tell me that part, and I forgot to ask her about it last night."

"That was a shocker—I still can't get over that he didn't tell any of us."

The coffeepot beeped, and Wren hopped up to pour a cup. She'd picked up a bottle of creamer last night on the way home.

"How long has he been married?" Wren asked.

"Close to a year. He's going to hear about this when I reach him."

Wren opened her mouth, then stopped. She wanted to tell Barb how they should all get along, but Barb wouldn't listen to her anyway. It might actually make it worse.

"And now we're just supposed to go along with this plan of Grandma's and all gather at Fern House for a happy little get-together?" Barb sounded like she was moving around as she spoke.

"She's turning ninety, what else can we do? I'm trying to get her to consider some other venues in town that might be nicer." Wren took a sip of coffee, savoring the taste on her tongue.

"Get on that, will you? A family reunion on the property sounds like a nightmare to me."

Wren had to keep from snickering. One thing her sister could be counted on for was her honest opinion. Wren could relate, but she felt guilty feeling that way. They were her family after all; it seemed wrong to dread the gathering.

"So if we end up at the property, where is everybody sleeping?"

"I haven't planned that far."

"I bet Jack and this Megan woman will want the main house."

Wren set her coffee mug on the counter. Did Barb want to sleep in the main house? The last time they'd talked, Barb had complained about the service at the Four Seasons in Hawaii. Wren had only eaten appetizers at a Four Seasons hotel. Fern House was over a hundred years old, with creaky floors, drafty rooms, and appliances that hadn't been updated since the sixties—and those were the most modern ones.

"Jack might want to stay in town, I have no idea. But if you both want to stay in the main house, you can all share it. There are five bedrooms."

Barb blew out a huff that reminded Wren of

their childhood horse Shogun, who would blow out snot all over them. "I know how many bedrooms there are. But no thank you."

Wren bit the inside of her cheek as she did whenever she talked to Barb. If they communicated more often, Wren would probably have a hole chewed through her cheek.

"We'll just have to bring up the RV."

"You have an RV?" Just when Wren thought she had Barb figured out, she completely surprised her.

"Logan. He's set on exploring America. Long story, I'll explain later."

"Don't you need some kind of hookups for an RV?"

"Yes, of course. I'll have Logan figure out what to do. We can get power and water from the house. Drainage is the issue. But maybe we're okay if it's just a day or two."

"Okay." This plan destroyed the hope that they'd stay somewhere else.

"And who else is coming?"

"I don't know. Grandma and I haven't sat down and worked on all of the details. Mom and Howard can't make it."

"Of course not. You talked to her?"

"Grandma told me. I haven't talked to Mom since the middle of summer. She was in Italy when she e-mailed."

"She called me from Greece. If we knew what

was going on with this party, maybe she could come. When will you have it planned?"

"I just found out about this like you did. And things are a little hectic around here. I had hoped everyone would help."

"Uh-huh. The library getting stressful?"

"Nice, Barb."

"What? Why are you being so snippy with me?"

"Me?"

"Yes, you. Haven't had your morning coffee yet?"

Wren placed her hands on the cool countertop, closed her eyes, and breathed deeply. They had to get through this party, and if she and Barb started it off wrong even before she arrived, there'd be little hope to salvage the event.

"Anyway," Barb said, laughing to herself. "We'll be there."

"You and Logan?"

"And we're most likely bringing Bradley. It depends on how he behaves. He just came home from one of those wilderness programs."

"Wilderness programs?"

"For at-risk rich kids. They show up and haul kids off to a camp in Idaho and teach them how to survive and stuff. It's supposed to shape them up. We'll see if he can go back to school next semester."

Barb relayed this news as if she were talking about her dog needing obedience training. Wren didn't know her nephew well. She'd tried harder when he was younger, but she couldn't connect with him. He didn't like to read, so none of the books she sent were opened. Then after two consecutive years of him telling her that the Christmas gifts she mailed him were for babies, she started sending gift cards that he surely saw as miniscule compared to the wealth of gifts Barb and Logan bestowed upon him. They spent more on their son at Christmas than Wren spent on Charlie all year.

"I didn't know you were having problems with him." Wren thought of Charlie being exposed to Bradley.

"The usual teen stuff. We caught him smoking pot, grades dropping, a few unauthorized piercings, he started hating us. But I'm not putting up with that, so one day he skipped school, and when he came home a van was waiting to take him away."

"He didn't know they were coming?"

"Oh no, that's part of the strategy. He was stunned. It was hard on Logan, seeing Brad cry as they hauled him off, but I knew it was the best thing for him."

Wren didn't know such a thing was legal. It sounded extreme, but then she didn't know the situation.

"How long was he gone?"

"Three months. He's improved so far since

getting home, but we'll see how it goes."

Barb continued to talk about Bradley, how he'd made them miss a trip to Bermuda because of a parent weekend they had to attend in Idaho.

We live such different lives.

Their differences were fine from a distance, but with them all together, the differences were going to be hard to manage.

"So I take it you haven't talked to Jack yet," Barb said.

"Not in three years, and I haven't seen him since Mom and Howard's wedding, which was what—eight years ago?"

"Well, it's been two and a half for me. That brother of ours. I don't know what's wrong with him. I think we were all adopted—there's no way three children could be this different and all from the same parents."

Wren agreed and glanced at the clock, wanting to wrap up this conversation.

"Does Grandma have Jack's number?"

"I'll ask when she gets up."

"Okay. Get the number and text it to me today. I just got a page from the hospital. Get the plans ironed out soon. I need to get the time off and can't leave my patients hanging." Barb's tone was condescending, as if her work was more important than everyone else's. She'd always been a bossy older sister, but the arrogance had grown along the way. Wren remembered years earlier when she and her sister had been close, sleeping in the same bed, wearing matching outfits, building tents in the living room, and roller skating through the house. They treated Jack like a baby doll created for them to dress, feed, and change his diapers. Barb took the role as oldest seriously, driving everyone crazy with her bossiness. But she was fun too, and Wren had looked up to her big sister.

Wren set the phone down and stood gazing out the breakfast nook window toward the back lawn. Their relationship had changed as Barb became a teenager, but the dramatic shift came the weekend of the family reunion. Did Barb ever think about how they were as kids? Did she long for a relationship with her sister again?

Wren had let go of all expectations or wishes for what might have been. She'd tried in her late twenties to bring her siblings close again, but it had backfired, making their relationships worse as more painful words were hurled at one another. It had been difficult for Wren to let go of her wish for a close family for herself and for Charlie. He could have had an aunt and uncle who loved him. But she couldn't change her siblings, so Wren changed herself.

Wren sat for a while, then straightened up with her thoughts lost in the past. When Charlie walked out in his pajamas, his hair sticking up on one side of his head, Wren realized how much of the morning had passed. He rubbed his eyes and yawned.

"Must have cereal," he said and headed straight for the cupboard.

"And I have to get ready," Wren said, smiling; she loved how young he looked when he first woke and was wearing his pajamas.

Charlie was pouring his cereal when she remembered she'd planned to make French toast.

She rubbed the top of his head as she passed him, which elicited a mumbled, "Hey," from his cereal-stuffed mouth. She put the eggs back in the refrigerator. No French toast today.

As Wren folded the blankets on the couch, her Bible fell from within the folds. How quickly the late-night prayer disappeared as the daytime thoughts overtook her. She set her Bible on the end table on top of the novel she was reading and decided right then that she'd pray continuously for the next few days about the Derek situation, her job, and the party.

"This day is yours, God. Help me know when to talk and when to be silent."

7

Sue came around the cubicle and set a Village Brew coffee cup onto Wren's desk.

"It is officially autumn," she said, motioning toward the cup.

Wren's expression questioned the older woman, who smiled smugly with her bright red lips.

"Autumn isn't here for a few more weeks . . . wait, is this what I think it is?"

"Yes, it is." Her heavily lined eyebrows lifted as she spoke.

"Pumpkin pie latte," they said in unison.

"Wow, it *is* autumn then," Wren said.

"Yes, and this is yours. I have my own on my desk."

"You are a gift." Wren reached for the cup and breathed in the scent of nutmeg, cinnamon, ginger, and coffee, making her mouth water.

"I'm hoping this inspires you to make that harvest nut bread for all of your adoring coworkers."

Wren leaned back in her chair and folded her arms. "Sorry, but I baked that last year because I was new, and I wanted you all to like me. The honeymoon is over."

Sue narrowed her eyes. "That's just wrong. I can turn all of your coworkers against you . . . and forget to print your next paycheck."

"Okay, okay, harvest nut bread coming soon." Wren took a sip of the latte and sighed deeply. "So good."

"Hey, before I get back to the factory grind, how's it going with Grandma Ruth?"

"I love having her here," Wren said.

"Oh, I'm sure you do," Sue said, scrutinizing her. "Who would mind having a relative show up on the doorstep asking for a party?"

"I admit it was a shock. It's taking some adjustment, but we made it through the first day. There are much worse things than having my grandmother show up." Wren wasn't about to tell Sue about the Derek situation.

"Yeah, I heard about the budget cuts. I think I'm the only one not worried, since the accountant is usually the last to go. But back to your grandmother, I have this feeling that there's more to this party and her showing up."

"What do you mean?"

"Sweet grandmothers are always hiding things."

"You haven't even met my grandmother."

"I don't have to. I had one, so believe me. She was adorable and I loved her, but she could cause some havoc, I tell you. Mark my word, start asking questions and you'll suddenly realize that your grandma is much more than you think. And no woman gets to ninety years old without secrets and at least a few skeletons stuffed in the closet."

Wren couldn't imagine Ruth having dark secrets hidden in her past. She'd always been the sweet, doting grandmother who offered wise advice and had a resilient faith in God that never seemed to waver. Of course, Wren didn't know everything about her grandmother. But what kind of secrets could she be hiding? Sue was being dramatic as usual, though Wren felt a sudden curiosity toward Ruth. It was easy to think of her as just a grandma, but not really as a woman.

"I guess we look at our parents and grandparents as if they aren't people."

"Think of her as if she's a character in a book."

"Am I really that transparent?"

"Bookworms speak their own language."

"Well, if I think of my grandmother as a character in a book, it does add a level of intrigue, and I realize I may not know her as well as I think."

"Exactly."

Maybe Wren needed to see this surprise visit as the opportunity to get to know Ruth better. The intrusion of Ruth's arrival had made Wren wish the next weeks would pass as quickly as possible. But she was looking at it all wrong. Ruth's age should have made her realize this was a rare opportunity to spend time with her grandmother. Wren had longed for Charlie to have more family in his life, and the answer had come knocking on the door with luggage packed, yet Wren had wanted it to go away as fast as possible.

"So . . . the plot thickens," Sue said with a mischievous grin. "And speaking of plots, I heard some news about our—or rather my—favorite man to watch."

"Who?" Wren glanced back at her computer screen, suddenly ready for this conversation to end. She needed to get back to scheduling an event about disability awareness.

"You know I'm talking about Paul Callahan. He's sure been in the library a lot."

Wren had thought the same thing. Few business owners came into the library, especially during the day. "I saw him yesterday. He met with Dr. James, but I don't know why."

"I saw him earlier today too. But, as cute as he is, I'm beginning to wonder about him. I think he has a thing for you, whether you see it or not. I've caught him watching you at the film nights, and now he's conveniently at the library all the time. But I had it confirmed by my friend Janice that Paul and Christine Meyers are dating."

"There you go then, no more Paul Callahan. Might as well give it up, Sue." Wren started to type and realized her fingers were on all the wrong keys. Christine Meyers? The newspaper writer had seemed nice enough when she interviewed Wren about the film night, but she didn't seem the right fit for Paul.

"I feel badly for Christine—she's had a rough time. Her husband was killed several years ago. He was a fisherman for Paul's company. Still, it's disappointing. My gut feeling was that the two of you would make a great couple."

"We'd make a terrible couple."

"And why do you say that?" Sue set one hand on her round hip.

"Because I . . . he . . . we . . . I don't know because I don't even know him."

"Exactly. But I know him, and I know you, and let me just tell you, that's one sweet match."

Wren pushed back in her chair. Maybe she should head up early to the reference desk.

"Haven't you learned your lesson from setting up Janice and that UPS driver who was stealing packages?"

"I never learn my lesson, I simply adjust my strategy. Giving up is for quitters—unlike you, who gave up on dating over a few bad experiences."

"I didn't fully quit."

Sue moved in close and took Wren's face with two hands. "Listen, Wren. I know you're religious and everything—it's my one grievance between us."

Wren never liked being called "religious," but she didn't interrupt Sue to correct her.

"With this lovely face and that body—unlike my lumpy one—you just need to cut loose and get some action. I don't want you becoming some old spinster lady without any memory of her special skills . . . if you know what I mean." Sue released Wren's face and crossed her arms at her chest.

"I don't *want* to know what you mean. And spinsterhood gets a bad rap. It's not like in the Victorian era when a woman needed a man to survive."

"Oh, I think a woman needs a man to survive."

"Who are you and what year is this?"

"I think a man needs a woman to survive as well, so it's not like I'm a male chauvinist in a female body."

"You had me worried there for a moment. But really, how many happily married people do you know? I'd rather stay a spinster than be stuck in a miserable marriage. It's not exactly safe fooling around with random people—and I don't say that just because I'm a Christian."

"You have a point there. My marriage might be boring, but I don't want out. You, however—I have big plans for your love life. You're my new hobby."

"What's wrong with scrapbooking?"

"Dream on. Enjoy your cup of autumn. I need to get back to payroll. Remember we have that technology thingie this afternoon."

Wren groaned. She'd completely forgotten about the workshop and had hoped to talk to Charlie after school about Derek. It would have to wait until tonight. This waiting was killing her, but maybe it was for the best since she was supposed to be praying about it first.

Wren turned back to her computer as Sue disappeared around the cubicle wall.

"Good morning, Wren." Paul Callahan waved as he passed her desk, going down the hall toward Dr. James' office.

Sue slid in her chair around the corner and gave Wren a long, low whistle.

Wren glared at her. "What? He just said hello. He's dating someone, remember?"

Technology. Wren wanted none of it. Well, not exactly *none* of it; she had to admit that some technology was quite convenient and useful. But it was getting out of control, and it changed so fast that keeping up was like catching leaves on a blustery day.

The library had updated its systems before Wren had arrived, and it was pretty easy to learn, but all the cell phones, computers, e-readers, tablets, music devices . . . even the cars and televisions were so techie it took research or a college class to distinguish between them all, let alone use them to capacity. Wren mentally lamented that the afternoon would be spent in such a workshop instead of going home at two o'clock like she usually did on Thursdays. Charlie would have to go to Franklin's after school. Wren took her phone to the break room.

She hesitated a moment before calling, feeling guilty that she hadn't called Missy about Franklin's school incident already. But she had to make the call.

"Working late?" Missy asked after they greeted one another.

"I have a technology workshop. Is it okay for Charlie to come over after school?"

"Of course. Franklin will be happy to have him."

Wren thought she detected something off in Missy's tone.

"I've been meaning to call you, but my grandmother came to town unexpectedly. Charlie told me about Franklin having a few problems at school."

Missy sighed, and Wren glanced at the clock wanting to give Missy time to talk, but the workshop was starting soon.

"You could call it that. Until now, I've been pretty happy with Franklin in public school. Mrs. Radcliffe was great last year because her son is autistic, so she took the time to really learn what's going on with Franklin. This year, well, it hasn't been like that at all."

"Have you talked to Mrs. Bailey?"

"Yes. I think the staff dreads seeing me walk up the steps of that school. I know it's hard and everything, being a teacher. But I'm just not sure what else to do. I don't think Franklin would do well homeschooling. He loves the interaction with other children, except that the children are becoming increasingly difficult for him. Kids are just mean-spirited."

Wren wished she could hug Missy. It was one of those fears of all mothers—their child's feelings being hurt by other children. "I wish our schools had curriculum for teaching kids how to be kind people with good morals. That would benefit the world more than basic academics."

"It's not going to happen. But we can dream." Wren waved at Jasmine as she arrived and put her satchel in the staff cubby. Jasmine pointed that she'd head up to the reference desk. "Charlie said Franklin had an incident yesterday."

"Yes, and it really upset him. But he's back today, and I haven't had a call from the school so far. I can't let myself think about it until he's home."

Wren wondered what Missy meant by that.

"I know that sounds cold," Missy said, as if reading Wren's thoughts.

"Not cold, just hard to do."

"It seems all I *can* do. I was so protective over my first son. I wanted him to wear the best clothes and have all the nice things so that kids wouldn't tease him the way that I was teased. Then the accident happened, and I couldn't protect him after all. Now I have Franklin. The best clothes and nice things don't keep him from being teased. I have to let him go into God's hands in many respects. I'm trying to trust that he'll be okay. I can't follow him around and protect him from everything and everyone as much as I want to. But I know God is with him even when I can't be."

Wren was speechless, as she always felt whenever she thought about Missy's first son's death. It wasn't a subject her friend brought up very often, and she'd only once told Wren about the rafting accident. It reminded Wren of just how light her troubles were in comparison. She didn't know how she'd survive the loss of Charlie.

"That's so hard," Wren whispered. She tried protecting Charlie from the world, and though she didn't want to be overly protective, she struggled with the balance. When he was hurt in any way —physically, mentally, emotionally—Wren wanted to soothe it away or harm the culprit. But no mother could save her child from everything. It was the most terrifying part of being a parent.

"I'm sure you need to get back to work. I'll see you when you pick Charlie up. And coffee tomorrow morning?"

"Perfect."

Wren stared at her cell phone for a moment after she and Missy ended the call. She noticed another afternoon intern arriving, which reminded Wren of the time. She quickly called Charlie's school. "Hi, Lisa, this is Wren, Charlie's mom."

"Hello, Wren. Tomorrow's the last film in the park?"

"Yep!"

"We've really enjoyed them, though we missed a few during our vacation. What movie is it this week?"

"It's *The Princess Bride*." Wren was constantly surprised at how many people commented on the films in the park. The idea wasn't original— numerous other cities had similar events, but it had become a community hit in its first year.

"I'm so excited. My kids haven't seen that

movie yet. But I suppose you weren't calling to be my personal movie guide. What's up?"

"Charlie will be going to the Johnsons' house after school. But I needed to talk to Charlie about it too. Would it be all right for him to call me at his next recess?"

"Sure, I'll get a message down to his teacher. Everything okay?"

"Yes," Wren said, not wanting to explain the situation.

She ended the call and checked the time. Three minutes till the workshop started. Wren dialed home and walked from the break room through the library toward the hallway in front of the community room where the workshop would be.

"Grandma, are you there? It's Wren. Grandma, pick up the phone."

"Hello?" Ruth's voice echoed loudly over the phone and through the answering machine.

"Hi, Grandma. Push the blinking button—"

"What? Where? Is this you, Wren?"

"Listen, Grandma, I'll call you in a few hours. But I'll be a little later than I thought. Okay? Did you hear me?"

"Yes, yes, I heard, you . . . oh, this darn phone is making such a ruckus, my word!"

"I'm going to hang up now, okay?"

"Okay, I've kept myself busy and I'm just having some tea. I don't know if you can even hear me."

"Bye, Grandma."

Wren turned around to the stares of several library patrons and realized she'd been practically yelling.

"I'm sorry," she said, covering her mouth and feeling her face flush with embarrassment.

"I thought it was supposed to be silent in the library," an older woman muttered as she tottered out the door.

Wren picked up the outline to the workshop from the pile at the doorway to the community room. The schedule read that there was another workshop for the other half of the library staff in the early evening. At least she could come to the early one.

"New Trends in Technology and How Libraries Can Remain Relevant"

"How libraries can remain relevant?" she muttered, immediately irritated, as she found an empty seat beside Sue.

"I know, huh?" Sue said, rolling her eyes.

The implication that libraries might not be relevant in the technological age didn't sit well with Wren. She believed in books. She couldn't imagine snuggling in bed with an electronic device. She was convinced that in ten years, doctors would report how all the gadgets people used caused cancer from the electrical waves buzzing through the human body. Suddenly everyone would be returning to real things . . . like books.

Dr. James entered the room with a guy who looked to be in his early thirties, dressed in dark blue jeans and a long-sleeved, button-up shirt with hair that appeared rumpled in that slick I'm-a-cool-musician style.

"He's nice on the eyes, at least," Sue said, leaning toward her.

Dr. James stood in front of the podium. "Thanks for coming, everyone. I know some of you don't love our subject today, but I'm confident you'll all get something out of it. I first met today's speaker at the National Library Conference, and I was quite impressed with his forward thinking —much more forward than my own. I'm happy to present Mr. Jeremy Bass."

Jeremy gave Dr. James a hearty pat on the back, then took over the podium, gripping the edges with two hands.

"Thank you, Dr. James. And please, if everyone will call me Jeremy, then I won't be looking around for my father, Mr. Bass, who was a math and science teacher."

Several people chuckled at his joke. Wren wasn't one of them.

"It's great to be in Maine at such a beautiful time of year. I've been working in technology within the library system for about four years now, and I recently started a consulting firm out of Boston. I specialize in helping libraries change with the times. Now, since I'm standing here with a library staff, I'm going to assume you love books. Am I correct?"

People murmured in agreement, and Wren had to remind herself not to dislike the speaker just because he had a topic she hated and a ridiculous title for his workshop.

"Ah, but none of you would admit to disliking books even if it were true." He laughed at his own joke.

"So let's talk about books. Take, for example, one of our beloved classics." Jeremy held up a thick hardcover edition of *Paradise Lost* by John Milton. He bent beneath the table and picked up a small trashcan. "Say good-bye to Milton." He dropped the book into the bucket.

Wren wanted to leap up and grab the book from the trashcan—or the guy by the neck. Obviously he was trying to provoke them, and it was working—on her, at least. He picked up another book with an embossed hardcover.

"*King Arthur and His Knights of the Round Table*." Jeremy dropped it into the trash.

"*Arabian Nights*."

"*Charlotte's Web*."

"Please, stop!" One of Wren's older coworkers, Edith Wampler, stood up, looking stricken and near tears.

"I'm sorry for the dramatics." Jeremy appeared quite pleased with himself and not sorry at all. Did Dr. James know what kind of guy he'd brought into their library? Their director treasured books, collecting first editions like fine paintings. This guy might know technology, but he clearly didn't have any respect for books.

Edith sat back down, but Wren could see her hands were still shaking.

Jeremy moved around the podium and sat on the edge of the front table. "Major changes are com-ing . . . and some have already arrived."

"So what you're telling us is that books and libraries are dead?" said a voice sarcastically from behind Wren.

Wren leaned back in her seat. They'd been hearing these ideas for a while now. Schools were eliminating libraries and textbooks, everything was going electronic, and rumors were flying that publishing was dead. Wren didn't believe it. Sure, fewer books might be printed and people could enjoy their gadgets, but there was no way books were going away. This talk was probably hitting them harder because of the budget cuts and the fear that the library might truly be in jeopardy.

"You've got it—libraries might be dead. Who in this room disagrees with me and believes books will always be in existence?"

Several in the room raised their hands, including Wren, but not everyone as she expected.

"How many think the age of print books is ending?" More hands went up, which stunned her. These were library people, not the average public. They all loved books, yet they predicted a gloomy future?

"Last week I was at a technology high school that eliminated the physical library three years ago and replaced it with an extensive online library. Now the room that once housed shelves of mostly unread books is being used as a creative photography lab. I'm seeing this all over—change is either being debated or has already occurred. This isn't the future, it's the here and now."

Jeremy continued as he walked up and down the aisles. "We have to address this in our libraries and be sure we aren't left behind. If we don't grow and evolve with technology, then libraries will become obsolete."

"Maybe they should," said Edith in a shaky voice. "Maybe we're all irrelevant. Maybe we should just shrivel up and go away."

"Now hold on, it's not that bad. I know change is tough."

Another of the older library staff, Roland Sorenson, raised his hand. "So what do you envision? Our libraries filled with computer screens instead of books?"

Jeremy sat again at his perch on the edge of the front table and leaned in like he was the wise master teaching his ignorant students. "No, I don't see that at all. Libraries should be—and I hope they always will be—warehouses for stories. So libraries need to offer more e-books, computer classes, and help for people to find the information or stories they need. No longer will libraries just be buildings lined with bookcases and offering children's story hour."

Wren wanted to inform Jeremy of the many diverse programs they offered at Cottage Cove Public Library and at every library she'd worked at since college. The way he said "children's story hour" was condescending, but the kids loved it, and they fell in love with books because of the early introduction. The library offered teen events, literacy classes, senior computer workshops, assistance with searches in genealogy— she could go on and on.

"Things will get more complex as the past meets the future." Jeremy pulled out one of the books from the trash and set it on the table. "It's about retaining traditions."

He took another book out and held it to his chest. "It's about modernization as well."

Instead of setting the book on top of the other, he put it behind the podium and brought out an e-reader that he set atop the first book.

"It's about making our libraries accessible to everyone as the years progress. When we offer options in our libraries instead of what is traditional and comfortable for us, then we move forward with the generations. In the best cases, we should lead the way rather than following reluctantly behind, don't you think?"

Jeremy went on to talk about the specifics of updating library technologies and offering digital and community resources, while still maintaining their status as the repository for civilization's knowledge, wisdom, and stories. He finished and the room broke into applause. Sue and Wren looked at one another with flat expressions, and Sue motioned with her head for them to get out of there.

When they reached the hallway, Sue made a huffing sound. "That stuff may be true, but nothing says I have to like it."

"Quite dramatic, wasn't he?"

"Seemed like people really liked him. Did you see everyone gathering around him at the end?"

"The entire thing was strange. He sort of treated us like imbeciles."

"I need a drink. And I'm not talking about a pumpkin latte."

Wren laughed. "I'm heading upstairs to finish up before I leave. What a waste of time."

But as Wren walked up the stairway to the second floor, she felt an empty ache in her stomach. She loved the full rows of books that filled the building. She walked among them, knowing that each one held a treasure of stories and information. Was everything on the verge of change? Was nothing safe anymore?

Wren passed a mom and her daughter working at a table. There were several homeschooling families who regularly camped out for part of the day in one of the study rooms. This woman, Laura, had surprised Wren with her racy vampire novels tucked within the piles of educational books they carted down to checkout every week. Her daughter, Hannah, often sought out Wren to discuss her reading material. She was working her way through the British authors, and at age fourteen, Wren expected the girl would surpass her knowledge in a year or so.

Many people thought a library was dull. Her sister, Barb, was one of them. But Wren saw it as the world pressed and condensed into book-sized morsels. The people who wandered the aisles or specific sections were as unique as the books.

There was sweet little Mabel Jenkins and her addiction to romance novels, much like Indian businessman Ravi Jarrah, though he always said he was picking up the pirate romances for his wife.

The local drama teacher, Mrs. Bickley, was often seen with a teen novel tucked within her scripts and dramatic arts books.

Jenks Bledshoe didn't like to be disturbed or even to be looked at. "I like to be left alone!" was his reply on the only instance that Wren asked if he needed help finding anything. Jenks had no set schedule for coming into the library. There were several months during the summer when he'd disappeared, then one day he was there in his usual overstuffed chair by the floor-to-ceiling windows on the second floor that caught a glimpse of the blue Atlantic.

Once when Jenks arrived, Wren saw someone already seated in "his chair." Jenks wandered the aisles, circling back and hovering around the chair until the intruder became uncomfortable enough to leave. Jenks dove for the chair, setting down a worn vinyl satchel, his thermos, and the books he'd already picked up. He read mysteries, disappearing into the pages as if the outside world ceased to exist.

Then there were the self-help people. Sorena Sanchez borrowed every book about men, dating, and marriage that the library had until she requested interlibrary loans for even more books.

Mr. Ebenezer Stein asked for help finding a book about having a gay son, then later one for rekindling a marriage, and a how-to on building wooden sailboats.

Wren had noticed a girl who couldn't be over sixteen pick out books about pregnancy. There was also a woman who borrowed books on infertility and just months later on adoption.

One guy read books about building underground bunkers and survival techniques. He'd never check the books out, but made copious notes on thick yellow note pads. Wren's imagination conjured ideas about serial killers or a new Unabomber until she heard that he was preparing for the end of the world. He'd done the same before Y2K. *Oh, the end of the world, that's all,* she thought, smiling to herself.

Working in a library was similar to bartending or sitting in the confessional box. She'd see library patrons at the Friday film nights or around town and many treated her as if she knew all their secrets, based on the books they read, the ones they hated and the ones they loved.

Wren especially enjoyed when a child carried off a new library card, holding his or her head high as if some rite of passage had just occurred, which was exactly how she saw it. The books the patrons borrowed told their stories for them. Wren wondered how the changing of the library would change the people who came searching for books.

In one year at the Cottage Cove Public Library, she had fallen in love with the community like they were the family she longed for.

There were layers here, stories alive in the patrons who visited the library and stories through the characters of the books. The books breathed love, places, stories, cultures, mysteries, evils, beauty, the divine, the humble . . . everything of life was found here.

Wren sat at the courtesy desk while Jasmine went out to return books. She looked over the schedule for the community rooms but continued to think about Jeremy's workshop and how change might affect them here.

Some time later she glanced at the clock and closed down the desk computer. Over the intercom, Edith had announced several times the genealogy group meeting in one of the community rooms. From her peripheral vision, Wren saw someone approaching the courtesy desk just as she prepared to set out the closed sign on the counter.

"Excuse me?" he said.

Wren looked up to the wide, bleached smile of Jeremy, the workshop guy.

"Ah yes, hello." Wren remembered that he had the evening session still to teach.

"You were in my workshop," he said.

"Yes, I was. Is there something I can do to help you before I leave?" She hoped this would be quick. Charlie hadn't called her at recess, though Missy had sent her a text telling Wren they were safely at her house.

"Actually, I was looking for you." Jeremy leaned on the desk.

"Here I am." She frowned, unsure what was going on.

"Dr. James told me about your summer film project. Very impressive."

"Thank you. Dr. James is too humble, though. He was instrumental in pushing it through, and we've had a lot of help getting it off the ground."

"That's not what I hear. It's that kind of creativity that I was talking about in the workshop this afternoon."

Wren raised her eyebrow but kept her objections to herself.

"What did you think of my talk?" He studied her with his light-brown eyes. He was an attractive guy, but he reminded her of a shrewd car salesman.

"It provided food for thought. I disagreed with some of your projections, but the library does need to keep up with the times."

Jeremy crossed his arms at his chest. "You hated it."

"No," Wren said and knew her voice wasn't convincing as Jeremy laughed.

"I don't expect everyone to like it."

"It appeared that many did."

Jeremy's smile hadn't wavered. "But not you. I love that."

Wren frowned, unsure as to what Jeremy wanted. Did he want a critique of the workshop, a survey of how to improve it, a negative response so that he could address it for his new work-shops?

"So . . . I'll be coming back through next week. I have a workshop in Bangor. Would you like to get a cup of coffee then?"

Wren stared at him. "Why?"

He laughed. "Because that's what single people do to get to know each other. I heard you were single."

"Oh? Oh."

"That's an interesting response." Jeremy laughed again.

"I'm sorry, I thought you meant something about the library . . ."

"We can talk about the library if you want."

"O-kay," Wren said, not sure how to get out of this.

"Great. Can I have your number then, and I'll give you a call?"

"My number?"

"That's right." He talked as if she were a little slow. "So . . . that . . . I can call you and set up a time and place."

Wren stared at him with a straight face. "Considering your commitment to new technologies, don't you think calling is a little old fashioned? Maybe you should text me. Or better yet, Skype."

After a pause, Jeremy's face lit up. "Touché." He grinned. "Might as well give me your e-mail address and Twitter name while you're at it."

Wren shook her head and momentarily considered lying about her number, but she was never good at strategies like that. She grabbed a scrap of paper and scribbled her cell number.

"See you next week, I guess."

"Count on it." Jeremy took the paper and jogged down the stairs before Wren fully comprehended what had just happened. Had she agreed to a date?

8

When Wren pulled up at Missy's house, Charlie and Franklin were in the front yard playing pirates. They ran toward her laughing and chattering as if nothing had happened.

"We need to get home—Grandma Ruth's been alone all day," Wren told Charlie after greeting the boys and hearing their new pirate names.

Charlie raced inside to get his backpack from Franklin's room, while Wren peeked in to thank Missy and ask how Franklin was doing.

"So far, so good," Missy began, but the boys rushed back ending the conversation. "We'll talk at coffee in the morning? And you have a lot to catch me up on."

"You have no idea."

On the drive home, Charlie talked about an upcoming school field trip to a local farm that had wagon rides, a pumpkin patch, and a corn maze. Wren decided to ask him about Franklin later, though she noticed something seemed off, as if he were trying too hard to be cheerful.

She glanced at the clock and again had the impulse to bring up Derek, but with Ruth at home, she needed to wait again. Patience was not her best virtue, and she tried to replace the gnawing itch with a quick prayer. Maybe she should call Derek and confront the situation from that direction. *Prayer, prayer, prayer,* she reminded herself.

Please, God, help me time this just right and not mess it up by being hasty and impatient like I usually am.

They walked into the house and were enveloped in a delicious scent. A large pizza box sat closed on the kitchen counter.

"Perfect timing," Ruth said as she shut her laptop on the kitchen table.

"Yummy . . . Mom never orders pizza," Charlie said, jumping up onto a bar stool. He lifted the lid and breathed in the aroma.

"We get pizza once in a while," Wren protested, her stomach growling at the sight of pepperoni, bacon, and sausage. Half the pizza was plain cheese and the other half rose higher with meat and veggie goodies.

"Only those take-and-bake kind. This is the kind that Randall is always bragging about. Mario's Pizza Shack. It's supposed to be good."

Wren studied Charlie. "I thought you liked the take-and-bake kind."

"Not to be rude, Mom, but not really. You can have the first bite."

Charlie picked up a piece and brought it toward Wren's mouth, a long string of cheese dragging from the box through the air. The cheese stuck to her chin as she took a bite.

"Wow, you win. That's better than take-and-bake. But I'm sure it's more expensive as well."

Ruth handed Wren a paper plate that said *Mario's*. "My cooking skills are hopeless, so I decided to treat you two."

"With the day I've had, this is a treat indeed."

After dinner Charlie went to his room for his nightly violin practice, but instead, she heard the strum of his guitar. Wren did a load of laundry and talked to Ruth about the day, but her attention kept drifting to Charlie and the music he played in his room. Music she hadn't heard before.

She walked down the hallway to where his door was slightly ajar. He sat on the edge of his bed beside his violin with his guitar in his arms. His head moved slightly, bent down toward the instrument, and his eyes were closed as he strummed the lonesome tune. The image captured her. He looked beyond the child that he was, as if he'd transformed into something else altogether. He didn't just get lost in music, it was as if he became music.

The song ended and Charlie switched the guitar for the violin, lifting the bow and touching the strings into the same tune he'd played on the guitar. He paused, gazed up at the ceiling, and then touched his bow down again, bending forward and back as the song spilled out like a soulful cry of something ancient and beautiful.

Wren stepped away, not wanting to spy too long on what seemed such a private moment between her son and his art. Her steps were light down the hall, until she leaned against the wall and felt a cool tear slide down her face.

Ruth called from the living room, something about her reality TV show being on. Wren took a breath and headed that direction.

Ruth sat on the couch, waving Wren toward her and trying to catch her up on the different people who were competing in some kind of around-the-world race. Soon Charlie joined them, and Wren's eyes felt heavy not long into the show, though it wasn't even eight o'clock yet.

During commercials, Ruth talked about her web searches into local florists, table and chair rentals, and housecleaners for the main house. Wren knew she needed to process this information and try again to get the party moved before Barb called again, but everything she needed to do was piling up, and she wasn't doing any of it. Tomorrow was the final film night, so nothing would get done until the weekend. Wren blinked her burning eyes, trying not to nod off in her chair before Charlie's bedtime. She woke to Charlie kissing her good night, and Wren gave up on her usual routine though she hadn't checked Charlie's homework or done their usual reading and prayer time. It was all she could do to make up her bed on the lumpy couch, brush her teeth, and crash.

• • •

"Mom," came Charlie's whisper. Time had passed. She'd been sleeping, and the house was dark and silent. Charlie came toward her, his silhouette backlit from a light in the kitchen.

"What's wrong?" Wren asked, sitting up and kicking off the twisted blankets, suddenly awake. "Did you have a bad dream?"

"No," Charlie said, his voice sounding small as if he were much younger. "I can't sleep."

"Is something wrong?"

Wren turned on the lamp beside the couch. Charlie rubbed his eyes either from sleep or from crying, she couldn't tell. He shrugged his shoulders and said, "I don't know why I can't sleep."

"Maybe you need to tell me something?" The words slipped from her lips and something within her heart prayed, *God, if this is the time, help me with this talk.*

He looked up at her quickly and fidgeted with the hem of his pajama top.

"Something about your cell phone or maybe the flyer?"

He shook his head and stared at his lap.

"Charlie? It's about one of those? Or both?"

He nodded. "The flyer . . ."

Wren took Charlie's arm and gently pulled him to sit beside her. She brushed back hair from her face and saw the red around his eyes. "Where did you get it?"

"From Dad." Charlie looked up at her, waiting for her reaction. Hearing her son say the word *Dad* sent a shockwave through her. Wren suddenly thought she might throw up, even while she was relieved that Charlie was confessing this to her.

"You've been talking to your dad?" she asked, her voice shaking.

"Not really. He saw my name on Facebook and sent me a note."

"On Facebook? How did he find your name on Facebook?"

Charlie bit his bottom lip and that guilty expression returned. "Franklin showed me how to make a Facebook account so we could talk. Then all my friends asked to be my friend. Then I got the note from Dad. He said he'd been looking for us and wanted to talk to us. He gave me his phone number and told me to put it into my cell phone. I said I couldn't use my phone except for an emergency, but he told me to save it if I ever needed to reach him, like for an emergency, and—"

"Slow down," Wren said, trying to contend with the assault of information.

"I would have told you, but he asked me not to say anything 'cuz he wanted to talk to you himself first. He asked for your e-mail and phone number. I hope it's okay that I gave it to him."

"But how did you get the flyer?"

"Dad sent me a link. I printed it off the Internet."

"When did this happen?"

"Um, Monday. No, Tuesday. I wanted to tell you, but I didn't know what to do since he asked me to please wait."

Just a few days—it wasn't as bad as she'd feared. "It's okay, but next time, tell me. So what about the summer music program?"

"He was really excited about finding me. He heard that I'm good at the violin from somebody, I think Aunt Barb or someone."

Wren clenched her teeth together. Her sister was in touch with Derek?

"He lives in this city on an island. He wants me to come there next summer for that music school, and I could stay with him."

Wren detected the excitement in his voice, and it brought a sinking dread through every part of her body.

"We'll see, okay?"

"You aren't mad at me, are you?" His eyes were large and pleading.

"No."

"Are you mad at Dad?"

Wren opened her mouth and closed it. She feared speaking for what might come out. Her impulse was to call Derek now no matter what time it was in Malta and tell him to stay out of their lives forever. How dare he contact Charlie and tell him about the summer program, and worst of all, to ask him to keep it from her. He had abandoned her, he had abandoned Charlie, and now he sweeps in like some great guy ready to make up for it?

"Mom?" Charlie waited for her answer, staring at her face and continuing to play with his shirt hem.

"I'm not happy with how your dad handled this. But it's okay. We'll figure it out."

"I'm sorry," Charlie said, blinking his eyes rapidly but unable to stop the tears from streaming down his cheeks and off the edge of his chin.

"Come here. Really, it's all right. What did you say to me yesterday, everything is going to be okay?" He sniffed and nodded as Wren hugged him tightly. With his body against hers, Wren wished she could hold him close forever and ever. She moved over on the couch for him to lie down beside her.

"We'll work this out," she said, as he rested his head between her shoulder and the crook of her arm. His hair smelled like shampoo, and she marveled at how far his legs stretched down along hers now. No matter what, Wren was going to fight to keep her son safe, especially from a wayward and manipulative father.

The next morning, after dropping Charlie off at school, Wren found a small table in the corner of the Village Brew Coffeehouse. She checked the time on her watch, then spotted

Missy walking through the glass door.

Missy tucked her short, blond hair behind her ears as she wove around the tables. She wore her workout clothes—most likely she was headed to the gym where she taught water aerobics and a Zumba class. Missy's smile turned to concern as she approached.

"Do I look that bad?" Wren asked as Missy pulled out a chair and sat down.

"You don't look *bad*. But I'm guessing not much sleep and something is definitely up."

"More than one something. This week was an invasion. I haven't even been reading. So I need your unbiased, honest advice. I already ordered your coffee, and we're sharing a cinnamon roll."

"This is serious. Cinnamon roll serious."

Wren smiled at that and glanced again at her phone. "I have forty-five minutes till I need to get to work. And we need to talk about Franklin. How's he doing?"

"Franklin is fine for now, but with such little time, let's stick with you. What's happened?"

Wren took a deep breath.

"I had my meeting with Dr. James yesterday."

"That's right—sorry, I forgot with all of Franklin's stuff going on."

"Well, I'm not getting the new position because there's no longer a new position available, and no additional hours either. The library is having some problems. And I have that appointment at the Boston School of Music on the nineteenth with Charlie—oh, that's next week. I totally forgot it's next week." Wren looked up at the ceiling and sighed. "They want a non-refundable deposit if he's accepted into the program."

Missy opened her mouth to respond, but Wren held up her hands.

"There's more."

"Lay it on me then," Missy said, leaning back in her chair.

Wren stared at the table, and then let it all out.

"I already told you about Grandma Ruth's arrival, but not why. She wants a birthday party with my siblings attending."

"Oh. Not good. Where's that cinnamon roll? This might be too much without it."

Wren saw their coffees and cinnamon roll waiting at the bar. As they went to the pickup station, she saw Christine Meyers sitting in a corner, typing on her laptop. Wren knew little about the woman except that she worked at the local paper, and Sue had said Christine and Paul were dat- ing.

"So your grandmother just asked for a party?" Missy asked as she picked up the drinks and followed Wren with the giant cinnamon roll back to their table.

"Yes, and on a side note, I think I'm a man-hater too, but we'll save that for later. I haven't told you the big one."

Missy laughed out loud. "Nice side note. But all right, I'm holding on to my seat."

"Did you know Franklin and Charlie are on Facebook?"

"Oh no. I think that's our fault." Missy's face said that she already knew. "Bill showed Franklin how to open a Facebook account so the two of them could keep in touch while Bill's gone on business. They chat online and play some game on there. I just found out last night that Franklin helped Charlie open an account too. He didn't know he wasn't supposed to, but I should have been watching closer. They're only on the computer when I'm in the room, and I knew they were playing that farm game, but I didn't know about Charlie's account."

Wren knew her friend was genuinely apologetic and she didn't want to make her feel worse, but if not for the Facebook account Derek wouldn't have found Charlie.

"It's a minor issue that he's on it compared to what happened because of it."

"What?" Missy's eyes grew wide and Wren knew she was thinking the usual mom fears—cyber stalker or porn.

"Charlie's dad found him."

"What?" Missy nearly shouted, turning the heads of people at various tables in the room. Her hands flew to Wren's wrists, holding them with a strong grip as if to keep her from flying away.

Wren relayed the discovery on Charlie's cell phone, the flyer, her prayers, and Charlie's late-night confession. The grip on her arms only increased, and Wren nearly smiled at how intently Missy was taking all of it in. Somehow it made her feel slightly better.

"As furious as I am at Derek, it really hurt me that Charlie would keep it from me."

"I'm glad he told you before you asked him about it," Missy said, relaxing her grasp on her arms. "What are you going to do?"

"Confront Derek, I suppose." Wren wove her fingers together and stared into her cappuccino cup. "And my sister as well, which could spark a big enough fight to ruin my grandmother's party. I'm trying to be careful about this, and to pray first."

Missy was silent a few moments. "I can't believe this. And I'm so sorry for our role in it." She glanced at her cell phone. "And it's nearly time for you to go. It sounds like your spiritual life is good."

"Ah, the question." When Wren and Missy met in Bible study, the leader had paired them together. She commissioned the group to be honest with one another, helping to strengthen each other by going deeper, beyond the simple, "How are you?" to ask, "How is your spiritual life?"

"I have a hard time saying that my spiritual

life is good or bad." Wren wished there was a thermometer that gave an accurate reading. "But I've been reading my Bible and praying more. If I wasn't, then I would have lost it and called Derek immediately. Having him out of our life seems best, but is a lousy father better than no father? I don't know. And I guess there's the possibility that he's changed."

"Yes. But it's not right that he told Charlie not to tell you, and that he even told Charlie about the summer music program. He should have contacted you first." Missy wrapped her hands around the coffee cup.

"My thought exactly. But still, I've been praying about it instead of diving in on emotion the way I usually do."

Missy wove her fingers together. "This isn't some Christian platitude. God *will* be with you through all of these challenges with your family. It's not a coincidence that this is happening. Maybe it's time for healing."

Wren bit the inside of her cheek and winced at how sore it already was. "Some wounds don't fully heal. Some families don't ever function as a family. And I honestly don't know how to deal with Derek returning to our lives."

"But God can and will do great things for you and Charlie through this, even if your family is still just as dysfunctional as it is now, and no matter what happens with Derek. But I'm telling you, God's promises offer us shelter through everything life tosses our way. You can find hope in those promises."

"I'm listening. I'm willing to give it a try. It's just, well, how do I let God be with me? Sometimes I hear these things, but I don't fully know how to implement them. I pray, but nothing really happens, or maybe it is happening, and yet I'm not clear that it's Him helping or guiding or whatever He's doing. It's so confusing."

"You keep praying. You keep seeking God throughout your day. This week I've been reading the 27th Psalm. I'm reading it every day for a week. Why don't you do it as well? If you don't read anything other than that, be sure you read that psalm."

Wren didn't tell Missy just how hard it was to read her Bible. She always felt like it was something on her to-do list that she wanted to get through so she could get on to reading something more interesting, like one of the novels in the huge stack on her bedside table. When she'd read the Bible in the last couple of months, Wren fell asleep before she got far.

"Are you going to read Psalm 27? Because I'm going to ask you about it. Details. You might want to memorize it, like I am."

"You deserve a gold star," Wren said, teasing her friend.

"I do, I do deserve a gold star. I don't care how

many other great books you have to read, be sure that you read, study, and yeah, why don't you memorize the chapter while you're at it."

"You should work in a slave labor camp."

"With people like you running around loose in the world we need a few more labor camps." Missy smiled with the lines around her mouth deepening.

They rose to leave, picking up their cups.

"We didn't eat our cinnamon roll," Missy said.

"With all this free therapy, you take it. You're about to burn hundreds of calories in your workout, right?" Wren said.

"This can be my gold star," Missy said, picking it up.

As they walked out onto the sidewalk into the warming sea air, Missy asked, "So you're a man-hater now?"

Wren shrugged. "I think I might be. Whenever there's a cute guy around, I immediately dislike him and look for every fault I can find."

"Is this with all guys, or just good-looking single ones?"

Wren considered a moment. "Good-looking single ones."

"Now that makes sense."

"It does?"

Missy glanced at her phone again. "We'll take that up next time. Let's get together soon—maybe over the weekend?"

"Sure. You can meet Grandma Ruth. I can always use more therapy."

Missy turned and winked at Wren. "We need each other."

9

Wren glanced at the clock on the library wall for the umpteenth time, willing the morning to pass more quickly. Tonight was the final film night in the park, and Wren was excited but distracted, worried about the minor glitches that often arose. Usually most problems were curtailed during her Wednesday night review, but she'd skipped it this week with Ruth's arrival. And then the message from her sister kept replaying in her mind. Barb said that Jack had called, and now they both were waiting for details about the party. Would she please contact one of them by this evening?

Wren wouldn't be able to call Barb with tonight's event, and there weren't any details to give her sister anyway. For once, Barb and Jack would have to wait. Wren knew that wouldn't sit well with either of them, but it was best on many levels. Peace-making pact or not, Wren was going to ask about Barb's connection to Derek, and she wouldn't be able to deal with it until the weekend.

As Wren rounded an aisle, pushing the book

cart, she noticed a middle-aged woman at the courtesy desk glancing around as if she'd been there awhile. Jasmine was supposed to be manning the desk, but was nowhere in sight.

"Can I help you?" Wren said, parking the cart and walking toward the station.

"I hope so." The woman dropped several binders onto the tabletop, sending a file folder and loose papers across the desk and off the edge. "Oh, sorry—I'm such a klutz."

Wren helped pick up the papers with notes and diagrams scribbled across them.

"What is this, astrophysics?" Wren said, handing the papers back. The woman appeared close to her mother's age and wore horned-rimmed glasses and a sunhat. She seemed familiar, but Wren couldn't place her.

"It's for my astronomy class, and my professor gives us equations that an astrophysicist would use."

"That's tough."

"It is. I've just gone back to school. My kids are long grown, and I find that I don't want to go into my late years working at Wal-Mart as a greeter. So I'm finishing my degree."

"That's great. What are you going into?" Wren handed her the papers.

The woman laughed. "Haven't figured out that part yet. Liberal studies right now, but what does that mean?"

"I'm sure you'll figure it out."

"I hope so. When I was eighteen and didn't know what I wanted to be, that seemed okay. But at my age . . . the time is a-ticking as they say. How did you know you wanted to work in a library?"

The question surprised Wren. She didn't usually get asked about her life from the library patrons. "I didn't for a long time. But I love books, so I think it stemmed from there. Maybe think about what you love." Wren shifted from one leg to the other. She wasn't much into giving advice to strangers other than to suggest a book they might enjoy.

"That's a good idea. I need to figure this out soon, but today I need help with a paper I'm writing."

"What's your subject?"

"It's about Peter the Great and his reforms."

"Russian history." Wren turned to the computer on the desk.

"Yes. And all of this has been quite a challenge —I haven't written a research paper in forty years. Ask me to build a volcano or write a report on Wisconsin, I'm a pro. Helped four kids and now two grandkids with those projects."

Wren smiled as she typed on the keys of the computer. She liked this woman, even if she seemed a bit scattered. There was something about people stepping out of their comfort zone, continuing to grow and learn, that she admired even if she wasn't always the best at it herself.

"We have several books that would be helpful," Wren said, turning the computer screen to face the woman.

"Great."

"I'll print them out. We also have a number of e-books that you can access with your library card through the library system."

"Oh, e-books, that's nice. This is so helpful."

The woman studied the printout. Wren thought about the technology workshop and imagined Jeremy saying, "See? The future has arrived."

Jasmine came around the desk and leaned in. "Excuse me, Wren. Dr. James asked if you'd stop by his office when you get a chance."

"Okay, but where were you?" Wren asked her intern.

"I was on my fifteen-minute break."

"Be sure to let me know before you take a break. The desk needs covering at all times."

Jasmine apologized, and Wren assured her it was fine. She headed toward the stairs, but noticed the woman in the hat was still looking at her.

"Are you Wren Evans?"

She stopped. "Yes."

"Oh, I didn't recognize you!" she said, covering her mouth with her hand. "I knew you when you were a little girl. I'm Mrs. Carter. Ima Carter? Your mom and I were friends when we were younger, and I'd come out to Fern House to see all of you on your summer visits. You were just a wee one then."

Wren tried to remember, but she couldn't quite place her.

"I always came with cookies. Your favorites were the chocolate crinkles, if I remember correctly."

"With powdered sugar, I remember now. And you had kids."

"Yes, Ben and Samuel." Ima stood with arms full of her notebooks, gazing at Wren as if she were her long-lost grandchild. "How lovely. And you work here, so you live in town?"

"Yes, for the past year. My son and I are staying out in the caretaker's cottage."

"And your mom, is she here too?"

"No, she's traveling with her husband."

"That's great. Though I was so sorry to hear about your father." Ima put her hand on Wren's arm. Wren never knew what to say when people mentioned her father. Did she thank Ima, or agree that it was sad?

"I was happy they stayed together all those years. Sometimes bad things turn out to be good."

Wren frowned. "What do you mean?"

"The accident, when your dad got hurt."

"Yes, but what do you mean about being glad they stayed together?"

"Well, I . . . um, I just meant that . . . you know

how they were back then." She laughed nervously.

"No, I don't think I know what you mean."

"Oh, well, it was a long time ago." Ima frowned with two light eyebrows forming one, then smiled and shrugged. "But it's so very good to see you. I'd best get my paper done. Perhaps I'll see you again."

Wren hesitated, wanting to ask more, but not sure what to ask. Ima took that as her chance to flee, and Wren found herself staring after the woman, wondering what she'd missed.

"Um, Wren?" Jasmine approached. "This is going to make me sound like an airhead, but did I tell you that Mr. James wanted to see you, or did I just think that in my mind?"

Wren snapped out of her thoughts. "Yes, you did. Thanks for reminding me. I better get down there. And it's Dr. James, not mister."

"Oops, that's right."

Dr. James was on the floor of his office with his legs raised toward the ceiling when Wren walked in.

"I'm down here," he said as if Wren couldn't see him.

"Am I interrupting?"

Dr. James chuckled and rose slowly from the carpeted floor.

"My chiropractor told me to do stretches two to three times a day. When I follow those instructions, I feel much better."

"I'm sure you do. Exercise and stretching make everything better for me—maybe I need to be doing a bit more of that as well. Jasmine said you wished to speak with me?"

Dr. James found his eyeglasses on the desk. He looked oddly vacant without his specs, but he quickly returned to the old Dr. James.

"Yes, indeed, I want to talk to you. We've had a development."

"A development?"

"Indeed. But I must make my way to a luncheon at our illustrious country club. Will you walk with me to my car?"

"Of course. I needed to check on the setup for the film night anyway."

"Let us do that together then. I'd enjoy the walk, and I'm in no hurry to reach my luncheon. It's to honor a member of the country club, and I'm not sure why they find it necessary to honor each other so regularly." Dr. James pulled on his sports jacket and picked up his worn leather satchel. "There is something quite amusing about these events. The pretension could be cut with a knife, and the gossip is tantalizing. If I'd pursued my writing dreams, the attendees would be perfect character sketches for a novel."

Dr. James laughed. He reminded Wren of someone who would have been friends with Tolkien and C. S. Lewis. She pictured him taking long walks in the woods while he smoked a pipe and thought about philosophies and myths.

They exited the library from a side door near Dr. James' office.

Library Park surrounded the east and north sides of the library with the street in front and parking lot bordering its length and width. The back of the grounds spread out over ten acres toward the bay with an access road and parking for day-use visitors along the pebbly shore.

The grounds had been part of the original settlement of the town and were considered a historical site. Wren thought the town council's foresight centuries ago to preserve this land was ingenious and offered the area a rare jewel saved from commercial development.

She and Dr. James chatted about the luncheon as they walked, though Wren hoped they'd soon return to the topic of the "new development."

"Ah, look at the trees, do you see that?" Dr. James paused along the shady walkway and pointed upward. The green leaves in the birch and maple trees provided subtle hints that soon they would turn into a blazing assortment of autumn foliage.

"It's coming," Wren said with a shiver of excitement. The changes in the leaves and the slight scent of winter in the air reminded her of that feeling she had when the first snow or the first holiday carols provided the childlike anticipation of Christmas. Last September, Wren had considered remaining in Cottage Cove forever. There was something magical in the air as autumn burst across the mountains and valleys of New England. Smoke rose from chimneys, the sound of a chain saw cut through the afternoons, and the scent of burning leaves added to the coziness.

"We'll lose some of our usual patrons for a month or so with all the tourists arriving. It's either a time to hibernate or make some money," Dr. James said with his trademark chuckle.

Autumn in Maine was a major event, bringing tourists to the northeast from around the world. Nothing had prepared Wren for that consequence of the season. The narrow country roads became packed with cars and caravans of RVers as the restaurants and B&Bs burst to overflowing.

Locals knew to stock up on groceries, take the longer routes, and call for takeout food with plenty of time before pick up. Wren had gotten caught in the traffic once and learned what roads to avoid after a two-and-a-half-hour drive home from work.

They approached the amphitheater area of the park. Strings of lights had been hung around the sitting area at the beginning of the summer and were kept up all season for the Friday film nights. The area was surrounded by tall pines, oaks, birch, and maples where birds sang and fluttered to the ground enjoying the park as their own playground.

Wren waved toward Brandon and Jason, two

high school seniors who were earning community service credits by setting up the movie screen and being the popcorn and candy vendors during the event. They'd unpacked the movie screen and set up the projector for this evening's showing of *The Princess Bride*.

"Everything looks like it's going well. Thanks, guys," Wren told them.

"You boys have certainly earned your credits on this project," Dr. James said, admiring the equipment.

"We'll miss it after today," Brandon said, flipping back his hair.

"Yeah, we get out of school every Friday for two hours," Jason said, laughing as Brandon socked him in the arm. "And, um, yeah, it's an honor to do something for the community."

Wren and Dr. James laughed as the boys went back to work unloading a white van full of equipment.

"You really created something special for Cottage Cove." Dr. James sighed and gazed at her proudly. She appreciated that Dr. James often acted like an adopted father to her and grandfather to Charlie, and it felt nice to have him proud of her.

"Charlie and I enjoy it. I'm bringing my grandmother tonight." Wren realized she hadn't shared Ruth's arrival with him. It seemed like her grandmother had been there longer than a few days.

"Lovely. She's here for a visit?"

"Yes, it was a surprise, but we're happy to have her."

"I'll look forward to meeting her tonight. Are you disappointed that this will be the last show for the season?"

"Yes. I'm not sure what we'll do with ourselves on Fridays now."

"That brings us back to our interesting development."

"I was wondering when you'd get to that."

"Shall we?" Dr. James pointed to the first row of wooden benches.

They sat down, and Wren waited for Dr. James to continue.

"I'm going to preface this by telling you that I can't make promises, though this appears to be unfolding wonderfully."

"All right."

"I'm also sensitive to the fact that you spearheaded this event, and so I want you to be completely honest about this new idea."

Wren moved to the edge of the bench. "Sure."

"Paul Callahan met with me a few days ago with an idea to consider." Paul Callahan again—she was starting to suspect a conspiracy. "He proposed that we continue the Friday night films."

Wren glanced around at the amphitheater, confused about this being the "interesting development."

"I think our audience might dwindle when it starts snowing," Wren said with a smile.

"Of course, yes, I'm not giving the best presentation. Paul did a much better job. He was supposed to come by, but there was some kind of kitchen crisis this morning at the café." Dr. James chuckled and adjusted his sports jacket.

Wren waited again, feeling compelled to pat him on the back as if he needed to cough the information out. Sometimes it took patience waiting for Dr. James to get to the point.

"Paul believes he can get permission to have films held in the Old Town Theatre. He could include appetizers and desserts from his restaurant. A sort of dinner-and-a-movie night. All profits would go to the library."

Wren had a "Why didn't I think of that?" moment. Her only hesitation was that Paul Callahan had come up with it. "That *is* an interesting development."

"Isn't it? He was inspired by your summer films in the park and wished to see them continue. We ran some preliminary numbers, and even our lowest estimates bring some decent fund-raising dollars to the library. We don't want to oversaturate the community with it. But if we ran something in say January through March . . . what do you think?"

"We could have date-night movies maybe once a month, then some for families. And we could have food that corresponds with our films."

"Yes, yes! So you're on board?"

"I think it's a great idea."

"Excellent. Then I'll have you work with Paul to get it off the ground."

Wren felt her ideas come to a halt. "Paul and I will be working together?"

"Yes. He'll be in charge of the food and funding, and you can do what you did over the summer and coordinate with the theater director, or however you and Paul decide to organize it."

"O-kay," Wren said.

"And this time, you'll get paid for it. Did I forget to mention that? That was another exciting part since our general funds didn't allow that over the summer for your extended hours. You'll be paid for the planning and implementing of it. That will be included in the budget for expenses, separate from our poor struggling library."

"Really? It won't affect the library adversely?"

"Not at all."

"This is amazing—thank you, Dr. James." And just like that, her work problem seemed to be solved. Wren wondered if Missy had prayed about this already.

"Paul will hopefully stop by the library today and discuss it with you further."

"Okay."

"It's ideas like these that can help us save the library. We're far from out of the woods, but I'm hopeful. We're going to have to think in new areas that aren't altogether comfortable for us. Believe me, I'm an old man and the old way of doing things is perfect in my book. But keep that thinking cap of yours going, Wren. We're going to need it."

Dr. James looked at his watch and jumped slightly. "Oh my, it's time I bid you adieu. I will miss the food portion of the luncheon if I don't make my way there. And believe me, that's the only good part of the event."

Wren thanked Dr. James. They said good-bye as the pathway parted directions. Wren took her time walking back toward the library. She was on her lunch anyway and usually this was a favorite time for her to read her latest novel, but instead, she wanted to process this sudden change of events.

As she walked, she thought of her meeting with Missy this morning. Her mind jumped to her late-night prayers and also to the technology work-shop that she'd dismissed so quickly. God might be bringing the pieces together—pieces she'd ignored while asking for Him to work in her life.

Gratitude filled her. And sorrow for how quickly she allowed worry and disappointment to rise up around her. If she'd been given the extended hours, she might have not have been able to do this next film night project; it would have been too many hours away from Charlie. One closed door allowed another to open, and even if Paul was involved, Wren loved the film events better than simply working additional hours at the library. Charlie could even be with her at the film nights.

Did God do that for her? Wren believed He had, and she took the steps back toward the library as time to thank Him. While she was at it, she asked, *And if you could, help me know what to do with Charlie, Derek, and my family.* The prayer brought a strange mix of peace, excitement, and fear because with God, it seemed nothing stayed unshaken when He started to work.

10

That afternoon Paul was waiting at Wren's desk when she returned from the printer with warm copies of the program for film night. He rose from her chair and slid his BlackBerry into his pocket.

Sue walked by with dramatic eyebrows raised, and Wren knew she'd hear about this later.

"Dr. James said he spoke to you?" Paul asked after saying hello.

"He did. Why don't we meet in one of the study rooms?"

"I can't stay. I'm meeting a repairman at the café in about fifteen minutes, but I wanted to stop by and get your response. Dr. James sent me a text that you were onboard. But I didn't want you to think I was taking over your idea."

Wren had a sense of that, but she was trying to see this as God's provision for her—an answer to prayer. She might have asked God to use someone other than Paul to make this all happen, but Missy's question came to her about why she disliked only particular men. She was holding Paul's singleness and attractive personality against him. It was ridiculous, she knew, but it was a definite hurdle that she was having a hard time overcoming. Her past told her to be careful because a guy like Paul couldn't be trusted. But that was based on her former relationships. It was completely unfair to Paul, or Jeremy, or any guy.

"It sounds like a great idea and good for the community." She couldn't get comfortable beneath his searching gaze as if he were studying every thought and reaction.

"Good. If you have concerns, let me know. Here's my business card with my cell phone and e-mail. Dr. James gave me your contact info. Is it okay to e-mail and text you with ideas?"

"Sure."

"If you want, we can announce the plan tonight, maybe bring a sign-up sheet for people who want more information."

Wren nodded. "I'll print one up, and if you don't mind, I'll let you do the announcement."

"Don't like center stage?" Paul said, grinning.

"I avoid it whenever possible," Wren said.

"You do a good job at the opening of every film, but I did detect some stage fright."

"It shows?" Wren remembered from singing performances as a child the importance of not showing fear.

"No, no. It's just something I caught a glimpse of."

Less than a minute after Paul walked away, Sue popped up from behind the cubicle wall.

"He caught a glimpse of stage fright because he was studying your every move."

"You were there the entire time?"

"Yes, and I'd appreciate it if you'd speak a little louder next time. These cubicle walls may be thin, but I could barely hear you."

"I'm going to check on Jasmine now," Wren said, and headed off, shaking her head at Sue.

Charlie approached the car with a bounce in his step. So, he had a good day, she thought. Wren reached across and opened his door.

"Thanks, Mom. How was your day?"

"It was pretty good, how was yours?"

"Good, really good." Charlie closed the door and snapped on his seat belt.

"You and Franklin getting along?"

Charlie hesitated long enough for Wren to glance over at him as they came to the stop sign.

"Well . . . I didn't play with him today."

"Oh."

"I played dodge ball at recess."

"What did Franklin do?"

"He played with a fourth grader—I can't remember his name."

Wren considered that for a moment. The kids usually didn't play with kids younger than they were. "Was he upset that you didn't play with him?"

"I don't think so." Charlie didn't appear at all concerned, and that concerned Wren.

"Why wasn't he?"

Charlie shrugged, and then she detected it—the slight chink in his happiness armor. Wren drove and considered what to say.

"Okay, Charlie, what's going on?"

"Nothing. Can't I have a good day without playing with Franklin?"

"Of course you can. But usually you'd be worried about your friend."

"He's fine. But can I stay the night at Briton's house tonight? He sent a text message to his mom at lunch, and she said I could."

"Briton—which one is he? He has a cell phone that he uses at school?"

"Most of my friends have cell phones. Maybe I can get one that isn't for emergencies?"

"You're ten years old." Wren wondered where this was coming from.

"I know, that's what I mean. Anyway . . . Briton? You remember him, he was in my class last year too."

Wren couldn't place the name. "Do I know his parents? Wait, tonight's the last film in the park."

"He's coming with his parents. Then you could talk together, and I can go home with them."

Wren glanced over again to be sure she'd brought home the right child. Charlie rarely liked staying overnight at people's houses.

"This is pretty sudden. I have a lot on my mind for tonight, details to take care of. We need to run home and get Nana, and I'm missing another person for cleanup."

"What if we help with cleanup?"

Wren gripped the steering wheel. "You've only stayed at Franklin's house—what if you get homesick?"

"I don't get that anymore, Mom. And I always have the code word."

Wren sighed. They'd created the code word in case he ever needed a way out of something. Charlie had an answer for everything today, and she supposed it was good that he was getting more friends, though Wren worried what that would mean for Franklin. But staying the night?

"Have I met Briton's parents?"

"His mom was room mother last year. His dad was a hockey player when he was younger, and now has that store for sports stuff. It's over by Wal-Mart."

Wren remembered the couple now. They were involved in numerous community events and had donated sports equipment to the poorly funded girls' soccer team. She was running out of arguments for keeping him home, though she still toyed with a blanket negative.

"No promises. I need to talk to Briton's mom on the phone and then I want to meet them at the movie."

"Great!"

"That doesn't mean yes."

"Okay," Charlie said, but she knew he was expecting it.

Wren turned her attention back to the road as they turned onto the highway going north. Driving back and forth to and from the cottage several times a day was getting old, but they had to pick up Ruth. Her grandmother hadn't renewed her driver's license after a fender bender a decade or so earlier. She'd said she didn't want to be one of those old drivers everyone was annoyed at because they drove slowly or didn't know how to judge distance enough to stop at the crosswalk line. And at ninety, Wren wouldn't have wanted Ruth out on the road anyway. It wasn't for much longer, she reminded herself.

"Call your nana and tell her we're on our way."

"Okay." Charlie grabbed her phone. "Mom? Did you talk to Dad yet?"

From the corner of her eye, Wren could see Charlie staring at her. Her heart rate raised like a temperature gauge in her chest, but she kept her expression unchanged. "Not yet. Over the weekend probably."

"Okay. I just don't want you to be mad at him."

"We'll talk about that this weekend too."

Forty-five minutes later they hit the drive-through to pick up dinner. Charlie told Ruth that they never ate fast food, and between this and the pizza, maybe Nana should never leave. The hot french fries did taste good, Wren admitted as she grabbed a handful and hopped out of the car in the library parking lot, leaving Ruth and Charlie to eat while she took the programs to the amphitheater and checked on preparations.

Evening was getting shorter now, and the pathway of solar lights had already turned on with the shade of the trees overhead.

Nearly an hour later, people began to arrive. Families, couples young and old, and groups of friends walked from the parking lot to the amphitheater carrying blankets, fold-up chairs, ice chests, and seat cushions. Classical music played over the speakers.

Charlie pulled the fold-up chairs from their carriers and set them up near the front left side of the screen. Then he helped pass out programs to those arriving while Ruth chatted with an elderly couple.

Wren noticed Paul's arrival, curious that Christine Meyers wasn't at his side. He carried a small shoulder ice chest and a blanket. His sister,

Emma, and her small children walked with him, talking and laughing as they came. She wondered why Paul wasn't married. He had to be in his mid- to late thirties, and the family image of him walking with his sister fit him well.

The amphitheater was brimming with people. Wren was happy to see the biggest turnout of the season with more people walking in as it reached start time.

Dr. James and his wife sat in the front. He looked quite grandfatherly in his flannel shirt and bowlers cap.

"Should I begin?" Wren asked him, as they both looked at the time.

"Yes, go right ahead."

Wren waved to get Paul's attention. He rubbed the top of his young nephew's head as he passed him, eliciting a loud "Hey" from the boy.

"I'll just introduce the film, and then pass it over to you," Wren said.

"Works for me."

Wren walked to the front of the blank screen and gave Brandon the signal to lower the music and raise the lights a few degrees.

The audience quieted and turned their attention toward Wren. She had to mentally count backward to calm her nerves, yet her heartbeat was so hard in her chest that Wren feared—like every week—that she might pass out in front of everyone. She smoothed her black vintage lace blouse over her jeans, then unfolded the paper in her hand and took a deep breath.

"Thank you all for coming tonight. Because of you, we've had a great first season of Film Night in the Park."

The audience clapped and a few people whistled, making Wren smile as she glanced around. She caught Ruth and Charlie beaming as they looked at her and the other many smiles turned toward her.

"Tonight we have possibly my favorite film of all time. It's one of the most often-quoted films. If you have not seen it, you are in for a treat, and if you have, try to minimize quoting lines aloud as much as possible, though I understand how hard that can be."

Sporadic laughter broke out among the audience.

"Inconceivable!" someone shouted, raising more laughter and mutterings of the quotes.

"In just a moment, our movie will begin. First released in 1987, the film is based on the book by William Goldman."

Wren glanced at the paper in her hand. Though she remembered the information, it helped her to have it there.

"It was directed by Rob Reiner and stars Peter Falk, a young Fred Savage, Robin Wright before she became Robin Wright Penn, Cary Elwes, Mandy Patinkin, and Andre the Giant, among a diverse and illustrious cast. Billy Crystal is barely distinguishable in his character, but look for him in the third act of the movie. I've included a website and more information on the back of your program about the film. Before we begin, Paul Callahan has an exciting announcement. Paul."

Paul took Wren's place as she walked toward Charlie and Ruth.

"Before my announcement, I believe we all owe a debt of gratitude to Wren Evans for her hard work and creativity this summer in making this weekly event happen."

The audience erupted into applause and cheers, jumping up from their blankets and seats to clap wildly.

"Mom, you got a standing ovation!" Charlie said with pride in his voice. Wren could feel her face flush, and she waved graciously toward the crowd, recognizing dozens of faces smiling and cheering for her.

Ruth laced her arm through Wren's. "Sweetie, I had no idea. I'm so proud of you."

Paul continued as the crowd quieted. "To me, this is one of the best things to happen in Cottage Cove in a long time. And because of that, we're hoping to keep it going instead of having a long winter wait until next summer."

Wren noticed a few people glancing at each other.

"Yes, I'm aware of the coming winter. Wren,

144

Dr. James, and I are working together, exploring the idea. We are looking at a few venues in town, and if everything pulls together, we'll be doing an indoor winter series that will include food and a movie together."

The audience clapped loudly once again.

"We're passing around a clipboard with a sign-up sheet to get more information, so look for it before you leave tonight. If you want to volunteer to help, there's room on the sign-up sheet for that too. Remember, every name on the list will get e-mail updates and be entered into tonight's raffle. You could win a dinner for two at Callahan's—I hear they have great food."

People laughed and Wren marveled at how easily Paul spoke and interacted with the audience. Her heart was still beating overtime after her brief introduction.

"But most importantly, the profits from these events support our local library. And now, enough of me . . . let the movie begin!"

More applause as the lights dropped and the blank screen flickered to life. Wren loved this part, when the crowd silenced and everyone waited for the moment the film began. She liked looking at the faces with their eyes on the screen. The light made their faces glow, their expressions held anticipation, and most everyone was engaged in the moment. She'd noticed this moment on the first summer movie night when she was glancing around the audience. As her gaze swept the amphitheater, her eyes had caught the rows of faces. They were each unique, running the gamut of age and race, yet together they would smile, laugh, lean in intently, jump back, or wipe tears as if they'd all been trained in a choreographed presentation. Wren had spent much of the film time watching the people with a sense of enjoyment and satisfaction that she'd been part of making this happen.

"I'll be right back," Wren whispered to Charlie and Ruth.

"Kettle corn?" Charlie asked, rubbing his hands together.

"Of course."

Wren walked to the back of the amphitheater, behind the bench seats and lawn area where people had spread blankets and set out ice chests.

"I remember the first time I watched this movie," she heard a man tell his boy sitting beside him.

An entire family leaned together to whisper, "As you wish . . ."

Wren would miss these Friday nights beneath the stars, though the idea of the winter films lessened the missing. It had started as a simple idea. Wren and Charlie had gone to a movie in the park while still in Chicago. Before moving to Maine, Wren had been researching how to implement an event at the small suburban town they lived in outside of Chicago, but it wasn't until Cottage Cove that she fully dove into the project. She'd presented the idea to Dr. James, who immediately jumped on it. The amphitheater was the perfect venue. The pieces fell together and, before she knew it, the event was on.

In the rush to launch and keep it going through the summer, Wren hadn't slowed down to fully take it all in. She'd been so busy with the doing that she missed the real point. These people were the point. Community, commonality, family and friends together, love and laughter, giving something to others . . . she'd missed the point of what she'd been doing all summer long.

Wren stood on a rise of grass and studied each section of the amphitheater. She recognized many in the audience, including Sue and her husband, Paul, with his small niece in his lap, numerous library patrons, her pastor and the minister of another church, one of her favorite grocery store clerks, Margaret from the bakery, and the front desk secretary at Charlie's school, as well as several teachers. Dotted among the faces she knew, there were dozens of people she'd yet to meet.

"This is amazing," she whispered to herself, wrapping her arms together at her chest as a shiver ran up her back.

Wren looked up at the stars, and the crowd chuckled as the boy on the screen interrupted his grandfather's fairy tale to say, "What is this? Are you trying to trick me? Where's the sports? Is this a kissing book?"

Wren's heart whispered, "Thank you." And she knew God heard her and understood what she meant.

And in that moment, Wren knew she wanted to do more, to bring more of this to the people in this community. She wanted to help save the library for the patrons who came in, never suspecting that one day the library might actually be closed to them. What this meant, Wren didn't know. So many things were up in the air, including whether they moved to Boston next year or not. But in this moment, a purpose stirred within her that she couldn't deny.

Wren returned to watch the movie with Charlie and Ruth and a bag of kettle corn. Charlie had pulled out drinks from their small ice chest.

At the closing credits, the audience stood and cheered. The lights were raised over the amphitheater as people gathered up their belongings and the summer of films concluded.

"You can come meet Briton's parents now," Charlie said as if he might burst at the seams if he had to wait any longer.

Ruth took Wren's arm before she walked away.

"Let me say it again, I'm so proud of you, my darling," Ruth said. "What an amazing gift to this town."

"Thank you, Grandma," Wren said, surprised at how good it felt to have her grandmother proud of her. She realized that her parents hadn't acted proud of her since childhood, and this warmed her more than it should for someone her age.

"Mom, Mom, come on."

"Duty calls. I'll be right back," Wren said to Ruth.

Briton's parents were folding up seat cushions with their initials printed onto the back. Wren noticed how their belongings—purse, ice chest, seat cushions, and clothing—were all designer brands. They had two other children who helped pick up trash, even the trash from someone who'd been sitting nearby. Charlie and Briton had agreed to help with cleanup as well, but Wren had been contacted by some high school students trying to get their extra credit in community service.

Briton's parents, Tisha and Brian, greeted Wren, and she knew they were all sizing each other up, trying to assess what kind of parents they each were, what kind of social status and moral standing they all possessed. In mere seconds, Wren was forced to decide if Briton's parents were the type of people she'd trust with her son. Their earlier phone call had helped, of course, but face-to-face and intuition were the real tipping points. Wren was getting the same inspection. Once the staying over began, it often went the other way.

Tisha was put together perfectly, friendly and warm. "We're going straight home, and I'll have them in bed soon after. Briton usually goes to bed pretty early. Tomorrow we were going to the salmon festival—if you don't mind, we'd love for Charlie to come with us."

Charlie and Briton leaned in, watching them, and now started jumping up and down nodding and whispering, "Please, please."

"Sure, that would be fine." Wren wanted to say no, but she couldn't find a valid excuse, and it would give her and Ruth more time to plan out the party. She could feel her stomach knotting, and she wished she could hide in the bushes to make a 911 phone call to Missy. Wren suddenly realized that Missy and Franklin hadn't come to the film night.

"I can pick him up when you get back—just give me a call," Wren said to Tisha, the knot in her stomach twisting tightly.

This transition into a more independent Charlie was not going to be easy. She politely chatted while fighting the urge to grab Charlie and run for the car.

"Charlie, I'd like you to call me before bed, okay?" She now saw the value of kids having cell phones, but his emergency one was still in the Subaru. She didn't want Charlie calling his dad without talking to her about it. What if he was in danger and couldn't get to a phone?

"Sure, Mom." Charlie then whispered, "And if I say *stomach ache,* then you know what I mean."

Wren nodded at their code word.

Tisha stood nearby taking in the scene. "I'll remind him. Has he stayed anywhere else overnight?"

"Just with his friend Franklin. Charlie doesn't even have grandparents that he visits, so this is all pretty new to both of us."

Tisha smiled and nodded as if she understood. "It'll be harder on you, I'm sure. Briton hasn't stayed with anyone other than family yet." That Tisha and Brian sounded protective as well brought Wren some comfort. "Next month he might be attending his first slumber party, so I'll be in your shoes soon enough."

Wren smiled, glancing at the boys who acted like they were going to Disneyland. At least Tisha understood how Wren felt, though of course she could just be a very good serial killer.

"If you have any concerns whatsoever, call any time, no matter how late."

"I might take you up on that."

Wren watched her little boy walk away without a backward glance. He was off to his own activity, with his own friend and his own plan. Wren knew she'd be watching this dynamic in different scenarios for the rest of her life, but oh how she wished to hold on tight and never let him go.

That night Wren slept in Charlie's bed. She

enjoyed the break from the couch, but mostly she just missed her son being safely under her roof. As she curled on her side with the phone beside her and pulled up his sailboat bedspread, Wren gazed up at Charlie's glow-in-the-dark stars. A few tears fell as she restlessly drifted off to sleep.

In the night, Wren tossed and turned in Charlie's bed. Finally, she wrapped her robe around her, slipped her feet into her slippers, and went toward the kitchen for some water. On impulse, she made a turn toward the nook where she opened her laptop. The clock read 3:23 a.m.

Wren wanted to pour out some initial thoughts onto the page, words to either write or say when she spoke with Derek.

If this were just about her, she could leave Derek Holmes to the past where he belonged. But whether he'd abandoned them or not, Derek would always be Charlie's father.

After Wren wrote some initial thoughts, she popped open her inbox. An e-mail address caught her attention. The subject line read, "Long Time."

"No." Wren stared at the name in the e-mail address; her hand froze on the mouse, and she quickly shut the laptop.

So he beat her to it. Derek had written her.

After a long hesitation to the tune of the refrigerator humming and the living room clock ticking so loudly Wren heard it in the breakfast nook, she opened the laptop again. She moved the cursor over to the e-mail and clicked on it to load.

Wren,

It is my hope that this reaches you and finds you and our son well.

"Our son?" Wren muttered bitterly. She pushed away from the desk. After all these years, one sentence from Derek and she was fuming. She worked her chair back toward the glowing screen.

Wren,

It is my hope that this reaches you and finds you and our son well.

It's taken me awhile to find you, but then you never liked techie things so of course you wouldn't be on the usual social media sites. I found Charlie and received your contact info from him—in retrospect, I'm sure that won't make you happy, and I apologize for not contacting you first. Don't be upset at him. I asked him not to tell you that I'd written him. I wanted to tell you that myself.

I've written you a hundred letters over the years, but haven't sent them. I've picked up the phone to call you, but I didn't have the number. To be honest, I didn't try very hard either. It's been too long and as time passed, it became harder.

When I left you and Charlie I believed it was for a short time, just to get my head around the fact that I was really a father. I never wanted to be a bad father, my own was such a monster, as you know. But I kept making bad decisions that took me further away. When I married Rene, she had a jealous nature and became angry when I talked about seeing Charlie. She couldn't have children. We were married for six years and recently divorced.

I'm not making excuses for myself. I left you and my son. I know that, and I can only ask that you forgive me someday.

I will be coming back to the States over the holidays. I hear that you are now in Maine. I don't want to cause problems, but I hope to slowly get to know Charlie and to be the father I should have been all this time. There's also an incredible music program here in Malta that I'd like to discuss with you.

Wren couldn't believe what she was reading. For years, she had tried to prepare herself for something like this, and when it hadn't happened, she pictured the eventual day when Charlie was an adult and wished to seek out his father. But that was a long way off. Wren had become comfortable in their lives without Derek, and out of the blue, he wanted to be part of Charlie's life.

Wren covered her mouth with her hand as she read further.

Perhaps there is hope for you and me as well.

"What?" she said aloud, then looked around in the dark, knowing Ruth wouldn't wake. *Is he insane?*

I know that sounds crazy after everything, but miracles sometimes happen. Charlie said that you haven't remarried and aren't dat-ing anyone. My memories of our two years together are still vivid, and I regret my fears that destroyed us.

I have always loved you, and hope you forgive me.

Please do respond, even if you want to cuss me out, as I deserve.

Derek

Wren closed her laptop and laid her forehead on top of it. What was she going to do? She padded back to Charlie's bed where her son's presence was so vivid and near.

Wren wondered where Derek was, right at this moment. Did he walk some ancient street in Malta, sit at an outdoor café drinking an espresso, or did he work somewhere . . . she had no clue about his life. But it seemed unfair. She'd always wanted to explore Europe, and it felt as if he'd hijacked her dream.

How often had he thought about Charlie over the years? Did he wonder what he looked like or how big he'd grown? She couldn't understand how anyone could walk away from their own son—let alone this child, this gift of a boy. It made Wren both angry and brokenhearted for Charlie. He only rarely asked about Derek, but she had wondered how he felt to be on his little league team with the other dads helping, cheering, and tossing balls back and forth to their sons. At back-to-school night, did Charlie wish for two parents to meet his teacher and look at his schoolwork? Derek had never even heard Charlie play his violin.

Wren stared at the stars glowing on Charlie's ceiling and breathed in the scent of him. It didn't seem fair that Derek could walk away and then show up now that he was divorced and ready to be a father. Wren wanted to slam the door in his face and let him suffer for his decisions. But one question remained—what was best for Charlie?

11

Wren jumped awake as Charlie's robot alarm clock sprang into action, beeping and moving its arms. She gazed around from the perspective he had every morning. Her phone rested on his bedside table, but he hadn't called after his one good night call. He'd survived it, and somehow Wren had too.

Over coffee with Ruth, Wren announced, "Okay, let's plan your party."

"Great," Ruth said with a gleam in her eye. She disappeared down the hall and returned with a binder that she opened up as if she were a party planner. They spent the morning writing out to-dos, making a guest list, and talking over ideas. After several calls to other caterers, Wren couldn't find any reason not to have Paul's restaurant take care of the event.

"And you're certain you want the party here?" Wren asked, giving it one more try.

"Yes, but perhaps we should have it in the front area of the main house instead of the back garden. I love it there, but the fence around the cottage and the sea trail so close by make it both inconvenient and unsafe."

Wren agreed, and at least this was an improvement. The party wouldn't be in the exact location of the reunion disaster. In her calendar, Wren wrote the date for the party.

"Oh no," she said, staring at her calendar.

"What is it?"

"I don't know why I keep forgetting the date. Charlie and I have an appointment next Friday in Boston to tour a music school I'm trying to get him into."

"Oh, lovely."

"We've had it planned for months, but I lost track of the weeks."

"It happens to the best of us. And you were invaded by a little old lady." Ruth was writing notes in her binder at the kitchen table, and Wren smiled at her grandmother's constant positive attitude. The morning sun shone through the curtains warming the room, and in that light, Ruth's soft wrinkles, age spots, and veins that marked her ninety years appeared more evident in her hands, neck, and face. There was something beautiful and haunting about it. Wren was reminded of time's passage and that she'd one day look back on this moment at the table with fondness and longing.

"Why don't you come with us when we go? If you stay here, you'll be stuck in the house again."

"I don't mind, honey. Traveling up here about did me in. I'd like to stay and keep the party plans going. Plus I need to reconnect with some old friends before I invite them to my party."

Wren nodded, hoping it was really all right. The music school was selective in making their appointments for potential students, and she didn't want to harm Charlie's chances.

Ruth went to shower and Wren dialed Barb's number while asking God to help her say the right words. She quickly prayed that she'd know the difference between peacemaking and cowardice, righteous indignation and truthful confrontation. If her sister had really been talking to Derek, it was a terrible betrayal, and she knew this could end with them never speaking again.

Barb's voice mail came on and Wren left a message about the party plans, ending with, "And I need to talk to you about something else. Call me back."

So, God, did you just save me from a disastrous phone call?

A number she didn't recognize appeared on the screen as her phone rang.

"Hello?" Wren said, wondering if it might be Barb on another line or even that Jeremy guy.

"Wren?"

The voice was familiar—her brother, Jack. At first Wren couldn't respond.

"Hello, Jack."

"Hello."

She hadn't spoken to him in several years. She knew his voice like she knew Charlie's, yet Wren

159

knew nothing about his life or where to begin. Jack was a stranger.

Wren cleared her throat. "So you heard Grandma is here, and about her birthday?"

"Yes. We're planning to come up, just for the weekend and maybe a few days before."

"Okay. Would you and . . . your wife like to stay at the main house or will you stay in town?"

"I think the house, but we don't want to be an inconvenience."

We. My little brother uses "we" now?

"Ruth is having it cleaned and set up for the party either way."

"Then we'll stay there."

"Okay, and Barb is bringing her RV." If they were like normal siblings, that line might make them laugh and joke about their sister staying in something with wheels, since they knew each other's quirks and idiosyncrasies. But now it was just a statement that neither responded to.

"We want to cover the party," Jack said.

Wren thought of her meager savings. She had been debating what to do about that. She was saving for her and Charlie's move back to Boston, but it was wrong for Ruth to pay for her own birthday party.

"We can split it between the three of us," Wren said.

"I'll discuss it with Grandma, but I want to do this for her."

160

"You might want to hear what kind of party she's planning." Wren chuckled a little at that, but Jack remained silent.

"Is Grandma there?"

"She's in the shower. I'll have her call you."

"Thanks. If you need anything, call me. I'll be more available. Sorry I haven't called before now."

"It's okay," Wren said, and then wished she hadn't. It wasn't okay with her. For years she'd felt angry about his withdrawal, especially after she had Charlie. The kid didn't have a dad; it would have been nice for him to have an uncle. She had just let Jack off the hook as if it had been nothing.

They ended the conversation, and Wren decided to take a quick run to clear her head. She hadn't been running in a month. As she walked along the gravel road, stretching her legs, she stopped at the gate to the main house. It was here that her mother said the words that had haunted her for years, perhaps even continued to haunt her.

"Why weren't you watching your brother? If something happened to him, it's your fault."

Wren heard her mother's voice as if she were standing there at that moment. Jack had disappeared for two full nights, and when he returned he acted differently than the eight-year-old boy he'd been. Every relationship in the family was different after that weekend, and she and Jack

161

grew apart, though it was years until they were fully estranged. Time and their father's failing health strained their affection until Jack withdrew completely. She'd once written him a letter asking him to forgive her for not watching him better that day. He never responded. Wren tried to tell herself that she'd done her part in trying to mend their relationship. What more could she do?

Wren started running down the gravel road. She wished she could run from the past, really put it behind her and never look back. She'd been running from that weekend all her life. But now it was catching up with her.

The next day Wren, Charlie, and Ruth attended church at the historic white building near the center of town. The inside shone with high beams and stained glass that filled the sanctuary with light. Wren had attended churches from many denominations, but she'd chosen this one because Charlie loved their children's program and Wren enjoyed the teaching, hymns, and the church's social and community involvement.

After church Wren found a text from Missy on her phone asking if she and Franklin could drop by in the afternoon. They'd gone to the earlier church service and wanted to bring over some homemade bread after going on a baking rampage the night before. Missy often did projects like that when she was missing her husband. Once she'd repainted her bathroom, hall, and mud-room in one weekend.

"Hello, Miss Wren!" Franklin said as he burst into the house several hours later. His voice carried through the room, reminding Wren of a radio announcer. He carried in a loaf of bread that made Wren's mouth water at the scent of it.

"Thank you, Franklin. You can follow the music to find Charlie—I think he's in his room."

"Cool!" Franklin said and ran down the hall like a small herd of elephants.

"I think my son was given the gift of noise," Missy said with a laugh as she walked into the kitchen. "I've told him he could do television, radio, or sports announcing. Or better yet, he should get a job with DreamWorks doing the voices for their animations."

"He'd love that," Wren said as she put on a kettle to make tea, then pulled out a cutting board to slice the bread.

"I'm he-e-ere!" Franklin's voice echoed down the hall from Charlie's room.

"He's going to break Charlie's ear drums," Missy said with a sigh. Wren often wondered what it would be like if the tables were turned. Franklin was certainly a gifted, yet challenging child. Wren tried to be supportive and never allow Franklin to annoy her as he surely did others.

Ruth came around the corner, rubbing her eyes.

"I'm so sorry," Missy said. "Did Franklin

wake you up? Of course he did."

"Sorry, Grandma, I forgot you were taking a nap."

"No, no, I was awake already and telling myself it was time to get up. You have the most comfortable bed I've ever slept in."

Wren smiled. "It has a feather top on the mattress. Grandma, this is my friend Missy."

They exchanged greetings as Wren pulled down teacups for each of them.

Wren had hoped to talk to Missy privately at some point. For some reason, she wasn't ready to tell Ruth about Derek's e-mail, but she was dying to tell Missy about it.

Missy turned to Ruth. "Wren told me about your party. I've made centerpieces for several weddings in town and I'd love to provide them for your party—that is, if you're looking for something like that."

"That would be lovely," Ruth said.

"If you give me your e-mail address, I'll send you some photos of what I've done and we can work together to create the perfect look for your party."

"This is very exciting. Wren, I didn't know you had such a talented friend." Ruth wrote down her e-mail address on a sticky note and gave it to Missy.

"She never fails to surprise me," Wren said as she dropped several tea bags into her favorite bone china teapot.

"Mom! He broke my statue." Charlie stood in the doorway, holding pieces of the small Mozart statue he'd bought at a museum in Chicago. Wren had always thought it was an odd treasure for a boy, but Charlie loved it. He'd put hats on it, and sometimes even took Mozart on car trips with them. For a while he'd played only Mozart after getting it. The statue was one of his most treasured possessions.

"Oh no," Wren muttered, taking the pieces from Charlie's hands. It wasn't just broken but shattered.

"Franklin!" Missy called, and a sheepish Frank- lin entered the room. "What did you do?"

"I didn't mean to. I'm sorry. Charlie, I really didn't mean to."

"You stepped on it on purpose!"

"I was just going to pretend to step on it, and then I accidentally did."

Wren looked at the crestfallen faces of both boys and didn't know what to say.

"Can we fix it?" Charlie asked in a quiet voice with his eyes blinking.

Ruth leaned toward it from her perch at the counter. "It sure doesn't look like it."

Charlie took the pieces and walked back down the hall, closing his door soundly behind him.

"Wren, I'm so sorry," Missy said. "Franklin, go apologize, right now. That was his special statue."

Wren sighed. They had no idea just how special it was to Charlie.

"I really didn't mean to," Franklin told his mother.

"You need to tell him that."

"It's probably better if we give Charlie a little time first," Wren suggested.

The boy had his head bent down. "Why do I always mess everything up?" he shouted and ran for the front door. "Everybody hates me!"

"I'm sorry, Wren. Is there a place we can buy a new one?" Missy appeared nearly as upset as Franklin.

"I don't know. We bought it years ago, and these things just happen."

"I'll just take Franklin home for now. Sorry to ruin our afternoon."

"It's all right. Let me walk you out."

Wren and Missy left the house in silence. Franklin was sitting in the car with his head bowed toward his lap and his hands over his head.

When Missy opened the car door, Wren leaned in.

"Franklin?" He tightened the hold over his head. "I want you to know that Charlie and I will never hate you. We love you very much. Charlie is upset, but it'll be okay."

Franklin didn't respond.

"I'll call you later," Wren said to Missy, giving her a tight hug.

"Thanks, and sorry."

Wren watched them drive away while trying to figure out what to say to Charlie.

When she walked back inside, Ruth was pouring hot water into the tea pot. "That little guy needs some discipline. He's a bit of a ruffian."

"He doesn't mean to be. He has a disorder."

"I hear that so much, but so many children are medicated or their bad behavior is excused by some disorder or another."

Wren sighed and leaned on the counter.

"Franklin really is a great kid, and his disorder is real. I've been around him enough to see how he struggles with it. I don't know what will happen to him."

Charlie was in bed with the covers over his head.

Wren sat beside him. She didn't know what to say or how to begin. If only her favorite literature included more mothers and had more parenting issues to resolve instead of just relationship turmoil. Jane Austen didn't become a mother, nor did many of the great classic female writers.

"I don't want to be Franklin's friend anymore." Charlie's voice was muffled under the covers, but Wren knew his crying voice.

Charlie had a sensitive heart. She always feared for his feelings and emotions. She'd been given the same tenderness toward people, and even at thirty-five, Wren hadn't decided if it was a curse or a blessing. Her sister, Barbara, certainly didn't suffer from it. As a child, Wren had her feelings hurt constantly. Her dad said she wore her feelings on the outside where everything pricked and poked at them. Wren got the distinct impression that this was a bad thing, so she tried stuffing them inside, not letting them be the basis for her life.

But Wren could also understand the feelings of others pretty easily. She could walk a mile in other people's shoes with little effort. Charlie was the same way. She'd tried to prepare him for the world outside, but she also didn't want him to lose his tender heart.

"People all have their strengths and weaknesses," she'd told him. "Your strength is that you understand people and their feelings very easily. But most people can't do that very well. They're good at other things. So if they don't understand you and aren't sensitive in the way that you are, it's not because they are bad, or they don't care about you, it's because they just don't think that way."

Charlie took these chats in like water disappearing into the sand. Wren wondered how much really stuck with him. Franklin was a hundred times Charlie's sensitivity and emotional instability. Wren wondered how to explain it since she didn't quite understand it herself.

She opted not to say anything right now. No

wise motherly words were coming anyway.

"I told him not to play with my statue. I told him that last time he was here too. He kept asking to hold it, and I knew he might break it so I told him no. Then he comes in and yells in my ear while I'm playing my violin."

"That's partly my fault. I told him he could surprise you."

"But you didn't tell him to shout in my ear. He snuck up and just yelled. My ear still hurts. He does stuff like this all the time. So then he starts joking around that he's going to drop my statue. I told him to put it down. So he put it on the ground and acted like he was going to step on it. Then he fell right on it."

"Oh," Wren muttered.

"Why does he always have to act like that? It seems like he's getting worse and worse. Do I have to be his friend, Mom? Do I?"

Charlie popped through the covers after that last line, searching her face for a response.

"No, you don't." Wren was trying for something to say.

"Good," Charlie said, sitting up in bed.

"But, Charlie. Franklin has been your friend for a year now. He was your first friend in Cottage Cove. I know it's hard, but you two also have a lot of fun sometimes."

"Not lately. And I just don't know how I'll get over this one."

Wren pursed her lips together to keep her smile at bay after that last line.

"Before you make a definite decision, take some time to really think about this. And . . . pray about it."

Charlie sighed and crossed his arms at his chest. "Why did you have to say the pray part?"

"Because you'd say that to me, and it's true."

"What if God wants me to be his friend?"

"Do you think He does?"

Charlie shrugged his shoulders.

"What about you? Do you really want to stop being his friend?"

He slid down in the bed, plopping his head on his pillow, and stared at the bookshelf on the side of his bed Mozart had inhabited.

"Do you want to think more about it?"

Charlie nodded.

"Okay. I'm going to warm up Miss Missy's homemade bread. You can help or come in a little bit."

"I'll come in a little bit if that's okay."

"Sure."

The new week began. Charlie played dodge ball at recess and didn't talk to Franklin at school. Wren and Missy's conversations had an underlying strain, especially when Wren mentioned that she'd have Charlie stay at the afterschool program that week on the days he usually went to their house. The four of them needed to find some solutions and talk it out. Usually Wren allowed friendships to fade when conflict or tension rose, but Missy's friendship and their spiritual connection prompted her to hang on to this one. It was time to stop running away, especially from things that meant something to her.

Wren saw the library differently as well. She noticed the patrons and her coworkers even more, and the sense of urgency to keep the library alive continued to grow in her.

Despite Ruth's assurances that she was fine at the house all day with plenty of party planning, her Sudoku book, her mah-jongg computer game, and her friends to e-mail, Wren tried to think of ways she could help Ruth get out more. She was relieved when Ruth informed her that several old church friends would pick her up to attend a senior luncheon.

On Wednesday afternoon, Dr. James gave Wren a few hours away from the upstairs courtesy desk to meet with Paul Callahan. Wren arrived five minutes early, glancing around the Village Brew, but no Paul. Her mom had tried teaching Wren to make an entrance by arriving a few minutes late to any social event. Wren found it impossible. It was in her DNA to arrive at least five minutes early everywhere.

She wondered if she should order her drink or wait for him, but if she waited he might think she expected him to get hers. Should she buy his since this was about a library event and she was the representative? These were the details that kept her from dating. If there was a rulebook to follow, that everyone knew and attended to, she could handle these situations better. Something along the lines of:

The Idiot's Guide to Meeting
with the Opposite Sex:
Business and Dating Situations

Wren was in line when Paul came up behind her. She always forgot how tall he was. He was smiling and smelling even better than the scent of coffee. Her instant defense shot up, though this time she was aware that it was from her past and had little to do with Paul. *Don't be a man-hater,* she told herself.

"What would you like?" Paul asked.

"I can get yours—I'll expense it at work."

"No, I'll treat."

"A small mocha please." Wren wondered if it sounded cheap to say she'd get reimbursed for two coffees and regretted saying it.

Paul looked up at the chalk-written menu on the wall and ordered her drink and a large Americano for him. Wren tried to soothe her ridiculous nerves. He was dating someone after all.

The same corner table was open where she and Missy had met the week before, and Wren wished they'd picked a different meeting place that wasn't so public. The last thing she wished for were rumors to spread about her and Paul. With all the quaint charm of a small town, the other side of the coin was the frivolous gossip.

Wren kept a stiff professional demeanor as she carried her satchel and laptop to the table. Paul said hello to several people along the way, then pulled out an electronic device that she hadn't noticed he carried. He set it on the table and opened up a file as Wren turned on her computer.

"First, let me reiterate that this is still your project."

"It's okay. I think it's a great idea. It'll have a different feel, being inside and offering food from your café, but it serves the same purpose for the community."

"Yes, exactly. We could have themes." Paul opened a file with a graph of his thoughts plotted out. "The themes could coincide with the library themes. For example, you have Women in Literature one month, we would match it up with coordinating movies. Don't you choose the monthly themes?"

"Usually, yes." Wren stared at his ideas on the screen. Did this man share her brain? It was starting to freak her out.

"What movies do you have in mind?" she asked, taking a sip of her mocha.

"I don't know. A few of those classic, slow,

no-action movies with a lot of tea, painting, and ballroom dancing. Those are always a hit with the ladies."

"Those movies have much more going on than that."

Paul smiled with a sly twinkle in his eye. "Yeah, I know. My sister is trying to make me appreciate the Victorian era, but I have to admit I keep falling asleep before I find out who ends up with whom and what nasty woman will get her due. My sister calls me a Neanderthal."

Wren laughed, then added, "I'll keep my thoughts to myself."

"Oh, I see, another one. Typical woman."

"Typical man."

"A few typical man movies would be nice. I also have a list of ideas that should please everyone."

"What are they?"

"*Sleepless in Seattle*—both men and women can appreciate or at least stomach that romantic com-edy. *WALL-E* for the kids. *Casablanca* because it's the best old classic of all time. In the newer classics category, I was thinking *Apocalypse Now* and *The Godfather*."

"We have a number of similar ideas, except your newer 'classics' as you call them—they aren't exactly date-night or family fodder."

Paul grinned wickedly. "We should have a few guy movie nights. Can't discriminate against our male audience."

"I guess that's fair. Maybe we can find some less violent guy films?"

"Then it's not really a guy movie, is it?"

Wren laughed. "I suppose not. I'll see what I can come up with."

"You know, something to think about long term. I've had this idea to start a local film festival, but it seemed too large of an undertaking. If our project goes well, would you be interested in helping to create that too?"

"A film festival? What kind of films?"

"I have a friend in a small town in California who started a fest there. They have local film students and amateur filmmakers submit their work for the festival. I've been talking with him about how they got it off the ground."

Wren's thoughts hopped to her plan to move to Boston. There was nothing definite, so she didn't bring it up.

"It couldn't hurt to do some research on it. I have a number of people who come into the library to check out books about filmmaking. I'd thought about trying to put on a literary festival in the summer, but as you said, it seemed like too large of an undertaking right now."

Paul seemed to consider that. "I'm a film guy first and foremost, but I appreciate a good book. Maybe we could make it a film and literary festival."

"Interesting."

Images of the event started rolling through her thoughts: outdoor tents with authors doing readings, stacks of books, flower petals floating in the fountain, films in the amphitheater, evening readings and bonfires, an opening and closing gala event. They could get local products for the food and decorating, children's authors could read on the lawn with maybe a picnic theme . . .

"Hello?" Paul said.

"I love this idea."

"Great, so first we tackle the winter movies. If you want to come with me this evening, I'm meeting the theater curator to discuss the Friday film nights."

"That would be the perfect location."

"I agree. They can be quite protective since the restoration, however, so we'll see. We need the approval of the board as well."

"Okay, but I can't come tonight. My grandmother is visiting and I really need to spend time with her. I've been so busy since she got here."

"That's right, she and I met. I believe we'll be catering her birthday party."

"Looks that way."

Paul leaned back and took a long sip of his drink. "So what do you love most about your job?"

"My job?" Wren's guard popped up at the personal question.

"Yeah, is it the books? You're a big reader, right?"

Wren wasn't sure how personal to get, and her gauge felt broken around Paul. "I am. The books are a big part of it, but I also really like the people."

"The people? It's such a quiet environment."

"The people are loud if you pay attention. Look around next time you're there. See what people are reading, what their kids are excited to take home, how long they're in there, how many books they take or how few. You discover a lot about people."

"Interesting. I thought people worked in the library to hide away from the world."

Wren gazed at her coffee lid. "I guess I do a little. But books were why I went this direction. I was a literature major and felt comfortable with dead British writers as my closest confidants."

"That's what I imagined." He studied her thoughtfully.

Wren tried to ignore what his clear blue eyes were doing to her stomach. "I've worked in a lot of libraries, but it's only since coming to Cottage Cove that I've really started to see the people. It's my favorite part of the job now. I love it when someone comes back and tells me how much they enjoyed a book I recommended or that something helped them through a hard time or get a good grade on a paper."

"Sounds rewarding."

"I'm sure your dual careers are rewarding as

well." Wren was more than ready to get the topic away from her.

"They are."

"Which do you enjoy more—the restaurant or the sea?"

Paul sighed as he considered the question. "They offer different rewards. My father didn't want me to a chef—he said only women liked to cook. But I didn't want to follow in the family fishing business. Once I got over myself, I found there's something to be said about heritage and continuing what my grandfather started. I love the sea, and it's rewarding to keep my guys working and knowing that supports their families. And the restaurant was my dream, so I suppose I get the best of both worlds, though they keep me busy and somewhat stressed out."

"And so you add a few things to your plate, like winter movie nights and a film festival."

"Well, I have great employees. It took time to get to that place. And these ideas are fun for me. I can also get to know you in the meantime, since you usually won't give me the time of day."

Wren bit her lip as Paul chuckled. Was he teasing her, or serious?

"If I came in and asked for help with a book, I'm sure you'd be much more friendly."

"Have I really been that rude?"

"Rude, no? You're always the picture of polite-ness."

Wren couldn't help but laugh at herself. She hadn't realized she'd been so transparent.

"If I did come in, what would you recommend for me? I bet you think you can nail people's preferences pretty fast."

"It is a gift," she said with mock seriousness. "Next time you are in, I'll have a few books set aside."

"What if I don't like what you pick?"

"You will. I think I can figure out your favorite books."

"I doubt it."

Wren knew she had an unfair head start after overhearing Paul and Dr. James talking about Thoreau and Hemingway.

"You doubt my literary skills?"

"I doubt your skills in reading me. My guess is that you've been wrong about me from the second you met me."

Wren denied it, but inwardly she had to consider that he might be right.

"I'll give you ten selections to try to discover my favorite."

"You have a specific book in mind?"

"Yes, and if you guess the author, who wrote a number of books—hint, hint—then that will be close enough."

"People do tend to surprise me. But I accept the challenge."

"What will we wager?"

Wren shrugged. "I generally don't wager."

"Loser buys coffee next time we meet?"

Paul's phone made a slight rumble. He glanced down, tapped a button, and slid it into his pocket. Wren wondered if it was Christine Meyers. A sudden tension came over her. It felt as if they'd come close to crossing a line from being professional to something else. She didn't know what to think.

Wren and Charlie arrived home late afternoon with groceries stuffed in the back of the Subaru. Charlie raced toward the house with two grocery bags in his arms as Wren was still getting out of the car.

"Mom!" Charlie's voice called from the house but she couldn't see him. She raced toward the door.

"Mom!"

"What is it?"

Charlie was staring at the doormat with the grocery bags on the ground beside him. She stepped forward, wondering what had stopped him. There weren't usually snakes or reptiles hanging around this time of year.

"Look."

Sitting on the doorstep was a handmade statue and a card underneath. Wren recognized the attempt at Mozart in the hair and nose. Charlie bent down and carefully picked it up. He turned it over one way and then another.

"That was nice," Wren said, glancing at Charlie to see how he was taking the peace offering. "Do you want to open the note?"

Charlie nodded and opened the paper. He passed the paper to Wren. The only words written on the page were: *I'm sorry.*

Wren held it against her chest, thinking of Franklin writing that out, then setting it on the doormat. It broke her heart to think of the pain he was in.

"I want to tell him it's okay. But I don't know what to say. Do I have to go to school tomorrow?"

"Yes, you do."

Charlie turned the clay statue over in his hands again. Then he smiled. "It's kind of ugly, huh?"

Wren laughed. "Yes, it is. But it was also very nice."

"Yeah."

Ruth appeared at the door and together they unloaded groceries and put them away. Wren stopped by Charlie's room to give him a signed permission slip for the pumpkin patch. Before she left the room, she spotted Franklin's Mozart statue on the shelf beside Charlie's bed, right where the old one had been.

That night as Wren made spaghetti and Charlie played his violin for Ruth, she went back over her conversation with Paul. She didn't want any problems with Christine—even though she didn't know the woman—and she hoped Paul was the decent guy that everyone said he was. She'd been out of the dating world for so long that she didn't trust her ability to detect a player, a nice guy, or a guy who was actually interested in her. She would have thought Paul was showing interest, but he had a girlfriend—so perhaps it was just normal friendliness. Wren sighed. Being a man-hater seemed so much easier.

Her history of dating was enough to turn anyone away from men for good. After Derek left, she had many years of one focus only—her new baby.

As time passed, her friends were compelled to "get her back out there" and set her up with every nice guy they knew. At first, she was adamant about not dating, that she wasn't ready, but with the passage of time her excuses no longer kept her helpful friends at bay.

For a time, Fred from a Chicago accounting firm called regularly and sent text messages despite the fact that Wren came up with some excuse or another as to why she couldn't meet him. She was slow at responding, so he'd text again and again. Then he started coming into the library where she worked, though it was restricted to the students at the private university. Security became involved, only a slight scuffle that embarrassed Wren but didn't seem to bother Fred, and still he persisted. Finally Wren told him she'd met someone, and the next day someone keyed the entire length of her Subaru.

Wren's married friends seemed to live vicariously through her, continuing to seek out prospective men for her. She'd heard all kinds of stories.

"His wife died of cancer, and he stayed by her bedside until her last breath. She was the love of his life, and he's not ready to get out there again since it's only been a few months, but he wants some female company."

"He went through a nasty divorce. His wife cheated and left him with three children that he's raising by himself. He's really attractive once you get to know him. He's not really over his ex, but maybe you two could start out as friends?"

"I used to think he was gay, but then I heard he'd been married before . . ."

Good-intentioned people, but it made her wonder what pathetic story had been told about her.

"Her husband left her so he could fool around in Europe. She's raising her little boy alone. She has no hobbies or real ambitions that I can see, but she's very nice and when she tries, she cleans up quite well."

Wren set up some dating ground rules and e-mailed the list to every friend, coworker, church member, or acquaintance who had mentioned knowing "a really nice guy." Her ideas weren't fully her own, of course. Some of them came from the perils of literary heroines like Emma, others from divorce memoirs that were both inspiring and irksome, because, seriously, how hard would it be to heal and have self-discoveries if she could escape reality for a year abroad? The list read:

1. No recently separated or divorced men.
2. No one under age 30.
3. Please don't give out my number or e-mail without permission.
4. No blind dates.
5. Prefer no more than 2 children.
6. Must like books.
7. No former professional athletes—really, it's just not for me.
8. Inform him that he won't be meeting Charlie unless we get serious.
9. No signing me up for *The Bachelor* or *The Bachelorette*.
10. If the best thing you can say is that he's "nice," then no offense, I'll pass.
11. No stalkers (or men named Fred).
12. No arrogant men who only talk about themselves.
13. No guy who is still trying to find himself.

Most of the people who responded to her list cracked jokes and added to it as if she was kidding. Wren later tried finding sympathy from a single coworker who dated regularly. Wren told about her list, the responses, and what she really wanted.

"I want a guy who is secure in himself, established, or at least somewhat stable. He can't be hung up on some other woman, I mean, who wants to deal with that? I'd like him to have his own faith in God, not just that he checks Christian on his Facebook status. And it would be nice if he likes to read, especially aloud and to me, but that's optional."

Her coworker Melissa responded with, "This guy you're looking for, he's already married."

"I'm beginning to realize that."

"Actually, I was wrong—this guy doesn't exist at all." This from Melissa who was twenty-five, worked out five days a week, had no baggage like Wren, and grew tired of all the successful men calling her.

"It shouldn't be too much to ask."

"And you've been out in the dating world for how long?"

When it came to Wren's rule about Charlie not meeting any of her dates, she found it was more complicated than she realized. Some single friends said it would be impossible to get serious with anyone until she saw how they interacted with her son. Since Wren didn't get beyond a first date, it didn't seem to matter. Until she joined a church singles group.

Martin was a single dad and one hot commodity in the group. Wren attended a few of their events, but it was more like a dating service with God stuck in. When they put on a family picnic, it seemed innocuous enough. All the single parents brought their kids for fellowship, food, and games. It turned out to be an enjoyable day, and Martin's interest in Wren became evident—much to the chagrin of several other single moms, or so her friend Celia told her.

Martin spent the afternoon teaching Charlie how to play horseshoes and acting like the male role model her son needed. Charlie talked about Martin for days.

A few weeks later Martin volunteered to come over and help with a leak in her roof. The guys in the singles group were doing repairs and handyman services like that for the single moms. It seemed like such a Christian thing to do.

Martin brought his ladder and tools. They were supposed to come in a team of at least two—the pastor's idea to keep everything on the up and up. But Martin was alone. No big deal, Wren thought, especially when he apologized and said his buddy had been called in to work that morning.

Wren planned to invite Martin in for coffee and brownies after he finished, a casual way to get to know him better and thank him for his work. While she went inside to start the coffeepot, Martin said Charlie could hand him tools. She'd never leave Charlie alone with anyone, no matter how Christian or brotherly they appeared, but this was for five minutes.

She put the coffee on in record time. Her paranoid-mom thoughts went into overtime, and as she walked back outside, she met Charlie coming toward her.

As Wren now stirred the spaghetti sauce and checked on the pasta boiling in the kettle, she felt a stab through her heart remembering the scene. Charlie's face was something she'd never forget.

Charlie had walked toward her, his hands cupped, his face contorted in pain, and his shoulders convulsed in sobs.

"What happened?" she cried out in horror, rushing to Charlie. Then she saw what was in his hands—a tiny creature, a baby bird, dead.

The nest in the tree outside Charlie's window had recently awoken with baby birds that raised their heads up as their parents brought worms and bugs to feed them.

"We found it on the ground. It was dead. But he just threw him away. Like it was nothing."

Martin walked up behind Charlie. "He shouldn't hold that thing. It might have a disease or something."

"We've been watching those birds every morning from Charlie's window."

Charlie continued to cup the bird in his hands and Wren bent down, looking at the bare little bird with its eyes still undeveloped.

Martin stared at them like they were insane. But Wren knew exactly how Charlie's mind worked, because it was how her mind worked, especially when she was a child. Charlie would reenact the scene in his mind, picturing the poor baby bird moving around in search of food and then falling from its nest—alone and vulnerable. He'd confer human emotions onto the little thing, knowing it would be hungry, terrified, alone, and in pain until it slowly died there at the bottom of the tree. She ached for her son who had feelings too tender for his age. Why did life have to be so painful so soon?

Martin returned to the roof.

"Mom, I found the baby bird and showed Martin. He picked it up with this tool thing and threw it into the trash can."

"He didn't know—most people don't understand stuff like this."

"It's just a baby bird. It's the little runt one, remember?"

"I remember."

Wren and Charlie had a funeral in the back yard. It was the first big loss that Charlie was old enough to understand, so they made it a serious affair.

A few hours later Martin was packing up his tools and putting her ladder back in the garage. Wren went outside to thank him. He smelled like leather and chewing tobacco.

"Well, I'm done," Martin said, not really looking at her.

"Thank you for fixing the leak." She brought

Martin's brownies wrapped in a container for him to take with him. Charlie was inside drinking hot cocoa with marshmallows and listening to a CD while playing with his Legos.

"No problem, that's what this ministry is for."

"Helping us helpless females, huh?"

"Exactly," he said with a light chuckle.

There was that moment of awkward silence with Martin glancing everywhere but directly at her.

"I'm sorry. I didn't know those birds were so special to you and Charlie." But Martin wasn't really sorry, just defensive.

"You didn't know, and it's not like you made it die. Charlie is sensitive to things like that."

"Well, he's a boy. When I was his age, I was torturing ants and frogs."

Wren stared at Martin, and they didn't need to say the words to know it was done before it had started.

"You know, he'll never be a real man if you baby him like that."

"If you mean him being a real man by killing helpless creatures, then I hope he never is that."

It wasn't nice of her, but did he really think it was okay and normal for boys to torture things? Martin left without Wren offering him the brownies. She avoided him at church, and she suspected he did the same. She quit the singles group, but Martin's words did nag at her, and she picked up some books from the self-help section about raising boys. She signed Charlie up for little league the next spring, after her roof leaked all winter long.

"Spaghetti's ready," Wren called to Ruth and Charlie. That was three years ago. Wren later heard Martin married a woman from the singles group.

Wren realized the longing for someone in her life was growing. Derek hinted at the possibility that they might try again. It had seemed preposterous at first. But what if he really had changed? What if she did fully forgive him? Couldn't God do something like that? Couldn't God even change the cold hardness she felt for Derek and change it into love?

Could He make them a family again?

12

Wren skimmed her e-mail inbox at her cubicle and saw the confirmation of their appointment at the Boston School of Music. She wrote a quick e-mail back as a text came through her phone. She hoped it wasn't Barb. Paul's name was displayed.

PAUL: Want to meet again? I met with the theater people. And have you figured out my books yet?

WREN: Not yet. Going to Boston tomorrow.
Charlie touring a music school. Next week?
PAUL: You moving?
WREN: Maybe. Been looking for something
like this for Charlie.
PAUL: He is very good. I was at the spring
concert and saw his violin solo. Enjoy the
trip.
WREN: Thanks. Next week then. Meeting and
books.
PAUL: It's a . . . appointment.

She laughed as she slid her phone back into her purse before heading upstairs. Paul could be a friend, she decided. Wasn't she mature enough to have an attractive single male who was dating someone else as a friend?

Wren and Charlie packed their suitcases and Charlie's violin into the Subaru the next evening and said good-bye to Ruth with one last invitation for her to come along.

"I have plenty to keep me busy and it's only two nights. Hazel Stuckney is picking me up for Bingo tomorrow, and I have the house cleaners starting on the main house."

Wren felt satisfied that Ruth was taken care of. Her original plan had been to spend the entire weekend in the city on a mini vacation of sorts. They shortened the trip with Ruth at home, but

Wren still hoped to pack the time with some fun activities together.

Wren estimated a four- to five-hour drive south to Boston depending on the traffic she encountered. The time passed quickly as they listened to a playlist of classical music that Charlie had put together. It was like a soundtrack as they drove through the late afternoon of forested mountains and open fields from Maine to Massachusetts.

The city skyline rose out of the darkness as they approached. Boston drew her in with its history and beauty. There was an unmistakable pulse beneath the surface, perhaps from the many books Wren had read about the city, or the unique culture of the locals.

The West End, Chinatown, Charlestown, Boston Common, the north end dubbed Little Italy, Fenway Park, Cambridge with Harvard University . . . there was so much they could explore. The city was alive with quaint restaurants, historical sites, conservatories, universities, tourist locations. It was a place where academia met blue collar, where gourmet cuisine met pizza, and perhaps where Wren and Charlie would meet their future.

Every visit made Wren wish for more time in the city. Her trips here were always too short with glimpses at what she longed to explore and savor. This was where the nation began with the Boston Tea Party, Paul Revere, the Battle of

Bunker Hill. The city hadn't forgotten its history, but it didn't live in the past either. It had taken on centuries of change and development, like a European city, she guessed.

She wished she could take a side trip to Walden, to walk the woods where Thoreau had contemplated life and nature, or to Hawthorne's House of Seven Gables in Salem. The area was full of literary tourist spots that Wren had yet to explore.

She leaned forward as they approached the city, taking it all in.

"Are we still going to the aquarium tomorrow night?" Charlie asked, turning down the music.

"Yes, if you want to. Are you nervous about tomorrow?"

"No. I just hope they aren't a bunch of boring kids."

Wren glanced at Charlie. She knew he was nervous despite what he said. "Why would they be boring?"

"You know some kids who are into music. They seem kind of stuck up and boring."

"Would you want other kids to think of you that way?"

"No. But I'm not."

"Well, give these kids a chance too."

Charlie didn't say anything for a few minutes. "I'm a little bit nervous."

"I would be too, but that's normal. I'd be worried if you weren't nervous. No matter what happens, we'll go to the aquarium and still have a great trip."

"Yeah, you're right. This is a good trip."

Wren watched the signs on the freeway.

"And . . . I got a hotel with a swimming pool."

Charlie whipped his head toward her. "No way! I didn't bring my swimsuit."

"I brought it for you."

"You're the best mom in the world. Can we swim tonight?"

"Of course. Look at that," Wren said, pointing at the tall skyscrapers and the Zakim Bunker Hill Bridge with its massive white cables glowing against the dark sky.

"Wow, it would be cool to move here." Charlie gazed out his window. "At least, I think it would be."

Wren knew exactly what he meant.

The next morning Wren couldn't get the butterflies out of her stomach, though she kept her outer calm for Charlie's sake. They ate an early breakfast at the hotel, then walked in the fresh morning the two blocks to the school. She had the urge to hold Charlie's hand but knew he'd never go for that. He carried his violin case and walked with purpose as if he belonged.

The sidewalks were wide and crowded with people carrying coffee cups and laptop bags, some dressed for business, others casual. Charlie watched a group of children carrying backpacks walking together across a street with one adult leading the way. The morning traffic filled the streets with an occasional honk from an anxious driver. Wren checked the time on a large clock tower mixed in with the modern architecture.

The music school was in the heart of Boston, blocks from the public library, parks, gardens, and economic center. Cottage Cove was quaint in its history, but this city was grand.

"I love Boston," Wren muttered to herself.

"Me too, it's cool."

"Yes, it is cool," Wren said with a smile. She could picture them here, her walking him to school and then going off to work wherever she could get a job—hopefully a city or university library. But it was such a big step. Was this the right plan for them?

They stopped at the front gate before a large plaque that read Boston School of Music. They stared up at the building.

Charlie whistled. "This looks like the White House."

The shape of the building was nothing like the White House, but there was that colonial grandeur in the white building and white columns along the front. The school felt pristine and austere, impressive and intimidating at the same time. Wren wondered how Charlie felt. He appeared excited and awed, while Wren had a sick feeling in her stomach. She looked over their clothing and Charlie's worn violin case, wondering if they were underdressed.

"Here we go," Wren said, reaching for Charlie's hand.

"Mom," Charlie said sternly, giving her the what-are-you-doing look.

"Sorry, it's habit."

"I haven't held your hand on the way into school since first grade."

"That wasn't all that long ago for me."

Students and adults walked toward the building. A few of the children peered at Charlie, but he kept his eyes straight ahead.

The grand front doors opened to an elegant entryway with marble hallways, a chandelier hanging in the center, and the sound of children —not the usual, loud school sound, but a more cultured environment. Was this for Charlie?

They followed a sign to the administration area on the first floor. Wren gave her name to the polite woman greeting them at the front desk.

"Dr. Mitchell will see you now." Dr. Mitchell rose from her desk as Charlie and Wren entered her office.

"Good morning. It's lovely to meet you, Ms. Evans, and you, Charles." She reached out warmly to shake their hands.

"We appreciate you taking the time to see us." The window behind Dr. Mitchell's desk revealed a green lawn and garden area.

"It's our pleasure to have you. I've been quite impressed with Charles' talent. I hope we find that the school and Charles are a perfect fit."

"He usually goes by Charlie," Wren said.

"It's all right, Mom. Charles is good too."

Wren glanced at Charlie, then back to Dr. Mitchell, who smiled knowingly at her.

"Are you ready to shadow the classroom?"

"Sure," Charlie said.

Dr. Mitchell leaned toward a small intercom on the wall. "Janice, please send Jacob to join us in my office."

"You'll like Jacob, Charles."

There was a light knock on the door and a boy Charlie's age walked in. He wore slacks and a button-up shirt, but he didn't appear overly mature or serious as Wren feared the children here might be.

"Hey," Jacob said to Charlie.

"Hi."

After brief introductions and Dr. Mitchell's explanation of what his day would be like, Jacob and Charlie were ready to leave.

"If you have any trouble, just come to my office or talk to one of the instructors. I'll check in on you at lunch."

"Have a good day, Char-lie," Wren stuttered over what to call him.

"Bye, Mom."

Wren watched Charlie walk out the door,

and she felt both pride and anxiety for him.

"He'll be in good hands."

Wren nodded as they sat down once again.

"We have gifted children here from all over the country as well as a few international students. I was impressed with Charles' story and his love of music. We've had influential parents bring their children into our school because of the parents' love of music or their own unfulfilled dreams. But here at Boston School of Music, we want students who have their own passion for music. Of course, passion isn't enough, but from the demos Charles' music teacher sent, it's obvious that he's also very gifted."

"He loves music. He says it's in his head all the time, but I guess not many people would notice. He has other hobbies as well—he really enjoyed little league this summer and we like bird watching. Most people would see him as quite normal." Wren knew she might be harming Charlie's chances of being admitted to the school by straying away from his music, but she wanted to be sure Dr. Mitchell had a clear understanding of who her son was.

Dr. Mitchell nodded. "That's refreshing to hear. We want our students to excel in their gifts, but also to have a broad range of interests. I understand your situation and admire the life you're giving Charles. It would certainly be a sacrifice for Charles to attend here. But we have scholarship programs that can help. I've included every-thing in this packet."

She handed Wren a white folder with the school emblem on the front. Pictures of happy children playing violins, bass, trumpets, and pianos decorated the inside flap of the folder.

"Would you like to follow me through my morning rounds?"

"I'd enjoy that."

Wren and Dr. Mitchell walked down the hall-ways and in and out of classrooms where they greeted teachers and students. The rooms were full of light from tall windows, and music sounded down the hallways from the practice rooms.

In an auditorium, a man played a piano while the students sat on the floor of the stage. Wren scanned the children. They weren't hitting one another or joking around. They were focused on the music.

The song ended with the pianist lifting his hands and the last notes echoed through the building. Wren joined the children and Dr. Mitchell in clapping.

"That brings us to Wagner," the man said. Wren assumed he was their teacher.

Now that the music had ended, the children became children again. One boy took the ends of a girl's braids and flapped them upward, then laughed behind his covered hand when the girl squealed and received a hard reprimand in the teacher's expression. Wren smiled when the boy shaped up. At least they really were children. She wouldn't let Charlie lose his childhood to a pretentious school of snobs. But it didn't appear to be the case at the Boston School of Music.

In one classroom, Wren spotted Charlie sitting in a chair beside Jacob and looking as if he already fit right in. She wanted to remain in the literature class, but continued after Dr. Mitchell.

One of Wren's favorite rooms was the beautiful library, with books in floor-to-ceiling bookcases. *Take that, Jeremy,* she thought.

At the end of the tour, Dr. Mitchell invited her to stay at the school or explore on her own.

"I'd like to look around. Thank you for the tour this morning. Charlie is finished at two thirty?"

"Yes. If you'd been here yesterday, you would have enjoyed a school recital with one of our alumni performing. If you fill out the information packet, we'll put you on our e-mail newsletter list and then perhaps you could come down for some of our concerts."

"We'd love that."

"I'll also e-mail you some names of other parents to discuss their experience with the school."

Wren thanked Dr. Mitchell and walked the school grounds, then out into the street.

She walked the streets and enjoyed the sights, finally sitting at an outside café and ordering a coffee. Wren tried to imagine this being their every day. But she loved Cottage Cove and felt comfortable there.

New things were always scary, she reminded herself. Ruth had told her numerous times when Wren was moving toward something different, "We have to grieve the closing of one door to enter a new one."

There would be grieving if they left the life they'd built in Maine. They'd be starting all over again. But this was the life they'd been wanting. Or at least, that Wren thought was the best for them. And God seemed to be providing it. Or was He?

"I filled out all the paperwork," Wren said, handing the packet to Dr. Mitchell. She watched the packet leave her hands and hoped she was doing the right thing. It wasn't like she had just signed Charlie up for the military, and this was far from a done deal.

Charlie trotted down the hall when he saw her.

"Bye, Charlie!" an Asian girl said, peering out of a classroom doorway.

"She was cute," Wren said as they walked outside.

"Mom!"

"Well, she was."

Charlie shrugged and had a smile on his face. "She was nice."

"So, what did you think?"

"I didn't do very well."

"You didn't? What happened? How was the audition?"

"It didn't seem like an audition. They just asked me to play, and they were a lot better than me. I don't want to talk about it."

Wren wanted to pummel him with questions about every detail.

"Can we go swimming at the hotel tonight?"

"Only if you'll tell me about today. But first we have the aquarium, unless you're too tired."

"No way. They have this huge penguin exhibit and we have to see the whales too. I can't wait."

"Let's go then." They were quiet for a moment as they continued walking toward the hotel. "So . . . do you think you'd want to go to the school?"

Charlie shrugged. "Sure. But I don't think they'll want me now."

"You're probably being too hard on yourself."

"Maybe. I did like it there. A lot. But I like a lot of things at home too."

Wren nodded, wishing she'd get all the right answers for their lives delivered in a letter to her.

"Are you hungry? I'm so hungry I could eat Fenway Park with all the Red Sox inside of it!"

The next day they drove out of Boston going north, and Wren glanced in her rearview mirror at the silhouette of Boston's downtown. She wondered if this time next year the city would be home. Usually she had a gut feeling about what to do, but her intuition acted as if it were already hibernating for the winter. She'd sent a text to Missy asking her to pray about the trip, and now she needed to pray about the decision. Perhaps with everything happening at home, it wasn't time to know about this decision yet. Besides, it would be several weeks before the school let them know whether Charlie was accepted. Having patience and faith had always been a challenge.

Her cell phone rang, and Wren put in her Bluetooth earpiece. Charlie was listening to the soundtrack to the movie *Iron Man* on his iPod.

"Hi, Barb."

"Where are you? I tried calling the house this morning, twice."

"I'm in Boston."

"Why are you in Boston? Where's Ruth?"

"She's at home."

"Why are you in Boston when the party is in two weeks?"

"Charlie and I had something scheduled."

"What?"

Wren wanted to turn off the phone and act like it was a dropped call. Her sister had no sense of boundaries.

"An appointment at a school."

"For whom?"

"Charlie. He was invited to tour a music school."

"You might move to Boston?"

"I don't know. Maybe. What's going on?" Wren watched the signs to be sure she was heading the right direction.

"I'm trying to find out what's going on. Getting a plan figured out with you is harder than getting it from our ninety-year-old grandmother."

"Did you get my voice message and e-mail?"

"Yes."

"Then you have the information, the date, the caterer's name and web address, and the invitation list. The location is the house. We're renting tables, chairs, and tablecloths. My friend Missy is making the centerpieces, and we'll have a string quartet for music with Charlie doing a special song. You said you were staying in your RV, and Jack and his wife will be in the main house. What more do you need to know?"

Barb actually stuttered. "I don't know. It seems like you'd want to communicate with me more about this."

"There *is* something I want to talk to you about, but I can't right now." Wren glanced over at Charlie; he didn't seem to be listening, but Wren wouldn't risk it.

"What is it?"

"I'm in the car with Charlie right now."

"What's it about?"

Wren hesitated, glancing at her son once again.

"It's about you talking to a specific person without telling me about it."

"So you finally talked to Derek?"

"What do you mean, finally talked to him? Why are you talking to him?"

"He e-mailed me about a month ago."

"I haven't talked to him yet, but he contacted a certain person without first talking to me."

Wren heard Barb's sigh over the phone. "He's been afraid to contact you. You aren't the easiest person to talk to, you know."

"What does that mean, and why didn't you tell me?" Wren wasn't controlling her tone as well as she wished.

"He asked me to wait because he wanted to talk to you first. I would have told you when I got there. He was getting information about some music program for Charlie."

"Like I'd let that happen."

"Wren, kids need to know their fathers, and with Charlie's talent, you should give him every opportunity possible. If my kid had any talent, I'd ship him off to Europe ASAP."

"I need to go." Wren's body was shaking.

"As usual. I'll be there next weekend."

"You will? The party's not for two weeks." Panic shot through her.

"I'd like to spend some time with Grandma and help the week before the party. By the way, Logan and I want to pay for it."

"Jack wants to pay for it. I suggested we split it."

"Funny, Wren. We both know you aren't in that kind of a position. If Jack wants to pay, let him pay. I'll talk to him about it."

Wren stared at the road after she hung up. Maybe Barb didn't realize just how much this party was going to cost. Not in actual dollars, but much more. Perhaps her siblings felt the same way.

Early Sunday morning Wren sat at the desk in the breakfast nook and searched the online Boston library system that had more than two dozen branches in the metro area. But when Wren clicked on "careers," there were no job listings. She wondered about the school and university libraries. Perhaps Boston wouldn't work out after all.

Wren yawned and rubbed her eyes. Fatigue begged her to go back to bed, but her lumpy couch had woken her in the first place.

The sound of feet padding down the hall turned Wren from the computer screen. Ruth peered into the living room with her bathrobe tied at her waist. Without her makeup or hair in its usual perfect coif, Ruth appeared older and more vulnerable than usual.

"You're up early. Did I wake you?" Wren asked.

"Oh no, darling. I usually wake somewhat early and spend some time with the Lord. But I felt perhaps the Lord wanted me to pop out and see if you were awake."

"Here I am. The coffee is ready, or I can make you some tea," Wren said, sliding away from the desk.

"Coffee would be lovely."

Wren poured Ruth a cup.

"Every time I see you, you're awake and doing something. Do you sleep?" Ruth asked, wrapping her hands around the mug.

"Occasionally."

"Not enough. I think you're worrying too much."

Wren smiled. "There's a lot to worry about."

"It sounds like an amazing school."

"Yes. It is."

"You don't sound sure about it," Ruth said, sitting down at the counter.

"I hate decisions like this. I go back and forth, weighing all the pros and cons, and this one's even harder because the decision's not all mine—the school hasn't accepted us yet. It's just . . . a lot of decisions are popping up lately."

"These decisions can change the course of your lives—for you and Charlie both."

"Thanks, Grandma, no pressure there."

"Take it off of your own shoulders, my dear."

"What do you mean?"

"Ask God's guidance, seek Him—really seek Him."

"I do, I am."

"No, you aren't really. You wouldn't be this concerned if you were."

Wren made a funny frown face to Ruth that made her laugh. "You're right. I find it hard to know how to seek God. Do I sit at my Bible all day, praying? It would be nice to run off to a monastery or some quiet place for a few weeks, but that's not going to happen. When I was younger, I used to spin the globe and ask God where He wanted me. I hope I'm not supposed to be living in Kyrgyzstan right now."

"Seek and seek some more. Seek and you will find. It's a promise."

"It seems right for us to go to Boston. If Charlie gets accepted, maybe that's God's way of saying He wants us to go."

"Sometimes the way that looks right is very wrong."

"Really?" Wren leaned on the counter.

"Other times it means that it's right. Sweetie, God is with us even when our life looks messy. Sometimes He wants us to trust Him through something that doesn't make sense until we get to the other side. Other times God makes it clear and simple."

"But that begs the question—how do you know which is which?"

"First you ask. You seek, and keep seeking. Then you listen. No one can answer it for you. Advice is great, but there's only One who has the right answer. Then you trust the answer—that is faith. And then you have to put action into that faith by making your decision and following it."

"Sounds so simple."

"It is."

Wren laughed. "I was being sarcastic. It doesn't seem simple to me."

"That's because you're still relying much too much on yourself, sweetie." Wren groaned.

"Oh, Grandma. Let's get ready for church— obviously I have a lot to learn."

13

Late Sunday afternoon Charlie knocked on the white door with Wren beside him. Missy opened the door with an expression of surprise.

"Well, hello. Come on in."

"I'd like to talk to Franklin if that's okay?" Charlie said before stepping through the door.

"He's in his room." She turned and Franklin appeared behind her.

"Hi," Charlie said.

"Hi."

"Why don't you guys come in?" Missy said, and Charlie and Wren walked inside.

"Thank you for the new statue and the note," Charlie said to Franklin. "That was really nice. And I'm sorry I've been ignoring you at school."

Wren and Missy glanced at each other.

"It's okay. I'd be mad at me too." Franklin's face reflected his sadness, then his face lit up considerably. "Do you want to see the other stuff I made from the statue clay?"

"Sure," Charlie said and followed Franklin.

Missy and Wren sat in the living room and talked while the boys played. Missy's husband was coming home in a few weeks, and she was excited and also a little nervous about the transition into having him home for a month. She asked Wren for any new updates about Derek.

"I need to write him back, but I don't know what to say. I've been praying about it," Wren said with a smile. "How is your spiritual life?"

"It's been a little harder for me lately," Missy said. "Things are difficult with Franklin. But I heard about a new therapy for sensory integration disorder, so Franklin and I are going there next month."

They talked awhile longer, then Wren rose to get back home to Ruth.

"Being a good friend is important," Charlie said when they got back into the car.

"You're right. It's not easy, but friends really make life better."

"Yeah. I still want to play dodge ball at recess though."

"Did you talk to Franklin about that?"

"Yeah, and he didn't like it, but he said it was okay."

"It won't be easy being Franklin's friend. It'll be harder sometimes than with other people. But I'm proud of you, and he does bring a lot of good things to our lives. He really loves God too."

"Yeah, and that's what is really important."

Wren rubbed Charlie's head. "You are one special kid, you know it?"

Wren was enjoying *Persuasion*, one of her favorite Jane Austen novels, while eating her lunch in Library Park when a text came through her phone.

Hey, it's Jeremy Bass—remember the workshop from hell? LOL. Can you do coffee Thursday afternoon?

Barely pausing to think, Wren typed back: *I don't think I can, sorry.*

Jenks Bledshoe pulled into a parking space in his old pickup. He climbed out and walked toward the library with his usual grouchy expression that made Wren smile. What would happen to Jenks if the library closed its doors?

Wren's phone rang.

"Hey, it's Jeremy Bass," the voice said.

"Hi, Jeremy."

"So, give it to me straight. You aren't interested."

"I, well, um . . ."

"It's all right. Either the chemistry is there or it's not, and I know when a girl isn't into me."

"I'm sorry. I'm not really dating right now."

"No problem. I still love that you hated my workshop. But you might not want to disregard everything I had to say."

Wren thought of Jenks and his solid faith that once he arrived at the library door it would open to him, and the books would be there along with his favorite chair.

"You know, Jeremy, if it's okay with you, I'd like some more information about what you were talking about in the workshop. Ways I could help our library stay *relevant,* as you say. Do you have a website or something?"

"Sure thing, Wren," Jeremy said with a laugh. "I'll send you some links and you can e-mail any questions you have. Then maybe later, you'll see how brilliant I am and agree to coffee."

That evening Wren drove home while Charlie had music practice. On Mondays, his teacher dropped him off at home since she had several students up the coast who received private lessons. Usually this gave Wren an extra two hours to catch up on housework or go out to coffee with Missy.

As she drove up the driveway, Wren noticed a ladder propped up against the main house and a white van parked in front of the walkway. The van said Green Home Cleaners, and its sliding door was open with buckets, mops, and cleaning supplies neatly organized inside.

Wren walked toward the main house. The front door was open, and she recognized Brenda Jacobs at the top of the ladder.

"You aren't afraid up there?" Wren asked the middle-aged woman.

"Hello there, Wren. Not afraid at all. My father was a window washer in New York. For a while, he worked at the Empire State Building. Hopping up on a roof is pretty mild compared to that."

"I guess, but my legs would probably get a bit wobbly. You can do that over at my place when you're done here," Wren called up.

"Really? We'll finish up here tomorrow. I'm about to go home right now."

"No, I'm kidding." She could only guess what Ruth was paying to have the entire house cleaned. Her house was tidy, but the deep cleaning kept getting put off.

Ruth was on the phone when Wren walked into the cottage. She heard the cleaning van shut its door and fire up the engine. Ruth continued talking, and the conversation sounded personal, so Wren walked back out toward the main house to inspect the progress.

Her sister and brother would be here soon—Barb in just a few days. Their arrival might turn everything upside down. Ruth's presence changed the dynamic, but in a pleasant way. Suddenly Wren was glad her reunion with her siblings would happen with Ruth around.

213

Wren walked up to the cleaned porch and noticed how the glass gleamed. She opened the front door. The house had a lived-in feeling, and it stopped her cold in the middle of the living room. When she and Charlie visited the house, it showed its age, acting abandoned and vacant like a ghost town.

Now, decorative cushions adorned the couches that had been uncovered and cleaned. White sheer curtains billowed out from shining windows. Vibrant rugs rested before the doorways, and it looked brighter inside as if they'd painted, though she knew they hadn't. The dusting, vacuuming, and cleaning had stripped away the musty scent of a pent-up house near the sea.

From somewhere, framed pictures had been found and lined up along the mantle. There were pictures from different eras, spanning four decades from post–World War II to the 1980s. There was a picture of Ruth and Grandpa Peter as a young couple on the beach. Ruth rested against her husband with one hand holding her sunhat.

Wren leaned in to study a photo of the family when she was about six. They were planting the maple tree in the front yard, replacing one that had fallen over during a winter storm. Wren remembered that day clearly and couldn't believe how young they all were. They were a family then. That maple tree had grown tall and strong, but their family had withered.

Were they as happy as she remembered, or was it a child's mind believing in fairy tales? Wren wanted it to be true, except then the tragedy of what they became was made even worse.

She thought of Ima Carter at the library and how she hinted at troubles between her parents. Should she dig up the past and ask Ruth or Barb what they remembered?

Another picture showed Wren and Barbara wearing matching sundresses that their mother had made for the Fourth of July. Wren's was blue and white, and Barbara's red and white. In the background, Jack was wearing a red corduroy shorts outfit that matched their dresses. He looked about four years old. Wren's old Barbie camping van and their dolls and tiny camping accessories were littered around the lawn. She remembered this day too.

Wren picked up the framed photo of her father, sitting in a lawn chair with his pipe dangling from the side of his mouth. He was thin and neatly dressed in casual slacks and a short-sleeved, button-up shirt. He'd pushed his sunglasses up to his forehead, and in his hand he held a tall glass that probably had scotch or some kind of mixed drink like he usually had in the summer evenings with Mom and their friends. He reminded her of a classic movie star.

Dad was gone now. Dead for over ten years. Sometimes it still seemed impossible. Her father had been such a strong force in their family, the center, the magnet, the core—until the accident that changed him into someone else. She stared at his face, deep into his dark eyes as if to find some answer to a question she couldn't remember.

In the kitchen, the refrigerator hummed loudly, and though far outdated, it shined clean and white. Wren opened it and found it full of organic groceries—milk, cheeses, Greek yogurt, Perrier, fruits and vegetables. The freezer had Cherry Garcia ice cream, and a coffeemaker and grinder sat on the counter with a bag of coffee beans from the Village Brew.

"Everything perfect for Jack," Wren muttered and felt instantly guilty for it. She hadn't heard when he was arriving, but the full refrigerator insinuated it would be soon.

Wren hesitated at the stairway, then marched up to inspect the rooms. There were four bedrooms upstairs and a small one downstairs. Two of the upstairs rooms had yet to be cleaned and uncovered. One appeared in progress, and another, the one that had been the kids' room during their summers, was clean and fresh like the downstairs rooms had been.

Wren didn't want to walk inside, but an unseen hand seemed to guide her toward the window seat that gazed out over the front yard, the driveway, and the blue rocky cove beyond the bushes and trees of the property.

For a moment, Wren could see the past clearly. The view from this window on the morning of the reunion had been full of excitement and hope. Relatives and old friends stuffed the house and some were camping on the lawn outside, with more coming for the afternoon event.

Mom had been stressed in the weeks prior, altering the mood at the vacation house significantly. Eight-year-old Jack started into the mayhem he pulled whenever their parents were distracted, working too many hours, or attending numerous social events. He ran wild through the house, wouldn't finish his food, pulled pranks, stole the girls' Barbies and hung them from the trees outside . . . whatever mischief he could think up.

As more people arrived, it seemed her parents forgot they had children, or at least the girls. Jack could always garner their attention in ways Barb and Wren hadn't figured out. He excelled at every sport, he could make them laugh, make them pull away from paperwork, arguments, and phone calls with a look of pride in their eyes. Did her parents truly love their son more than their daughters? Wren's attention-grabbing attempts fell flat at her parents' feet, with them reprimanding her for behaving like a child.

The reunion celebration began in the afternoon. Everyone gathered at the stage set up for the band. Mom welcomed everyone with perfect social grace once she had the microphone in her hand. She told a few jokes and introduced the song that Wren would sing.

It was her moment—when she sang, Dad seemed most proud of her and Mom noticed her. On this day, she sang her favorite hymn from church, "His Eye Is on the Sparrow."

Wren shut away the people around her—though she could see them somewhat, they were outside the safe bubble she created whenever singing in public. She sang and dwelled on the words of the song, letting them fill her small body and be released through her voice.

The applause surprised her and burst the protective bubble. She was on the stage again where she curtsied and hoped her face wasn't blazing red. Barb had told her that she blushed horribly at the end of singing.

After that, the party began. The band played and everyone had their fill of food and drinks. Wren ate and played with the other kids—some of whom were distant cousins, others town friends.

Wren was playing on the lawn, doing cartwheels, when she felt a hand grasp her arm.

"I need you and your sister to keep an eye on Jack." Mom's breath stunk like something Wren hadn't smelled before. It was probably from the drinks at the table Wren had been shooed away from. She'd been drawn to all the glass bottles of different heights and colors, the fruits stuck through skewers and cute little umbrellas that would be perfect for when she took her Barbie to the beach again. It all looked so elegant and sophisticated.

"Okay," Wren said, seeing Jack playing horse-shoes with Aunt Doris' date.

Mom disappeared and Wren saw the bartender wave her over.

"Have you had a Shirley Temple?" he asked.

"No. I'm only eleven and a half."

"You're in luck—it's only for people eleven and older. Want a cherry in it?"

"Yes, please. And an umbrella?"

"Of course."

Wren carried the drink, feeling six feet tall. Barb might tease her that she still played with Barbies, but Wren didn't care, and now her Barbies had a sun umbrella. Her younger cousins crowded around.

"It's a Shirley Temple drink," Wren bragged. "You have to be eleven or older to get one."

She savored her status until Barb walked by with several other teenagers from town and, upon spotting Wren, demanded to know what she was drinking.

"It's a Shirley Temple," one of their younger cousins announced as if to defend Wren.

Barb and her friends laughed. "Those are for little kids." She patted Wren on top of the head and walked away.

Wren felt torn between wanting to be with the older kids wearing mascara and talking about guys, or to play as a kid, building forts and playing make-believe games. Back home, Wren had one friend who had started her period, and Mom had taken Wren shopping for her first "training" bra, though she wasn't quite sure what was being trained.

The entire weekend had been a tug of war between childhood and adolescence. One major obstacle kept her from crossing over. Barb had become the gatekeeper, barring her from hanging out with the older kids.

"Go play or something," Barb would say when she realized Wren was on the periphery of conversations about parties, drinking, sex, and drugs. Wren tried not to act shocked by the profanities and experiences of her cousins, or that her older sister acted as if it were normal and cool.

So finally, Wren succumbed to the pull of childhood. She let her hair go wild in the breeze, not caring that one barrette had fallen out or that she had dirt under her nails. They made tunnel forts through the thick bushes bordering the fence line near enough to the party so that whenever a parent remembered he or she was a parent and called out one of their names, it was only a minute before that kid appeared without delay.

The parents became more and more distracted and significantly louder as the afternoon went on.

Mom and Dad were drinking a lot. Wren hadn't seen her parents like that before. She'd heard Mom talking to Dad about her stupid relatives and why was he dancing with some woman who could barely keep her red bra from popping out of her top. The reunion for the parents seemed no fun at all, until they began dancing. They danced and drank and laughed. Aunt Doris fell over twice.

Wren had noticed Barbara flirting with the drummer in the band when she was searching the crowd for Jack. Her brother had been beside the dance floor—tossing ice cubes in between the adults' feet. She was going to stop him when Barb had taken him by the collar and shooed him and his mischievous sidekicks off.

"Listen, you're going to watch Jack," Barb said, stomping over to her.

"Mom said we both have to."

Barb glared at her. "I'll give you five bucks."

"Ten," Wren said, crossing her arms at her chest.

"Five! And only *after* you watch him."

"You won't pay me. I know you won't."

"I will, but it's in the house."

"Then go get it," Wren said.

"No. Just do it or I'll hurt you."

Barb hurried back to the dance floor and her friends with Wren calling after her, "I'm not watching him."

But Wren was the first to wonder where her

brother was. He'd been playing beneath the tables with the cousins. Wren realized that she'd been seeing the cousins for a while, but not Jack.

She stood from the grass where she and her cousin Tory were making hair wreaths out of flowers and vines. She brushed at the grass stains on her sundress and white tights.

"I'll be right back," Wren said and began a search under each table.

"Where's Jack?" she asked his playmates.

They shrugged or said they didn't know until Wren was sure he was definitely not with their cousins now. She turned around slowly, taking in the entire grounds. The dance floor with family members dancing and stumbling in front of the band, the tables where people sat talking with their hands on wine glasses, the buffet table that had reminded her of a king's feast but now appeared like an animal carcass torn apart. Wren thought for sure he'd be near the dessert table, hiding underneath, perhaps taking pieces of the cake and candies for himself.

Wren walked quickly that way, looking under more tablecloths.

"Jack?" she called once. It turned the head of a woman from town.

"What's wrong?" The woman acted more alarmed than Wren expected.

"Nothing, just my brother. He was here a minute ago."

"What's his name?"

"Jack?"

"What about Jack?" Mom emerged from nowhere, it seemed. "Where is he? Where is Jack?"

"I . . . don't know."

Mom's face contorted into something fearful.

"He was just here," Wren stuttered.

"Where is your sister?"

People were drawn toward them, asking what was wrong. Wren heard her sister say, "Wren was watching him."

"I asked you both to watch him."

"I know, but then I asked Wren 'cuz I had to go help do something."

Wren turned to see the innocent expression on her sister's face. She couldn't believe Barb would betray her like that.

"We'll figure out who's at fault later. Right now we need to just find him."

The band stopped playing. An announcement was made over the microphone.

"We're missing Jack, so if everyone will take a moment to look for him, then we'll get right back to the party."

Wren expected Jack to pop out at any second and felt like all this attention was too much, considering this was the kid who constantly pulled pranks on them. Why was a sense of hysteria mounting?

Mom and some of the other women ran toward

the house. Dad and several men headed toward the sea trail. Other people searched bushes and beneath tables as if it were an Easter egg hunt.

A half hour passed with another announcement. Everyone called out Jack's name as the search widened. Mom ran around the property frantically and then hysterically. She nearly fainted when Uncle Chuck ran up from the small rocky beach holding Jack's jacket in his hands.

"Call 911 and the Coast Guard," Uncle Chuck yelled to his wife. "All the men come with me. We need to search the rocks and water."

Evening dropped upon them. Fire trucks, police, and a red ambulance pulled in, parking haphazardly along the driveway, blocking the cars and RVs. The yard was littered with decorations, and the rising breeze rolled paper plates and napkins across the green grass. Angry gray clouds were like bulldozers driving in fast from the sea, whipping up the wind and tearing at the white party lights Dad and Jack had strung up along the fences and porch eaves.

Wren and Barb searched the house while the adults scoured the grounds outside, both still unable to grasp that Jack was out there in the cold and not tucked safely into some corner of the house. Maybe he'd fallen asleep in a hiding place, but that didn't explain his jacket down by the sea.

It was nearing dark when Wren heard Barb

gasp and saw her pressed up against the window of their room.

"What happened?"

"I don't know. I think someone got hurt or something."

They watched from the upper windows as paramedics rushed down the beach trail with a long board in their hands. The view was better than downstairs, and all the kids who hadn't left had been ordered to remain in the house. It seemed like forever before they saw any more movement. Uncle Chuck and their older cousins came running up the trail, then came the paramedics carrying someone on the board. Someone big, not small, not Jack.

"Who is it?"

Wren strained on her tiptoes, pressing her face to the glass, then wiping away the fog made by her breath.

"Daddy!" Barb shouted and turned from the window, running for the stairs.

Wren kept her face at the window, not believing her sister. Daddy didn't get hurt—what was Barbara talking about? It was beyond her imagining that her father could be the one on that board, being carried up the hill instead of running himself.

But then from the warping of the window, she saw his thick dark hair and the white button-up shirt he'd been wearing. Barb was already running across the lawn toward the ambulance, but Wren froze at the window. Dad tried to rise on the board, a terrible grimace on his face.

Mom was running behind Barb, screaming so loudly Wren could hear the wail above the wind and through the window as if she were right beside her.

Wren finally got her feet moving, and she raced down the stairs and out the front door, across the lawn to where the paramedics were loading Dad into the back of the ambulance. People rushed around, nearly knocking Wren over as she squeezed through to see what had happened to her father.

A painful vise gripped her arm causing Wren to cry out in pain. The hand didn't let go but pulled her away from Daddy. Her mother's face loomed close to hers.

"Get out of their way! What are you, stupid?"

Wren's mouth froze in a stunned gape. Her mother had never stared at her with such hatred in her eyes, such anger in the set of her mouth.

"Look at what you've done! You were supposed to be watching your brother. If something happened to him, that's your fault too."

The doors to the ambulance were slammed shut. Mom ran for her keys and purse, then toward their town car.

"Stay in the house, Wren. And for once, follow instructions. I'll be back later."

Wren didn't want to go back in the house. She wanted to ride with her father to the hospital, or to go out and help search for her brother.

"Go. Now!" Aunt Doris shouted to Wren.

Nightfall came. Wren felt like a prisoner, trapped in solitary confinement, while people moved in and out of the house, some quickly, some slowly. Coffee was made and remade for the search party scouring the peninsula through the night as the wind brought rain that beat against the windows. Neighbors brought food into the house, but few people ate. A command center was set up in the living room.

Wren crept to the top of the stairs, trying to overhear updates. She woke in the night cold and curled up against the top railing of the stairs.

Men were stomping the mud off their boots with the front door open, letting in a blast of cold air. It seemed impossible that the weather had changed so quickly. A freak storm sweeping in from Greenland, she'd heard some searchers say. They were working in shifts. Someone was always out in that storm, searching for Jack.

Why hadn't she watched Jack better? What if he was dead right now? Wren pictured him at Christmas time, running to his stocking in his footed pajamas with the button-down behind. He might act like a terror at times, but usually he was very sweet. When he got scared in the night, Jack sometimes came into her room and would whisper her name from her bedside until she woke up. He'd ask if he could sleep with her and would crawl under her covers as she lifted them, curling up at her back and sucking his thumb, though he didn't know she knew he did so. Wren had wondered why he never went to their parents' room or to Barb's. Maybe he trusted that she'd keep his fears a secret, while the rest of the house could believe he was brave and strong. When he was smaller, he had been her baby doll that she'd carry around, dress up, and feed. Dad was angry when she dressed him like a girl and he came out in her Easter bonnet and dress with white patent leather shoes.

"No son of mine is going to dress like a girl. Get him out of that!"

Jack loved Wren's shoes, though he learned not to wear them around Dad. He'd tromp around Wren's room, and they'd have tea parties and play with her Barbies. For a time, Barb would join them in playing Barbies. But Wren didn't like her sister playing with them. She liked to make Ken and Barbie kiss all the time and get into bed without their clothes on.

While Wren shivered at the top of the stairs, Ruth had found her.

"You need a blanket. Have you eaten anything, honey?"

Wren stared at her.

"They'll find your brother."

Wren took a deep breath and asked the other pressing question that she was almost too afraid to ask. "What about Dad?"

"Didn't anyone come tell you?"

Wren shook her head, cradling her arms together.

"He's going to have surgery in the morning. He hurt his back pretty badly, but the doctors are sure they can fix him up good as new. He'll be okay."

Wren stared at Ruth, trying to process it all. Her dad in surgery. His back hurt. But he'd be okay, everything would be okay, except that Jack was still gone.

Wren kept picturing her little brother out in the storm in his Christmas pajamas, not in the suit he'd been wearing during the party. She pictured him at her bedside asking to sleep with her, but then she saw his little body crushed on the sharp rocks or floating at the bottom of the ocean. Worse images came to her that included sharks and horrible men with yellow teeth, but Wren couldn't hold those in her head for long without wanting to scream and run out of the house.

In the gray morning, Wren heard a helicopter move up and down the shoreline. She sat at the bedroom window all the next day. Only Ruth came up to see her.

"We need to pray that God takes care of your brother."

Wren couldn't pray. No words would come

to her. She couldn't talk or eat or sleep.

Mom returned home, though Wren avoided her. She yelled at Barb, trying to blame her, but Barb yelled back, "This isn't my fault. You were smashed, and I already told you that Wren was watching him."

Wren had never spoken to her mother as Barb did.

Another grueling day and night and then at sunrise, the house came alive with shouts and tears that Wren thought were full of despair at first. Then she realized they were joy, not terror.

"They found him!" Ruth called up to her perch at the top of the stairs. "He's going to be okay."

Jack was flown to the same hospital where Dad was recovering from surgery.

Ruth said praise be to God, over and over again. Everyone was happy, hugging, thrilled. As Mom cried with a huge smile on her face, again picking up her purse and keys, she turned to hug the person beside her and saw that it was Wren. Her smile faded from joyous to a forced expression, and the hesitation before her embrace felt like an hour of deciding whether to bring Wren into her arms or not. Finally, Mom did reach for her, but her arms felt cold to Wren. They felt forever cold to her in the years after. Was that her own projection, or did her mother stop loving her that weekend? Had they all stopped loving her that weekend? One thing Wren knew for sure, their family was never the same.

They were decades beyond those days. Wren stood at the window of the kids' room. She could see the events almost as clearly as if they were happening again before her eyes. Now she could take it apart and know it wasn't really her fault. She couldn't imagine asking Charlie to be in charge of another child during a family reunion. And if she had, she'd never hold him responsible for what happened. She'd assure him that it wasn't his fault.

But no one had assured her, except for Ruth and a few of the other women. Even now, though Wren knew these things in her head, she had a hard time changing her heart and her painful memories. And the shame that she'd carried all those many years continued to plague her.

And now, there seemed no way to run from it.

14

On Saturday morning the repeated sound of a horn blowing brought Wren, Charlie, and Ruth tumbling from the house to see what was happening. Charlie let go of his ears to point to the massive silver RV rolling up to the cottage.

"Wow, look at that! It's like a giant toaster on wheels."

"It's Barbara," Ruth said, clapping her hands together. Wren could see her older sister in the passenger seat, waving at them. She waved back as Logan laid on the horn one more time, making them jump.

The door opened and Barb came out laughing. "You should have seen how you all jumped at that last one."

Wren hadn't seen Barb and Logan in over a year. Her sister's hair was a darker shade of auburn and cut short with one side slightly longer than the other. She wore tight designer jeans and a beaded shirt.

Grandma Ruth and Barb hugged as Logan hopped out. He bent down to say hello to Charlie first, then grabbed Wren into a bear hug.

"You look fabulous, Wren," he said, and Wren was reminded how much she always liked Logan. He acted more like a big brother than her own siblings did, but their visits were always overshadowed by Barb's strong personality.

"You look great too, Logan." Though he did look a bit tired, probably from his long drive.

"Sister," Barb said matter-of-factly, "it's about time we see one another."

Somehow Barb made it sound as if it was Wren's fault. *That road goes two ways,* Wren wanted to say, but she was keeping her defensive remarks from coming out. And it was good to see her sister.

"Yes, it's been too long."

"And Charlie. My, you look very much like your Uncle Jack at that age."

"I do? I don't know what Uncle Jack looks like."

"I'll have to show you some pictures, because with his balding head, you don't look so much like him now." Barbara laughed.

"I like your car," Charlie said.

Barbara put her hands on her hips and looked up at the mammoth vehicle. "I don't, but would you like a tour?"

"It's like an entire house that you get to take with you."

"It most certainly is. When I travel, I like to do it in style. You can call me your five-star auntie."

Charlie gave her a confused look.

"Of course, with your mom, you don't know what that means."

Wren smiled with her lips pursed together.

Barb leaned into the open RV door and yelled, "Bradley!"

"Bradley came?" Wren asked.

"He's in back with either his head stuck in a video game, online, listening to music, or all three. Fifteen—just you wait."

Wren glanced down at Charlie and dreaded her sweet kid transforming into a teenager.

"Come on inside." Barb walked up the stairs. Logan helped Ruth with the steps, then waited for Wren and Charlie to step inside. The RV looked like one of the tour buses for singers that Wren had seen in movies.

"Wow! Look at that, and that," Charlie exclaimed, pointing out the flat screen TV, the laptop, and plush interior. He hopped in a swivel seat and started to spin, but Wren pulled him back out with a shake of her head.

They followed Barb down the hallway, passing a tiny bathroom and bunk-bed area, and into the back master bedroom. Bradley was stretched out in the back room with his hood covering his head and headphones stuck in his ears. His eyes were closed and his hands tapped his stomach like it was a drum.

"Bradley," Barbara said loudly, nudging him hard in the shoulder. He jumped and sat up, rubbing his eyes as he took in the faces staring at him.

Wren hadn't seen her nephew in more than a year. He'd made a remarkable transformation from boy to teenager.

"Oh, hey," he said, as Barbara pulled the ear buds out of his ears.

"You don't have your contacts in, do you?" Barb asked her son.

"No. But I can see—mostly. Hi, Nana, Aunt Wren, and little kid next to her."

"That's Charlie," Barb said sarcastically.

"Hi, Charlie."

Charlie waved.

"Get up and out of your pajamas," Barb

ordered and then led the way out of the room.

"It's great to see you, Bradley," Wren said, but he already had his ear buds stuck back into his ears as he plopped back against the pillows once again. Wren wondered what he was like before the wilderness camp and if this was a great improvement.

Outside, Barb took in the property. Ruth stood beside her and Wren and patted their backs. "I'm so pleased to have two of my grandchildren and two of my great grandchildren together."

"I haven't been here in decades." Barb stared at the main house.

"It hasn't really changed much, has it?" Ruth said.

"It's smaller than I remember," Barbara said, then looked at Wren. "How's it been living here?"

"Good, nice. It was a little strange at first, but the cottage feels like home for me and Charlie now."

Barbara studied her.

"What?" Wren asked.

"What what?" Barbara said.

"What are you thinking?"

"Nothing really. Wondering how healthy it is for you to be living here after all these years and . . . well, everything. I just worry about my little sister, that's all."

"I didn't move here because I wanted to. It was sort of necessity. Mom offered it to me."

"Don't get defensive now. Sometimes we make our choices subconsciously, and I just want to be sure you've moved on. You've never been good at moving on."

Wren let her annoyance simmer. Barbara had taken a career path that insured financial security, and she'd married someone with money as well. She'd never know what it was like to struggle and wonder how to survive until the next paycheck. She truly believed people always had the choice in the matter, and they made their beds after all.

"I've been extremely proud of your sister," Ruth interjected with her usual kind way of soothing out tension.

"You're proud of us no matter what," Barb said.

"She's raising a wonderful son. And she's done amazing things in this community. She started film nights in the park that have been a huge hit."

"That is amazing," Barb said with just enough niceness to cover the sarcasm.

"Why don't we go inside for some coffee and tea," Wren said. Logan walked toward them.

"Coffee sounds great," he said.

"When's Jack coming?" Barb asked.

"Thursday—they couldn't come any earlier. I have to work at the beginning of the week, but I'm taking off Thursday and Friday."

"So we'll have plenty of time together. This could be great or disastrous."

For the first time, Wren and Barb agreed on something.

Wren didn't see Bradley for the rest of the morning. He seemed uninterested in Charlie and the rest of them. Barb seemed content to explore the grounds and sit around talking to Ruth while Logan napped, hung out inside the RV, and tinkered with the engine.

Wren had spoken to Charlie about being around Bradley. She didn't mention the wilderness camp, and she'd kept her warning general. But she worried about the dangers she couldn't say out loud—Internet porn, dirty jokes, or even drugs. She resolved to keep a close eye on Charlie this week.

In the afternoon Ruth went to take a nap, and Charlie followed Logan as they checked the fluids and tire pressure on the RV. Barb and Wren remained in the cottage, cleaning up after lunch and then sitting down to go over the guest list for the party.

"So—any man in your life?" Barb asked, probing her face with her eyes as they sat at the table with the laptop and a small stack of returned RSVP cards. Wren didn't have time to hide her discomfort with the question. Her immediate thought went to Paul, but there wasn't really anything between them.

"No," she said.

"There is." Barb's mouth dropped. "Tell me."

"No, there's not. Really."

237

"There certainly is."

"No, there's just . . . a friend. And another guy asked me out, but I'm not interested."

Barb continued to study her, and Wren shifted in her chair under the scrutiny. "The friend—that's the one I want to hear about. Is he single?"

"Yes, of course." Wren frowned at her sister's implication.

"Nowadays, you never know. Is he divorced? Any kids?"

"No, and no."

"How old?"

"Late thirties, I think."

"Cute?"

"Yeah."

"Job?"

"He owns a boating company and a café on the boardwalk—it's the one catering the party."

Barb opened Ruth's party binder and flipped through until she found the flyer for Callahan's Café and Catering. "That's interesting. Why hasn't he ever been married?"

"I don't know. We're just becoming friends. We're working on a project together—another film night program for the winter." Wren scrolled through the e-mails she'd received from distant relatives who mostly couldn't attend the party on such short notice.

"Oh, that's convenient."

"There's nothing more to say." Wren hoped

Barb would take the cue to change the subject.

"I'm going to ask Grandma about this."

"She doesn't know anything."

"Oh, I bet she knows more than you realize. She always does."

"You'll meet him at the party."

Barbara rubbed her hands together. "This is getting better. I was worried about some geriatric snoozer of a party."

Wren decided it was long past the time to turn the conversation toward her sister, though it surprised her that Barb was actually asking about her life at all.

"How's your practice?"

"Good, busy, thriving. But Logan wants us to retire in the next few years, or for me to take an extended sabbatical."

"You're only forty-one."

"He's fifty-four."

Logan didn't seem that much older, so Wren often forgot. She couldn't imagine Barb retiring from her medical practice after so many years of building it. "You're considering it?"

"Not at all. He thinks I am, but I didn't go through med school to retire when my practice is finally doing this well."

"What will Logan do?"

"I don't know. He's going through one of those guy things. He'll probably have an affair next, if he's not already having one."

"Are you serious?" Wren closed the laptop and stared at her sister. Barb shrugged it off as if her comment was nothing. Was this her act, or did she really not care?

"It's how things are, Wren. How people are. If our marriage survives for life, I'll be shocked. I never thought it would in the first place. Don't look so freaked out. I'm a practical woman, always have been. You were the dreamer, and that's what ends up hurting you. Life is *this*— the hard stuff. I expect the good and the bad, and I don't romanticize things."

"That seems so . . ."

"Sad, yeah, I know you think so. But it's not sad for me. It's okay, really. I get so much out of my work, my patients, and colleagues. My marriage is extra. I enjoy marriage and sharing life with Logan, but . . . *c'est la vie*, right?"

Wren couldn't believe her sister just said *c'est la vie* about her marriage.

"What about Bradley?"

She shrugged. "He'll be in college in three years."

Wren tried to rid herself of the growing sorrow. She wanted to grab on to her sister and hold her tightly. Her act was simply that—an act. It had to be. Wren knew the dreamer Barb had been as a child. Life might have crushed it out of her, but that little girl resided in her sister somewhere. Barb was an academic and a professional, but Wren had seen her stack of gaudy romance novels in the RV. There was a yearning in her for something more.

Barb was in pain. It was suddenly visible as if her sister wore a sign on her shirt, and it stunned Wren. Barb was so difficult to be around that Wren kept herself on the defensive, protecting herself without thinking about what her sister was actually feeling.

They went to work on the guest list, discussing different relatives and their memories of them. But Wren kept thinking about how the past haunted not only her but all of them. Wren had no clue what to do about it.

15

Wren rose early the next morning and slipped on her running shoes. She needed time alone and exercise always helped clear her head. Her favorite trail meandered in and out of the forest along the cliff edge above the rocky shoreline with scattered views of the coves, hidden beaches, and the open sea.

The morning was cool and foggy. The pines and cedars towered overhead with the green ferns crowding the trail. The colors in the deciduous trees were definitely turning, fading toward gold and sienna tones, and soon the forest would blaze with colors. In a meadow, a stand of aspens was halfway toward gold. Their small heart-shaped leaves sounded like bells jingling in the breeze. Wren breathed in the fresh-forested scent mixed with the sea, and her overactive thoughts fell away.

Nature reminded her of the greatness of God and of how temporary her immediate worries were. She ran at a brisk pace, her movement and presence small compared to the timelessness around her, the revolving of seasons, the growth toward the sun, the intricate balance of life and death that had been designed with precision. God was the designer, the God of nature and the God of her life. How easily she forgot Him. Why was it so difficult for her to integrate her faith into the details of life?

Wren slowed to a walk to take it all in. A sense of awe welled within her that reminded her of singing, how when she lost herself in a song it was like releasing something beautiful that had been bottled up. The desire to sing was rising within her, but instead, she prayed.

More of you, God. Give me more of you throughout my day, in my relationships, in my thoughts and heart.

The trail opened up from the forest to move along the cliff's edge. Someone was standing at the point, staring out toward the sea. Wren couldn't go along the path without passing where he stood, but she didn't want to interrupt someone else's escape. She was debating whether to go forward or turn back, when Logan turned from the ocean and spotted her. He waved and she walked the distance between them.

"Another early riser?" Logan said as she approached.

"Yes, we're kind of boring compared to those night owls."

"Some might say responsible. We're also getting exercise and fresh air—can't knock us for being health-conscious."

"That sounds just like me," Wren joked as she and Logan walked toward the view. Wren thought of what Barb had told her about her marriage, and the sadness crept through her. This time she tried releasing it and asking God to guide them.

"This is an amazing place. I'm really glad we came."

"Me too." And Wren was surprised to realize that she meant it, at least so far. "I hope you don't feel like you have to stay in the RV. Come inside whenever you want."

"I will. Yesterday was the Bears game, so it was a self-imposed seclusion."

"That makes me feel better. I thought you just didn't like me."

"There's that too." Logan and Wren laughed.

For a moment, they stared across the horizon

243

that was opening up as the fog thinned. The craggy rocks rose from the water with white-capped waves springing over them like fountains.

"It's beautiful here. I can certainly see why you like it. I'd never want to leave."

Wren had never spent much time with Logan. He seemed a pretty basic, uncomplicated guy, though he'd started a small business when he was still in high school and was a millionaire before thirty. It was computer software or something that Wren didn't understand. She realized she'd never tried to get to know her brother-in-law.

"Barb said that you'd like to retire."

He nodded, turning out toward the open sea again. A sudden sadness seemed to weigh him down. "Yeah, but she's not serious about it. Your sister placates my ideas with maybes. We have enough money, and she doesn't love what she does as much as she says. Between you and me, I think she hates it. For me, I've given my life to making money. And here I am with what to show for it, except a load of money? I gave up my high school years, college, all of my youth to be successful. I have an accomplished, stubborn wife and a gifted yet annoying son, both of whom I love like mad. But we don't know one another. We have everything we want, and nothing at all."

Wren shivered in the morning chill. Logan had given this a lot of thought, and what could she say? He was speaking the words she'd wondered about, but the honesty of saying them out into the air made her unable to respond. Did she give advice? And what would she say? Material things will never complete you? God is the answer? He can fulfill your life, though I haven't really let Him fulfill my life? The ideas sounded trite in her thoughts.

"I'm sorry," she muttered.

"No, don't be." Logan smiled and looked tired for a moment. "I think it's about to change. Maybe I'm going to lose everything or find everything. But I'm not going to keep living in this meaningless existence."

"What are you going to do?" His words sent a panic through her.

"I have no idea."

Wren touched his arm, and Logan turned with his expression changing, moving from sadness to confusion to something else. He faced her fully, reaching his hand toward her cheek and leaned toward her ever so slightly as if he might kiss her. Wren stepped back, surprised.

"Whoa," Logan said, taking a few steps back with his face taking on the flush of embarrassment. "I have no idea what just happened."

Wren stood several feet away and couldn't meet his eyes. "Me neither."

"I don't know what's wrong with me. But can we just forget about that? Rewind a few minutes."

"I'd like that very much," Wren said, and tried to reassure him with a smile.

"Thank you. I sincerely apologize." Logan made a slight bow. "Now, I should head back to the RV."

"And I better head down the trail and get some cardio."

Wren raced down the trail with her feet pounding the earth.

A text from Paul was waiting on her cell phone, inviting the family to go deep sea fishing on his boat that afternoon.

Charlie was ecstatic about the idea. He'd never been out in a boat on the ocean. Barb told Bradley he was going whether he liked it or not, but she was staying home with Ruth. Logan hated boats, so he excused himself, and Wren found herself taking Charlie and Bradley before she could think of a way to say no.

She packed the car with their backpacks filled with extra clothing, snacks, and waters, much like what she brought on their bird-watching outings.

Wren thought about her rule against introducing Charlie to a guy she was dating before it became serious. But it didn't apply here. First, Charlie already knew Paul. Second, they weren't dating. He supposedly was dating someone else, though Wren was beginning to wonder if that were true or not.

Plus, there would be other people coming along, and Bradley was one of them. Wren wished she could create some attachment or affection for her nephew, but it just wasn't there. She tried to be nice to him, searching for a connection, asking him about his music on their drive to the harbor. He gave one-word responses, though Charlie appeared to take an increasing interest in his cousin.

"I'm so excited to go out in a real boat," Charlie said when they got out at the harbor. He was decked out in his rain boots and rain jacket, and carried his fishing pole.

Wren tried to keep from laughing. She hadn't noticed all this when they'd loaded up. "Is there a forecast for rain?"

"Mom, haven't you watched those reality fishing shows on Discovery Channel? This is dangerous business and everyone gets really wet. You'd better have your rain gear too."

"I hope it's not that dangerous today."

Charlie glanced at Bradley to see if there was even a spark of interest. He stared blankly at the ocean as if still listening to his music, though Barb had insisted he leave his iPod at home.

"Oh, I think it will be."

"Mr. Callahan said we'll use the boat's fishing poles. Yours is for rivers—it would break in the ocean with the giant, dangerous fish we're going to catch."

"You are so right," Charlie said with a nod.

Paul waved to them as they approached. Wren had to admit he looked handsome in his thick jacket, stocking hat, and rain pants.

"Come aboard," he called to the boys. "I meant to ask if any of you get seasick and have the seasickness patch?"

"Oh, I didn't even think of that. I don't get car sick, but I'm not sure about seasick."

Paul offered her his hand as she climbed into the large fishing boat. Wren squeezed her hand closed after he released it, trying to rid herself of the tingle of electricity that ran from her fingers up her arm. Paul introduced her to another man, Harvey, who was going to captain the boat so Paul could help them fish.

They churned out of the harbor slowly and Cottage Cove grew smaller behind them, the tree-covered hills in their early autumn coats rising above the town. Charlie asked Paul questions about the boat, fishing, what kind of bait they'd be using. Wren enjoyed watching the excited expression on Charlie's face, yet it reminded her again of how her son longed for a father figure. Was she denying him in protecting him from his real father?

As soon as they increased speed and hit the rougher waters, Wren felt it. Her stomach lurched up and down, and her head began to hurt. She hoped when they stopped she'd feel better.

"Not feeling well?" Paul asked, suddenly beside her. Wren looked up from where she'd leaned her head against the railing of the boat.

Every up and down motion was making it worse by the second. She nodded, trying to paste on a smile.

"Let's get you back to shore."

She shook her head. "No, Charlie is so excited."

"We'll take him and Bradley back out."

"No, I couldn't ask you to do that." The boat dipped down and up again, and Wren knew it wouldn't be long before she was leaning over the side.

"Harvey, take us back in," Paul called with a motion of his hand. The spray from the water felt cool on her face, but Wren could hardly sit up with the sickness barreling through her.

The boat increased speed again, and Wren felt too sick to argue more. As the speed increased, the rolling motion decreased and her stomach somewhat settled.

As they returned to the harbor, they motored toward the dock slowly without a wake. The sea was smoother here.

"Mom, where are we going?"

"I'm sick. Paul is taking me back."

"Oh no. Do we have to leave? Can you take medicine or something?"

Wren glanced at Bradley, who was leaned back with his usual blank, hooded look.

"Charlie, do you want to drive the boat?" Paul called from the captain's deck.

"Yes!" He raced up the few stairs.

"Harv, turn it over to the kid."

"Captain Charlie, is it?" Harvey said with one hand on the wheel. Charlie grabbed the top with both hands as Harvey gave him instructions, pointing out the buoys and where they were heading.

"Is that all right?" Wren asked Paul as he sat beside her. She wished she could curl into a ball on the seat.

"Sure, Harvey will keep an eye on him. I didn't want to say this in front of Charlie. My sister drilled it into my thick skull that I don't ask the kids to do things before asking her first, and not in front of them. But I know Charlie will have a great day today, and I'd love to take him out. Bradley too, of course. I'll get him to catch some fish."

"I need to ask Barb, and I wouldn't normally—"

"Charlie will wear his life vest the entire time, and I'll watch him like he was my own."

Wren didn't have the energy to argue.

"Okay. Just please, be careful."

"I promise."

They pulled into the dock, and Wren couldn't wait to get out.

"Why don't I help you up to my office?"

"I'm okay."

"Uh-huh, right."

Paul turned to Charlie and Bradley. "You two sit tight, I'll be right back. Bradley, text your mom and make sure it's okay that you come out without your aunt."

"I already did. She said I have to."

"Bye, Mom. Thanks for letting me stay," Charlie said, wrapping his arms around her and squeezing.

"Give your mom a bit of air. She's not feeling very good right now."

"Oh, sorry."

Wren looked at Charlie as Paul guided her to the edge of the boat. "Keep your life vest on. Listen to Mr. Callahan and Mr. Harvey. Be careful. You too, Bradley."

"I will, Mom. Promise I will."

Bradley gave her an annoyed nod.

Paul hopped over the side of the boat onto the dock and then put one foot back on the boat to help her over. Her strong act was fading, and Wren wondered if she could even get far from the boat before collapsing. She just wanted to stop moving.

The dock rocked slightly under their feet. Paul glanced toward the boat, then slid his arm around her waist.

Wren wrenched her head around to check on Charlie and be sure he wasn't getting some wrong idea. But Charlie was inside the wheelhouse, and from the looks of it, getting a lesson in how to work the boat.

"Okay, good," she muttered and leaned in heavily against Paul.

He helped her up the stairway to an office that said CALLAHAN FISHING. Then he unlocked the door and led her inside. Wren barely glanced around as Paul helped her drop onto a soft leather couch. The room still spun and rocked.

"You should sleep a bit now that you're on steady ground."

He disappeared from view and returned with a water bottle, blanket, and box of crackers.

She sensed that he was kneeling beside her, but she couldn't open her eyes. If she didn't move or open her eyes, she felt somewhat better.

"I have more food in the little kitchen in there. Do you want me to stay with you?"

Wren shook her head ever so slightly.

"I don't mind. I'd enjoy it, actually."

That brought a faint smile to her lips. She cleared her throat and muttered, "I don't get car sick . . . didn't think I'd get seasick."

"Not many people are immune to it. We'll get you the patch before next time."

"Next time?"

Paul chuckled. "Okay, I won't mention a next time right now."

"Thanks. Go. With the boys. I'll be fine."

"Sure?"

"Yes. He'd be so disappointed." Her voice was just a whisper now.

"I'll make sure he has a great time. And I promise I'll keep him safe."

Wren realized how often Paul had emphasized how safe Charlie would be today. Was her protectiveness that apparent, or was he more perceptive than she'd realized? Right now, she just appreciated it and wanted to rest knowing that Charlie was safe and happy.

"We'll be back in the evening. I'll call you. Stay here if you want. Make yourself at home."

"Thank you."

Wren raised her hand with all the energy she could muster to wave good-bye. She heard the click of the door closing, and Paul's quick steps going down the stairs. She thought she heard the boat leaving the dock a few minutes later, and for a moment, a sense of panic shot through her. But she couldn't get up, and they were already gone.

Take care of him, Lord. Take care of all of them. Please, keep them safe. Harvey and Bradley too.

Wren woke some time later, at first unsure where she was. The afternoon shadows were long in the room as she remembered where she was. She sat up on the couch, and her seasickness was completely gone, not even a thread remaining.

Paul's three-room office was sparse and neat. A row of ships in bottles lined a shelf behind the front desk above a window that looked out onto the harbor. Some of the bottles appeared pretty old, and Wren wondered how long they'd been collected or if Paul made them as well.

She stood up, stretching as if coming out of a long hibernation. It was surprising how much better she felt. The other room had two desks—one with photos on it that made Wren believe it was Paul's sister's desk. There was a conference table in the center of the room and a small kitchen on the opposite end. Wren used the bathroom, then checked her phone, but there were no messages.

Back in the first room, Wren noticed a woodstove with several logs stacked up beside it. The office was old but remodeled in a minimalist design with several oil paintings of boats braving the rough sea on the wall. A large lone conch shell decorated the coffee table.

There was something about being in Paul's environment without him being here that drew her to him even more.

Bradley had a huge smile on his face that matched Charlie's when Wren met the boat at the dock. They held up large gray fish when they saw her, and Wren was assaulted by fishing stories.

"Paul is going to cook the fish for Nana's party. First, he's going to teach us how to clean them," Charlie said. Wren had only seen him this happy when he hit his first baseball after striking out the first three games.

"Thank you," Wren said to Paul after they cleaned the fish and packed up to leave.

"Any time," Paul said. Charlie gave him a tight squeeze and raced after Bradley up the dock toward the car. Both boys had thanked Paul and Harvey numerous times without even one prompt from Wren.

"This really meant a lot to them. And to me." She was suddenly hyper-aware of his presence.

"It meant a lot to me too. We'll have to do it again." The look in Paul's features drew her toward him and the air crackled between them.

Wren took a quick step back before she was completely swept away by this man.

"*The Old Man and the Sea*—that's your favorite book," she said, seeking some way to lighten things up.

Paul laughed. "Did you see that book in my office?"

"I might have. So I'm right?"

"Not at all. It's a favorite, but not my very favorite book or author."

"I'll get it eventually."

"I doubt it." He took a step toward her.

"I'd better get up to the car. The boys will be waiting." Wren said good-bye and strode up the dock. She glanced back once and saw Paul watching her leave. Wren sensed she was getting in over her head.

16

"Is that finally my little sister?"

Wren heard her sister's booming voice as she walked in the cottage. Barb would have made a great prison warden, Wren thought.

"Hi, Barbara."

"We have a problem."

Had Logan told Barb about them seeing each other on the forest trail? Wren had decided to brush the awkward moment off completely, though her concern for Barb and Logan's marriage had grown immensely. But Barb could make it into something much worse than it had been.

"Do you want to hear about the fishing trip?" Wren looked behind her for Bradley, who had spent most of the drive chattering about the fishing trip. When they pulled into the driveway, it was as if she'd turned Bradley into his old self when she shut off the engine. Now he'd disappeared toward the RV, even though Wren had invited him to come into the house for a shower. Barb was sitting at the kitchen table with Ruth's binder and numerous papers spread around her with diagrams and sketches covering them.

"I'll hear about that later," Barb said.

"Okay. Hey, Charlie, go take a shower—you

smell like fish." Charlie looked tired but happy, with his eyes heavy and cheeks pink from the sun. Wren sat at the table across from Barb and wondered where Ruth was.

"What is it?"

"I don't think we have enough decorations for the party. Your friend is doing centerpieces for the tables, but what else? This should look really nice. Maybe white lights, floral arrangements on stands, luminaria candles up the drive and pathways."

Wren stared at Barb as if she'd turned into their mother. "I think the decorations we planned are great. Are you volunteering to do all of this?"

Barb rolled her eyes. "I'm on vacation. Do you know how stressful it is to be a physician? When I get a break, I need to really take a break. This is not helping."

"Yes, but I'm not on a vacation. I'll be at work in the morning."

"So what are we going to do?"

"Listen, Barbara. I'm not going to do anything. I am not in charge of this party; I didn't even want this party in the first place."

Wren turned and saw Ruth standing in the archway with several photo albums in her hands. Her smile faded.

"Grandma."

"Nice," Barbara muttered under her breath.

Wren glared at Barbara, then stepped toward their grandmother.

"I'm sorry if this has inconvenienced all of you—and you especially, darling." Ruth set the albums on the counter.

"No, it's fine. I'm excited about it . . ." Wren wanted to rewind the last few minutes.

"I found where the old photo albums are located over at the main house. I brought just a few."

"I'll help you with the others."

Wren followed Ruth out of the cottage and across the drive toward the main house. They didn't speak until reaching the front porch.

"Grandma—"

Ruth put her hand on the railing for support and took a deep breath.

"Should you be walking this much?"

"Always using stairs is what's kept me in great shape for decades. I requested a second-story apartment at Shady Oaks for that reason. Don't worry."

"Grandma, I'm really sorry. I didn't mean what I said. Barb got me really upset, and it just came out." Wren slid her arm through Ruth's and walked up the steps with her.

"I know, sweetie. I also know it was unfair of me to dump this party on you without any announcement whatsoever. But I feared if I didn't just show up, you'd make a big deal about me coming for a visit and try to put if off until it was convenient for everyone. I decided to bypass all that and try to get my family together one more time."

"You're probably right to surprise me. I'm not very spontaneous, am I?"

Ruth put her hand over Wren's. "You never have been."

"I'm sorry. I am excited about your party. I'll admit, it wasn't easy when you first came, but I've really enjoyed the time we've had together."

"I have too, and I do understand what you're going through with Barb. I didn't have an older sister, but a younger one, and that relationship is tedious. It can also be wonderful."

"I need to communicate with Barb better. We're not on the same wavelength, and I get offended at everything she says to me."

"I'd say anyone would be offended by most everything she says." Ruth chuckled.

"Barb and I are just so different."

"You are in many ways, but you're tied together by blood and family. Don't let your differences tear apart what brings you together. I talk to her about these things as well, just so you know. But she's a tough one, and she's going through something—I don't know what it is."

"I just wish she'd get through it fast. By this weekend would be nice."

Later that night Wren knocked on the metal door of Barb and Logan's RV.

"Hey, what's up?" Logan asked, peering from where he crouched behind the back tires.

"I'm looking for my sister."

"She's inside. Go on in."

The door opened at that exact moment.

"What?" Barb stood, towering above with her hands on her hips.

"Just want to talk."

"I bet you've been sitting in the house for the past hour, trying to get up the nerve to march over here and give me a piece of your mind."

Barb's condescension was tearing down her resolve to make amends. Wren feared she'd get so angry, she'd cry the way she used to do as a child. Barb always found that hilarious and she'd no doubt think that again now.

Wren stared at her sister. "You know what? I'm done."

"You're done. That's the best you can do?"

Wren could feel herself shaking and hoped Barb wouldn't notice. She stared at her sister, her only sister, and felt such anger she wanted to scream or cuss or throw something. Her fury boiled up from deep within, pulling up all her frustrations with Barb from the past. But she wouldn't give in to it. Wren prayed as she stood there shaking, her sister staring down at her with a pompous smirk on her face. *God, help me, help me not explode and say all the things I want to say but know that I'll regret.*

"What? Go on. You're done."

"I am." Wren's voice was soft but firm.

"And what does that mean, exactly."

"It means that if you can't treat me with some semblance of respect, then after this weekend, I honestly don't see us having any relationship at all."

"Really."

"Yes. You can boss me around, but when you treat both Charlie and me with such disdain—it's inexcusable. You respect nothing about my life, and you constantly treat me poorly. I've tried to be patient, not let it bother me, just think of it as my sister being my sister."

"Oh, that's what you think?"

"I'm still talking. Don't interrupt me."

"Whoa, Wren acting tough."

"Barb. I'm serious."

"When are you not?"

Barb slammed the RV door closed, and Wren stared at it, trying to decide if she should knock on the door again. So far, she hadn't completely lost herself to her temper, but Wren didn't know how long she could control it if she stayed near her sister.

Someone clapping turned her toward the back of the RV. Logan walked forward, clapping his hands together.

"That was impressive."

"It didn't do anything."

"You'd be surprised."

"Why don't you stand up to her?"

"I do, once in a while. It seems easier to keep the peace."

"She thinks you might leave her," Wren told him, still shaking from the exchange.

"I might."

"Really?"

Logan crossed his arms, glanced up at the RV door, then motioned with his head for Wren to follow him. Wren hesitated, then joined Logan and they walked through the gate toward the lights of the cottage walkway. The chill of the night whispered over her skin.

"You can probably guess a number of reasons why I'd consider leaving your sister."

Wren nodded and a foreboding grew around her like a cold specter creeping through the forest. Wasn't that exactly what she was saying to Barb as well, that she was ending their relationship? Yet it seemed so much more final for Logan to leave his wife than for her to issue a sibling ultimatum.

Wren sat in one of the wrought iron chairs in the cottage front yard. She looked toward the RV with its windows ablaze with light, and then beyond it to the dark outline of the main house rising against the night sky.

"I love my sister."

Logan shoved his hands into his pockets and stood awkwardly staring at the RV as Wren had. "I do too. She doesn't give people many options, though. It's her way or else. I've done her way for a long time. We've been in counseling for a few months now, so I hope that helps us make progress. Your sister isn't as self-consumed and uncaring as she acts. She really does love you. She worries about you and Charlie."

"No, she doesn't."

"She does." Logan pulled the other chair away from Wren's and sat down.

Wren frowned, taking this in. "Is your family this much of a mess?"

"I was a foster kid," Logan said in a low tone. He leaned forward with his arms resting on his knees.

"Your parents passed away, right?"

"Mom died when I was seven. My father has life in prison. I've never met him, never even spoken to him."

"I didn't know that. Sorry I didn't." Why didn't she know about Logan's family? He was her brother-in-law, after all. As much as Wren sought to blame her family members for their dysfunctional relationships, she hadn't done much to change the dynamics either, not since the last big blow up. And here she was ready to dump her sister. Logan had been part of the family for nearly two decades, and Wren had always thought his parents had died—she even believed it was from a car accident, though she had no idea where that had come from.

"The thing is, I don't have a family, which is what it is. But that means I have no one but your sister and Bradley. Barb knows that, and I think

263

for years that made her feel safe. But I also see that having family can be worse than not having family."

"I suppose it can be. Since Charlie was born, I've distanced myself from the family because of that. It seemed better that he had little contact with relatives instead of having painful memories attached to them. Barb thinks you're having a midlife crisis."

"I'm beyond that. But I'm reevaluating my life and I bought an expensive vehicle—not a Corvette, but this baby"—he pointed across to the RV—"is the Corvette of motor homes. No younger women, don't worry. No other women at all. I just think everyone should stop and look at their lives now and then before we all end up old and full of regret."

"Yeah, reevaluating is usually good." Wren shivered. "That made me think of my mother. I don't think she's ever done that—evaluate her life. She runs from taking inventory of what she has, or more accurately, what she doesn't have."

"Barb could end up like that too."

"I hope not."

"We can't save those we love. We can try, but in the end, they have to do their own living."

Wren arrived home from work the next day after dropping Charlie at his music lesson, and before she could reach her front gate, the RV door swung open.

Barb leaned out. "You're home."

"Yep," Wren said. "Where's Grandma?"

"She's on the phone. I think she has a secret boyfriend."

"Really?"

Barb shrugged and walked down the stairs. "Maybe. There's some reason she's always on her cell phone and checking her e-mail. Anyway, I took her into town today, and we bought her a new dress for the party."

"That's nice." Interesting that Barb was talking to her after the night before.

"Logan heard a rainstorm is coming tomorrow. It'll only last a day."

"We get them now and then."

"You've only lived here a year, Wren. You act as if you're a native."

Wren stopped. "Does your sarcasm have an off switch? If so, maybe you should try to use it."

Barb laughed. "A comeback, I'm stunned."

"Well, you won't hear many. I'm not you. For some reason, I don't imagine you get compliments for your bedside manner at the hospital."

"How did you guess? But people don't care too much about bedside manner if I find out what's wrong with them. And I'm just going to say it—my job is more important than yours, and you aren't going to change my mind about that. I'm not being rude, just truthful. I'm sure you're important in your job too, helping

265

people find books to read and stuff like that."

Wren turned to walk away.

"Wait. I know I'm difficult. I speak everything on my mind, and my mind is a critical organ. It works well in trying to diagnose rare medical problems, but it's not so great for being a loving and generous person."

"This is your apology?"

"Sort of. What I do admire about you is how you are with Charlie."

This surprised her.

"Really?"

"You're a good mother. I wasn't, and well, we can all see the result of that." She laughed but with a bitter edge. "And the decorations will be fine."

Wren turned to Barb, who walked forward toward the house.

"They will?"

"Yes." Barb kept walking, and Wren realized that this was the best her sister's apology would get. She supposed that, for now, to make it through the weekend, it was enough.

A few hours later Wren sat at her computer desk in the nook while Barb and Logan cooked pasta for the family in Wren's kitchen. She was trying to pray every time she worried about them and their marriage. She didn't know how to talk to them about it, and Barb had never taken Wren's advice in the past, so prayer would have to do. Even as Wren thought that, she knew prayer was the best she could do.

Bradley and Charlie were playing Xbox in the RV, though Wren felt somewhat nervous about her son being around her nephew. His lack of respect for his parents and the rated M—for mature—games he wanted to play kept driving her to check on them every twenty minutes or so.

Paul had e-mailed. Wren felt excited to click it open. They hadn't talked since after the boating trip, and she found her thoughts wandering to him more often than she cared to admit.

I must be getting used to seeing or talking to you. Seems like a long time.

But business now, I've attached a draft pro- posal to present to the board at the theater. Read and revise when you can.

Wren closed his e-mail to open his other with the attachment when an e-mail from Derek caught her attention. The subject line read, "Please respond."

Wren,

If you received my e-mail, please let me know, even if you aren't ready to answer or talk further. I just want to know you received it. I've included it below in case it went to spam or something. If I don't hear from you soon, I'll try to call.

Take care,
Derek

"No." Wren stared at the e-mail. She certainly didn't want him to call.

"What?" Barb leaned from the counter.

"Nothing, sorry."

Wren glanced over her shoulder to be sure Barb returned to chopping up lettuce for a salad. Then she stared again at the e-mail.

She closed her laptop and joined Barb and Logan.

"Can I help?"

"No," Logan said at the same time that Barb said, "Yes."

"I hate cutting vegetables," Barb said, setting down the knife on the cutting board. "I'll finish the bread."

"Move over," Wren said.

Morning light filtered softly through Charlie's sailboat curtains as Wren sat on the edge of his bed. Charlie slept on his side with one hand tucked under his chin. She loved to watch him sleep. He didn't look ten years old with his face softened and round lips parted, but more like four or five. He rested in such sweet content-ment, unaware of the stress and worries that kept her from sleep.

The Derek situation couldn't be ignored, try as she might. Wren wondered what such an intrusion would do for her life and for Charlie's. Would he still be so innocent?

Wren jumped as Charlie's robot alarm clock came to life. Charlie moaned, and Wren bent to kiss him on the forehead.

"Time for school, sleepyhead," she whispered.

"Three more hours please?" Charlie groaned with his eyes still shut.

"How about five more minutes," she said with a smile.

"It's cold this morning."

"This is just the beginning of cold." And as Wren heard her own words, she feared how symbolic they might be.

Jack and his wife would be arriving in two days. She had to get herself mentally prepared. If she could just put thoughts of Derek away, pack them into some secret compartment of her mind that would keep her from returning to his letter and all the possibilities that might await them, then she'd deal with this after the party—unless he called first. She knew Derek had Charlie's cell number but wondered if Charlie had given him their home phone or her cell number. Ruth or Charlie might be the one to answer if he called. She needed to deal with this soon.

Throughout the morning and her drive to drop off Charlie, Wren pictured Derek picking up Charlie for the weekend, watching them drive away. *Joint custody* weren't words she'd had to deal with. Legally, she had full custody since Derek had signed away his parental rights. Yet, if he could be a good father, or even a semi-good father, how could she deny Charlie that because of her own resentment?

Scenario after scenario crossed her mind—the weekend visits, Derek coming to watch Charlie's recitals and bringing people into Charlie's life that she didn't know. Wren didn't want to control the entire situation, but she'd protect her son at all costs. What was wrong with that? Wasn't that a mom thing to do?

Working at the library, her mind continued to churn. Anger assaulted her next. How could Derek just pop into her life out of nowhere? How could he assert his role by saying "our son" as if she didn't know he had both of their blood running through his veins? He was the one who had seemed to forget.

Wren slammed down a stack of books, and all eyes turned toward her. She continued with the cart as if nothing had happened.

At lunch Wren went to the Village Brew more than ready to blurt everything out to Missy. She tapped the table and pulled the laptop from her bag. She'd nearly printed the e-mail, but Wren was too afraid to have a hard copy around in case someone found it.

"What's wrong?"

Paul was standing in front of her table.

"Oh, hi. Nothing's wrong." Wren's phone buzzed with a text from Missy.

I can't make it. Sorry. Will call tonight.

"Something is definitely wrong," Paul said as she set down her phone.

"Nothing, really, I'm fine."

Paul sat in the chair across from her. "Okay, you don't have to tell me. Can I get you a coffee?"

Wren could feel a rush of emotions rise up, and she feared if she spoke one word about it, she'd fall to pieces.

Paul stood. "I'll get you a mocha?"

"Pumpkin spice . . ." Wren could barely get the words out.

"Pumpkin spice latte, got it. Anything else?"

Wren shook her head. She wanted to tell someone about Derek's letter, but Paul wasn't the right person. Ruth wouldn't understand—she'd probably want Wren to forgive Derek and give him another chance. Barb would tell her how to respond and where Derek could go, and it would be full of colorful adjectives that would make a sailor blush. Missy had been her best bet.

Paul returned several minutes later, long enough for her to gather her emotions and stuff them back down.

"Is your family okay?"

"Fine. I think we're ready for the party."

Paul studied her face. And she thought, *Why not? He's a friend, right?*

She opened her e-mail account and found Derek's original e-mail.

"Charlie's dad wrote me." Wren turned the laptop toward Paul.

Think about something else, something that isn't this. Wren tried remembering a joke or something funny Charlie had done that week, but her mind was blank. Everything kept returning to Derek.

Paul whistled and leaned back in his chair. "That's shocking. Are you okay?"

The emotion welled up again and Wren shrugged.

"Seems your ex-husband has impeccable timing."

This struck a humorous cord in her for some reason. Her laughter was enough to release the tension that threatened to make her burst into tears.

Paul turned the laptop back toward her and leaned his arms on the table.

"What do you want to do?"

"I want that letter to disappear from my memory. But last night, he wrote again asking me to respond so that he knows I got the e-mail."

"And do you . . . have any feelings for him?" Wren glanced up at Paul. He stared at his coffee cup instead of looking at her.

"You mean like hatred?" She smiled.

Paul grinned. "Not exactly."

Wren thought it through for a moment, then explained, "I don't hate him, though I have hateful feelings toward him, that's for sure. But no, I don't have other feelings for him. I haven't for nearly ten years. But I always get in a mess over what's the right thing, and what's the best thing for Charlie. If I could ignore that, then this letter would mean nothing to me."

Paul nodded.

"You haven't written back?"

"No. I've hardly talked to anyone about this."

"I want to do the guy thing and tell you my opinion on how to solve this, but Emma would tell me that women don't really like that."

"I think your sister and I would get along very well."

"No doubt about it. She's certainly enlightened me to a lot of my mistakes in the past."

There was a moment of silence. Wren wasn't sure what to say next, but she didn't really want advice yet. She just wanted someone to know. Then later, soon, she might ask for Paul's opinion, though she'd likely regret telling him about this in the first place. This was getting too personal for her, this thing—friendship or whatever it was —between them.

"What are you thinking about now?"

Wren wondered if he could read her mind.

"Nothing."

"You may not know this, but when you're over-thinking, you crunch your eyebrows together until you nearly have a uni-brow." Paul touched the space between her eyes. "Right there."

"I do?" The imprint of Paul's finger tingled.

"Yes. It's pretty cute actually."

Wren tried to ignore his comment and not over-think that too.

"Before this month everything was going along so well."

"Was it?" He looked at her as if he didn't believe her, and she didn't quite understand what he meant. Her life had been less messy.

Boring. Protected. Stagnant. Complacent.

The words came from that place she tried to ignore.

"Your mind is in overdrive right now, I'm guessing."

Wren touched between her eyes and felt how her eyebrows came together.

"I tend to try working out every possible scene that might happen."

"And probably none of those scenes will actually happen."

Wren took her first sip of pumpkin latte, savoring the taste of spices on her tongue. Paul was right. None of her worried imaginings happened exactly the way she envisioned; they rarely happened at all. It seemed it might prepare her for disaster, but instead it only drained away the life she was living.

"Thank you," she said.

"Any time. So, you still haven't figured out my favorite book, or at least, my favorite author?"

"Not yet. But this week for sure."

17

On Tuesday evening Wren returned to the library to get ahead on some projects after taking Charlie home, since she'd be working a short week.

Paul and Dr. James were meeting about progress on the winter film nights, so Wren joined them. The plans were coming together even more smoothly than the summer series. The board at the community theater was expected to approve the event at their October meeting. The budget needed some adjustments, but continued to look appealing. Finally Dr. James picked up his coat and hat, and Wren realized it was already past eight. They said good-bye to one another, and Wren returned to her cubicle to gather her belongings.

She stepped out the door of the library and pulled the handle to assure it was locked. Rain poured off the eaves. Paul and Dr. James had already gone. She reached into her purse for her keys, digging around the bottom searching for them.

She kept telling herself to put her keys and cell phone in the little side pouches so she wasn't always digging through her entire purse every time a call came or she needed to drive some-where. It was a habit she'd yet to master.

The rain spattered off the concrete and onto her shoes and ankles. Logan had said a rainstorm was coming, and this was quite a downpour.

She bent down with her purse on her knees and dug through every crevice and crease again and again, then searched the lining for a hole in the seam. Nothing in her coat pockets, and she had no pockets in her skirt or jacket. Where were her keys? What if she'd left them inside or locked them in her car? Wren glanced up at the water pounding down at angles. And then Paul emerged through the sheets of rain and was standing under the eaves beside her.

"It's really coming down. I was waiting to make sure your car started, but you never made it to the car. Is everything all right?" he asked, brushing off his wet face.

"I can't find my keys."

"That's a problem. I brought this." He turned on a small flashlight.

"Great."

"Is that them?" Paul pointed the flashlight through the glass where a set of keys could be seen sitting on a chair.

"Oh no. I must have set them down when I was doing the alarm."

"Why don't I give you a ride, and you can get your keys in the morning." The rain forced them into the small space under the front eaves at the entrance. Paul's closeness was distracting.

"Uh, let me think, um, maybe. But I won't have a ride back. Maybe I should call someone with a key. Or . . . I could ask my sister to give me a ride in the morning."

Wren's legs were shaking and soaked from the splatters of water off the walkway. The wind whipped rain across them as they stood there.

"I can come out in the morning and pick you up if you can't find a ride. Right now, though, let's just get you out of the rain."

"Wait," Wren said, unsure how to ask what she wanted to ask.

"Wait?"

"I . . . are you . . . what would . . ." She took a deep breath. "Will your girlfriend care that you're giving me a ride? I don't want to cause trouble."

"My girlfriend? Wren, I don't have a girl-friend." Paul laughed and Wren could see his smile from the light of a street lamp.

"But . . . I heard you were dating Christine Meyers."

"Christine, no. She's a friend, and I try to be there to help ever since her husband died. Let's talk about this in the car, before you freeze."

"All right." She wanted to strangle Sue at that moment and felt embarrassed for asking Paul in the first place. She opened her umbrella, know-ing the wind might pop it inside out, but she took her chances.

Paul took her arm, and they stepped through

the stream of water into the whipping rain.

"I don't think your umbrella—" Paul was cut off by a gust of wind that whipped Wren's umbrella inside out and then right out of her hands.

"Oh no," she cried out, stumbling to chase after it.

"You get to the car, I'll get it," Paul shouted.

Before Wren could get far in her shoes on the wet walkway, Paul's arm was back, this time around her waist half guiding, half carrying her toward the car. He deposited her into the SUV that was running and warm, then raced around to the driver's side. Wren didn't move; her clothes, hair, and purse were soaked.

"This is some crazy weather." Paul was soaked as well. He set her umbrella in the back seat. "Do you mind if we stop by the café and get some dry clothes? I have some stuff you can wear too."

"Sure," Wren said, glad to not have to travel the twenty minutes home like a drowned rat, but she also wondered what kind of clothes he had for her.

Paul chuckled to himself.

"What's so funny?"

"You. So you thought I was dating Christine Meyers. Is that why you always give me the cold shoulder?"

Wren bit her lip. "I didn't give you the cold shoulder."

He laughed and said, "Right."

Minutes later Paul pulled down an alley to the

back of the café. He opened the door and held it for Wren to walk inside. They were in a small brick office with a desk, file cabinets, safe, and a basketball hoop on the back of the door.

"I have extra clothes since I practically live here or at the harbor office. There's a clean sweatshirt on the hook, and Emma keeps an extra pair of workout clothes in the closet for those rare chances she gets to run to the gym. You can borrow them. There's a small bathroom behind that door. I'll use the café's. Follow this hallway to the kitchen after you change."

He scooped up extra clothes.

Wren watched him go and shut the door to his office. She stripped off her wet coat, shivering from the cold. Paul's sweatshirt hung on a hook. She hesitated, feeling it might be too familiar wearing a guy's sweatshirt, but her teeth chattering made the decision. Her skirt had been a poor choice for today. In the closet she found some black sweats and running shoes that were a little big for her feet, but better than her wet flats.

After slipping the sweatshirt over her head, Wren read the logo that said CALLAHAN's. Wren looked at the framed pictures on Paul's desk beside the telephone. She recognized Emma and her kids in several. One was of a black Lab, another was of Paul holding up a huge marlin in some tropical loca- tion, and another was an old photograph of a couple—his parents, she surmised.

Wren gazed at a bulletin board over Paul's desk. The Film Night in the Park flyer was tacked up there as well as a scripture written on a three-by-five card, and several child's drawings, one with an arrow pointing to a boy figure that read: *Uncle Paul, I love you! xoxoxo Izzy*

One look in the bathroom mirror made Wren gasp. Drowned rat was an accurate description. Her mascara had smudged below her eyes, and her hair was damp and soggy-looking. Wren ran her fingers through it, then crunched up the strands in an effort to make it curly. After wiping away the mascara, she applied a lip gloss and gave up on any other improvements.

Wren was walking down the dark hall when a light flipped on ahead and the stainless steel kitchen came to life.

"Is it all right that I'm using these shoes? I'll leave them in your car when you drop me off."

"Sure. Emma would be all too happy to help you out. She's been wanting to get to know you, but as you're well aware, the working single mom life is quite hectic. Are you hungry?"

"No," Wren said, wondering how Charlie was doing at home. Ruth might forget to remind Charlie of his music practice, and that she didn't want him playing too many video games with Bradley. Then her stomach growled loud enough for Paul to hear.

"Her mouth said no, her stomach said yes."

"Okay, maybe a little hungry. But I probably need to get home soon." She gazed around at the clean, empty kitchen—counters, burners, ovens, walk-in refrigerator.

"Pizza, pasta, soup, or anything on the menu."

"Pizza actually sounds great, but how long?"

"Twenty minutes."

"Let me check on things at home first. Can I use your phone? My battery is dead."

"Sure, there's one on the wall there."

She dialed the cottage, hoping Ruth would answer. It was already getting close to Charlie's bedtime. Ruth picked up after a few rings.

"I'm so glad it's you. We were getting worried," Ruth said after they said hello.

"I'm sorry I didn't call sooner. I was in a meeting, then my cell phone was dead."

"No problem. Barb is here and we're doing fine. It's only been the last ten minutes that I became concerned."

"I locked my keys inside the library, and Paul is bringing me home, but first we stopped by his café."

"Oh really?" Ruth then repeated to Barb, "She's with Paul."

"Oh really?" Barb said loudly.

"Well, no hurry. Charlie is already asleep."

"He is? He must have been tired. Okay, then I guess I'll be home after we eat something." This felt both strange and a little nice being out at night without Charlie. Everything revolved around their life together and she had forgotten what it felt like to just be herself.

"Take your time. We're chatting and watching a marathon showing of *NCIS*. That Mark Harmon is such a cutie. Oh, and Charlie did his hour of music, and I didn't let him be alone with Bradley for very long."

Wren heard Barb ask what that meant, and Wren groaned to herself.

"All right, thanks, Grandma. Will you ask Barb if she can give Charlie and me a ride into town in the morning?"

Barb had to know the entire story before agreeing to drive her, and Wren listened as Ruth explained. Finally, she hung up the phone and returned to the kitchen. Paul dropped a ball of dough onto the flour-dusted counter. He wore an apron and grinned.

"You have time for pizza?"

"It looks like it. And it looks like you already knew that."

"The kitchen echoes, and pizza is my specialty. We'll talk toppings after I get the dough and sauce on."

"I already know my favorite. The one with basil, mozzarella, and tomatoes."

"Good choice. You can hop up here or I'll pull you in a chair, just don't tell my sous chef. She's meticulous about the kitchen rules."

Wren hopped up onto the counter beside him. He glanced at the sweatshirt with a look of admiration and smiled.

"Are you warming up?"

"Yes, finally." Wren felt most of the heat in the kitchen emanating from a brick oven built into the wall.

Paul rolled out the dough as he talked.

"Do you like to cook?" he asked.

"I do, though I'm far from a gourmet cook. I enjoy baking best." She watched as he pressed the dough with his fingers into a flattened circle.

"So you don't toss the dough in the air like in the movies?"

"I'm getting to that," he said with a smile, taking a handful of flour and tossing it onto the board. He rolled the dough with a rolling pin until it was a bit wider. "Do you want to toss it?"

"I'd ruin it."

"You just take it like this." He took it in his hand and slapped it back and forth. "Now put your left hand into a fist and your right hand flat under the dough, and you just toss it. Toss and catch, toss and catch." He made it look easy and the circle grew wider. "See, easy. Here, catch."

"No, no." Wren put up her hands and hopped off the counter.

"It's coming." Paul tossed it to her, and Wren caught it, making it wobble and nearly fall to the floor.

He stood behind her and showed her how to use her flat right palm and then her left fist to hold it, and then spin it in the air. Wren felt awkward, but she laughed as she tried it.

"You have potential," Paul said after he took back the dough and finished up the tossing. He spread red sauce and toppings that he brought from the walk-in refrigerator.

"So you'd hire me?" Wren asked.

"I wouldn't go that far," Paul said with a laugh. He took a large wooden spatula-thing and slid the pizza into the oven.

"Is this what you always wanted to do?" Wren asked, feeling the warmth from the oven on her face.

He glanced at her as he cleaned up, pausing a moment, and nodded.

"I wanted to be a chef in France or Italy or Austria for a long time."

Paul turned on a stove burner and pulled a saucepan from a dangling hook overhead. He cut off a few squares of butter into the pot and went into a pantry, returning with a large chunk of chocolate. He brought out more containers and spices, adding them to the pot without looking at a recipe or hesitating as he talked.

"What happened to your plan?"

Wren warmed her hands in front of the brick oven. She could see the pizza cooking inside and smelled the scent of dough, sauce, and cheese that turned her stomach into a growling monster.

"I spent a year in culinary school in Paris and traveled all over the place. Have you been to Paris?"

"No. I used to dream about living in Europe, but that was a long time ago." It had been one of the first things that drew her and Derek together. He ended up getting their dream while she raised their son. "My ex-husband sort of hijacked the plan. He lives in Europe now."

"That doesn't mean you can't go."

"Oh, I know, I didn't mean it like that. But with Charlie, I guess it's pretty far down on the list of priorities."

"What is your list of priorities?"

"Well, um, I guess mainly I'm trying to give Charlie the best life possible. Lately I've wanted to be part of saving the library. If we don't go to Boston, then maybe that's what I'm called to do. But we were talking about you. Why did you come home from France?"

"I'd rather talk about you."

"You first. Why did you come home from France?"

"I think I told you about my falling out with my father. How he wanted me in the family business."

"Yes, that's right."

"After a year away, it started to nag at me. It had been nagging the entire time, but I was pretty good at ignoring it. I guess it was God and family duty, or both. My father became ill, so I came home."

"And took over the family business?"

"Yes. For about ten years, that's all I did. I became the fisherman that my father always wished I'd be." Paul stirred the ingredients in the saucepan over the stove.

"That's hard." Wren leaned onto the stainless steel counter, watching Paul.

"It was sometimes very hard. But when we do what God wants us to do, He works it out for us. Those years with my dad are something I'll never regret. He was proud of me, and we became closer than we'd ever been. Fishing was simple, hard work and created a bond with my family and this community that eventually helped me to open the café. It was my father who ended up asking me to do it before he died. He loved my chili, my soups, my foo-foo sandwiches."

"Foo-foo sandwiches?" Wren said with a laugh. Her opinion of Paul was changing with every sentence he spoke. She knew she'd misjudged him, but there was even more to Paul than she could have guessed. She'd judged him as a player and the stereotypical single guy who probably went to church to meet women. She realized that her judgments were as bad as Barb's. Wren mostly kept them in her head, but they were still there.

"Foo-foo is what Dad called anything that didn't have bacon and a slab of beef on it. He'd rib me for it, but he'd ask me to make my grilled apple chicken sandwich with brie and bacon every Sunday after church." Wren caught a hint of the bittersweet in Paul's smile.

"When did your father die?"

"Three years ago. I started the café plans right before, so he never saw us open the doors, but I know he'd be proud. And I still have the fishing company, though I'm mostly hands-off now. My sister is quite the office manager, and we have a great foreman, so my responsibilities have lessened considerably."

"So you can do more of what you love."

"Yes, like cooking and community work like our movies. Taste this," he said, holding out the spoon with his hand underneath to catch any drips.

"Yum," Wren exclaimed at the warm chocolate sauce with a touch of salty. "What is that?"

"Topping. We made up some vanilla bean ice cream this afternoon."

"I'd gain a lot of weight if I was around you for long."

"You could use some fattening up."

Wren gave him a frown. "Can I help?"

Paul seemed to consider a moment, then said, "Yes. Stir this for me while I get us a table ready."

"How often do I stir it?" Wren looked inside at the chocolate swirling around the bottom of the saucepan.

"Continuously."

"I'll try my best," she said, but stared at the chocolate sauce nervously.

Paul disappeared behind the double doors, and she saw a dim light go on in the dining area.

The chocolate was lightly bubbling. Wren stirred it and had a momentary image of more days like today with Paul. She could picture Charlie here in the kitchen too, sitting on the counter learning to cook . . .

She shook her head—what was she doing? This was exactly how her imagination took off and created all kinds of scenarios that were completely unrealistic. A few hours with a guy and she was marrying herself off to him, and this was Paul, the very guy she'd vowed to stay away from only weeks earlier.

Wren tried to release her mind's wild musings. She wanted to simply enjoy tonight, time with another adult who just happened to be a very interesting and attractive man. *Enjoy the moment,* she told herself. *Nothing more.*

It was a welcome epiphany over chocolate, she thought with a smile. The chocolate turned into a boil, and she hoped Paul returned soon—she didn't know what to do next.

Wren lifted the pot off the stove and carried it toward the double doors.

"Paul, it seems ready," she said, pushing through the doors and into the dining room.

Paul turned around fast with a long lighter in his hand. The room was lit by miniature white lights and candles flickered on nearly every table in the room.

"You caught me," he said with a sweet, embarrassed smile and Wren felt a surge of emotion for him, sudden and unexpected. "I wanted to surprise you."

"I was worried that the chocolate would burn. Chocolate can burn, right?"

"Yes, sorry, let me see." He leaned over the pot she carried. "It's ready."

Back in the kitchen, Paul took over again. The pizza was nearly done.

"So do you cook for all your dates?" Wren asked, her hand on her hip.

Paul put his hand over his heart. "You mean this is a date?"

"Uh, no . . . I mean . . ." Wren could feel her face flush hot, and Paul laughed as he wielded some knives and a variety of vegetables as if it were the simplest thing in the world. Within minutes, he'd created a salad that was bursting with color. He grated a white cheese over the top and sprinkled dried cranberries around the edges. On the stove, he heated another saucepan with a few drops of olive oil and dropped in slivered almonds.

By now, the smell of cooking pizza, the almonds on the stove, and the chocolate sauce were making her stomach roar with hunger and her mouth water. He pulled the pizza from the oven. The smell filled the kitchen.

"I don't think I've ever wanted to eat this badly in my life."

"I hope it's worth the wait."

Five minutes later they were seated at the table with the salad and pizza loading their plates.

"The cheese is hot, be careful."

He waited, watching her take a bite.

The flavors awoke in her mouth—the tangy sauce, a touch of sourdough in the crust, the cheeses, basil, and fresh tomato. "Oh," she said with her mouth full. "Mmmm."

"Good?"

"This is the best pizza I've ever had."

"You think?" he said and laughed. "You're just saying that to make me feel good."

"Oh no, it's really, really good. Incredibly good. I'm not usually a huge pizza person, it just sounded good tonight. But this is great."

He smiled and seemed nearly embarrassed by her praise. "I've done my job then—reeled in a new customer."

"Ah, that's it then." Wren squinted her eyes and tried to act angry.

"You bet. The only way I can get people in here is to make them fall in love with my food. It takes time to build a clientele. Dr. James especially loved the candles—we had quite the romantic evening and now he's hooked on my soups."

"Well, you make it easy for people to fall in love —with your food I mean." Wren glanced down at her plate, and Paul surprised her by not shooting back a joke that might embarrass her further.

He shifted in his seat and was silent a moment.

"Salad?"

"Sure, but pizza first, huh?"

"Always. So Charlie's dad—he isn't involved at all? And if my questions get too personal, just tell me."

"No, it's okay. Charlie's dad left when he was three months old. We haven't seen him since," Wren said, taking another bite of pizza. Her stomach and taste buds acted like the party had started.

"You have a lot to carry on those small shoulders." Paul studied her face, and Wren took a bite of salad.

"I have a lot to be thankful for. I need to remember that. My grandmother's been reminding me to worry less and have more faith."

"Sounds like a wise grandmother. I think there's a lot that's out of our control. Worry doesn't accomplish anything good."

A timer sounded from the kitchen.

"Ready for dessert?"

They talked about places they wanted to see. Wren explained how she enjoyed visiting the homes of authors, and Paul talked about returning to an alpine region of Austria. Then the conversation turned toward the single life.

"Have you tried the whole online dating thing?" Wren asked.

"Oh, that was a nightmare. Several of my waitresses convinced me to try it. I only lasted a few months and had one actual date."

"It all sounds terrible to me."

"The Internet dating was, but in other ways I've met some great people. I've also met some very scary people. When you throw in the church factor, that I'm a single guy there, well, I've had three women tell me that God told them we'd be getting married."

"You're kidding."

"I wish. I wanted to say that God didn't tell *me* we'd be getting married, but I tried to let them down a little softer than that."

"Why don't you give up?"

He shrugged. "I have at times. I've taken my focus off dating. But I want to share life with someone."

Wren felt an ache in her heart, not too far from the ache of hunger that had been in her stomach before they'd eaten. She didn't know if the ache was for Paul and his longing for someone, if it was her own ache to share life with someone, or if Paul himself was creating this wrinkle in her heart.

They drove home in a mostly comfortable silence, talking here and there. The heated seats in Paul's car wrapped her in warmth and the soft jazz music soothed her toward sleep. She couldn't remember a more enjoyable evening, except with Charlie, but that was something different. She wasn't in a mother role, but a woman role. It surprised her to feel like an individual, to be asked questions about her dreams, her worries, herself.

Once in their driveway, Paul hopped out quickly and came around to open her door.

"Thank you. This was a really fun night. It was great. The food, everything, was great."

Paul had his hands shoved into his pockets and looked at the ground, then up at her.

"It was great for me too. I guess I'll talk to you soon. Tell your grandmother and Charlie that I said hello."

"I will."

She turned toward the house when he called her name.

"Wren?"

She turned. He stood with his car door open and the light illuminating his face.

"I really had a great time. Thank you. And . . . well, I'll talk to you soon. And . . . I just said that, didn't I?"

Wren laughed. "You did."

"By the way. I've never cooked for one of my dates like that. A few have been in my restaurant, or I've dropped off food, or I've cooked for them, but not like tonight. And I have never let a date in my kitchen."

"Okay," she said, not sure what else to say. "That means a lot."

18

Wren woke at five thirty a.m. thinking about the night before with Paul, then other thoughts cascaded through her mind. Jack's arrival today . . . Derek's letter, which she hadn't answered and still had no idea what to write. She stretched out the kinks in her shoulder from the couch, then sat staring at the dimly lit room and taking in the quiet.

Missy had sent a text the night before that asked if she'd memorized Psalm 27 yet. Wren hadn't read it even once.

There was no better time than now, she decided, rising to get her Bible from her desk.

She was turning up the small lamp by the couch for better lighting when the idea came to bake some brownies for Charlie's lunch. He'd love that, and she could give some to Paul as a thank-you—though her boxed brownie mix might not be a welcome gift to a chef.

Two verses now, Wren told herself, realizing how easily distracted she was from her Bible.

¹The LORD is my light and my salvation—

Wren repeated the line to herself a few times. The second part of the verse said:
Whom shall I fear?

There seemed plenty to fear—"whoms" and otherwise. God didn't stop kids from being kidnapped, car accidents from happening, people from dying or getting harmed. But David had plenty of enemies to fear, and still he wrote these verses.

On to the next lines:

> *The LORD is the stronghold of my life—*
> *of whom shall I be afraid?*

Again, similar lines. Wren touched the word *stronghold* with her finger. Often she felt a lack of anchoring. A ship tossed on the sea. For David, the Lord was his stronghold. And there it was again, "of whom shall I be afraid?"

She decided to read a bit more, since the brownies really weren't a priority.

> *2When the wicked advance against me*
> *to devour me,*
> *it is my enemies and my foes*
> *who will stumble and fall.*
> *3Though an army besiege me,*
> *my heart will not fear;*
> *though war break out against me,*
> *even then I will be confident.*

Wren thought of the ups and downs of David's life. These were the cries of his heart—his songs and poems—not sermon notes for everyone to look at as an example. David's journal entries, in a sense.

> *4One thing I ask from the L*ORD*,*
> *this only do I seek:*
> *that I may dwell in the house of the L*ORD
> *all the days of my life,*
> *to gaze on the beauty of the L*ORD
> *and to seek him in his temple.*
> *5For in the day of trouble*
> *he will keep me safe in his dwelling;*
> *he will hide me in the shelter of his sacred tent*
> *and set me high upon a rock.*

Wren felt a surge of wonder within her heart at these verses. The image of God keeping her safe in His dwelling, in His arms.

> *6Then my head will be exalted*
> *above the enemies who surround me;*
> *at his sacred tent I will sacrifice with shouts of joy;*

Wren thought of the enemies around her—not people in particular. More and more she was seeing people as broken, but their actions were enemies surrounding her. Barb's constant verbal jabs. Derek's abandonment and sudden appearance. The past that was rising up to meet her this weekend.

Could she really find true shelter in God for all the challenges of life?

I will sing and make music to the LORD.

This line stopped her. She read it again and thought of her grandmother's request to sing at her party. Wren had successfully deflected the subject since first shooting it down, though over the years, sometimes Wren had the urge to sing again as if the wall she'd built around this childhood love had sprung a leak and come gushing up to the surface. Then just as quickly her life concerns and the busyness of single parenting made quick repair work of the wall, and it was sealed up tight once again. Sure, she sang on Sundays at church with the rest of the congregation, but that wasn't the all-consuming, from-her-soul expressing that she'd once known as a child.

Wren moved on in her reading, not ready to go too deeply into thinking about that one.

⁷Hear my voice when I call, LORD;
be merciful to me and answer me.
⁸My heart says of you, "Seek his face!"
Your face, LORD, I will seek.
⁹Do not hide your face from me,
do not turn your servant away in anger;
you have been my helper.

Wren felt tears on her cheeks. She'd been running from the past, from trusting others, from the weekend of her family reunion since she'd been a child. But what if God would truly be with her, in and through all things past, present, and future?

Do not reject me or forsake me,
God my Savior.
10Though my father and mother forsake me,
the LORD will receive me.

Wren's parents had forsaken her after that weekend. They might not have meant it, dealing with their own fears and pain, but Wren had gone from having a whole and happy family to feeling blamed for ending it. The shell of their family remained, but there was such emptiness inside all of them, in their relationships, in the falsehood of who they were.

The Lord would receive her? How fully had Wren allowed God to receive her? She thought she'd given her life to Him, but it was like jumping into a pool and clinging tightly to the side.

11Teach me your way, LORD;
lead me in a straight path
because of my oppressors.
12Do not turn me over to the desire of my
    foes,

for false witnesses rise up against me,
spouting malicious accusations.
13I remain confident of this:
I will see the goodness of the LORD
in the land of the living.
14Wait for the LORD;
be strong and take heart
and wait for the LORD.

In the stirring of dawn, Wren had a sudden image of a scene from C. S. Lewis' *The Magician's Nephew* when Aslan sang into being all of creation. His song brought everything to life.

Her chest filled with such longing and warmth, a sense of both excitement and peace. Her lips whispered her heart's cry: "Teach me your way, Lord. Lead me in a straight path. I put my confidence in you, that I will see your goodness in the land of this living. I wait for you, Lord, in my heart, soul, mind, and life, I will wait for you."

19

Jack rose from the driver's side of the rental car. He squinted and shielded his eyes against the late-afternoon sun. It had been eight years, and Jack wasn't the scrawny college student he'd been the last-time she saw him. He looked like a real man now, broader through the shoulders, no longer lanky but filled out.

Wren walked toward the car, grateful for once to have Barb beside her. They embraced one another politely. Jack appeared distracted, then turned to the woman coming around the car.

"Barb and Wren, my wife, Megan."

Megan moved toward Wren with as much warmth as Jack had coolness. They were like winter and summer. Megan's smile lit her entire face, and she carried herself with the grace of a dancer.

She wrapped Wren in a deep hug. "It is so good to finally meet you."

A little girl popped out of the backseat of the car. Wren stared at the girl who looked around seven with red hair in a cute, short bob and freckles on her nose.

"Hi!" the girl said.

Wren bent down and smiled at her. "And who are you?"

"This is my daughter, Lucy," Megan said. "And she thinks of Jack as her dad."

"He is my dad," Lucy said with a wide smile that matched her mother's.

"Hello, Lucy." Wren liked the girl immediately.

"This place is cool," she said, gazing around as if ready to run off and explore. Charlie was going to love his new cousin.

"Let me get your cousins out here to meet you."

She walked over to the RV where Charlie and Logan were watching *The Three Stooges* and Bradley was playing one of his video games.

"Barb, you had to get the most expensive RV on the road, huh?" Jack commented with a slight smile, the most Wren had seen on his face.

"Of course," she replied.

Wren opened the door to the RV and announced Jack's arrival.

Charlie came bounding out the door.

"Charlie, this is your Uncle Jack, Aunt Megan, and your cousin Lucy."

He gazed around with an excited expression and seemed unsure whom to hug first.

"Hi, everybody! This is cool. I have a big family now."

It sent an ache through Wren's heart, both of sadness and of joy that at least for this weekend her son had the experience of family.

Jack bent down to look Charlie in the eye. "The last time I saw you, you were carrying a bottle, and you lost my car keys down a drain pipe."

"Uh, sorry?" Charlie said, peering up at Jack.

Jack laughed, surprising Wren. He acted differently with Charlie than he did with her and Barb. "I forgive you, finally."

"You are younger than my mom, right?"

"Don't I look younger?"

"Uhhh . . ." Charlie looked from Jack to

Wren and back to Jack. "I'm not sure."

"I'm the baby of the family."

Wren nearly teased her brother about just how much he was babied, but that was treading toward the subjects they'd best avoid.

Lucy leaned against her mother and studied Charlie with interest.

"Charlie, you could show Lucy around."

"Okay. Do you want to see our house first?"

Lucy smiled. "Sure."

Logan popped out of the RV and walked down the stairs.

"Where's Bradley?" Barb asked.

"Guess." Logan motioned toward the RV with his head, then walked toward Jack and Megan.

After another round of greetings, Jack asked, "Is Grandma around?"

"Taking a nap," Barb said.

"So, is she okay or what?" Jack asked, sliding his arm around Megan, who gazed up at him with clear affection in her eyes.

"What do you mean?" Barb asked.

"The birthday party, insistence on us all coming here, the guilt trip."

"Jack," Megan chided, nudging him in the ribs.

"It was a guilt trip that only a grandmother could give. 'I'm turning ninety years old, and I want to be with my grandchildren.' " Jack did a decent impression of Ruth, making them all laugh. "I was worried she has cancer."

Barb crossed her arms at her chest. "I thought the same thing, but she denies any health problems, and after being around her for the past week, I believe her. Sometimes I think she has more energy than I do. And okay, I might have called her doctor as well."

Barb hadn't told Wren that.

"She loved her retirement community," Jack said. "She said so just a few months ago when Megan and I visited for a few days."

"You've been visiting Grandma?" Wren asked.

"Yeah. She didn't tell you?"

"No. She hasn't told me anything about Shady Oaks now that I think about it, or about much of anything else."

"I'll call Grandma's friend Lonnie tomorrow. We exchanged numbers in case anything happened to her," Barb said.

"Lonnie—a male friend?" Wren felt like her siblings knew so much more about Ruth than she did.

"Lonnie is sweet on your grandmother," Megan said.

"Do you think Grandma Ruth has a little romance going on?" Logan asked. He and Barb's distance was made more pronounced by the closeness of Jack and Megan. But they were still newlyweds, Wren reminded herself.

"I don't know, but she's here for a reason. We could have been guilted into this little reunion down at her place. They have a community center and park for events."

"That's right," Wren said, remembering the tour Ruth had given her and Charlie on their one visit a year before when they'd driven from Chicago to Maine. Ruth loved the gazebo beside the fish pond and fountain. This made Ruth's sudden arrival very curious.

"This place has hardly changed. It's like stepping back in time." Jack turned, looking around in the way Barb had when she first arrived. Wren supposed that she, too, had this reaction when she and Charlie showed up to live there. The first month had been challenging with memories following her every step.

"The main house is clean and ready for you. Grandma Ruth brought in cleaners and stocked everything."

"We considered staying at a hotel in town," Jack said, staring at the house with an expression Wren couldn't discern. "I suppose we'll stay here though."

"I wouldn't want to hurt your grandmother's feelings either. It'll be nice for Lucy to get to know Charlie." Megan spoke, looking up at Jack. He glanced down at her and his expression softened.

"You've been married a year?"

"One year and two months. We eloped with only Lucy along. Neither of us wanted a big wedding."

"I wanted her committed before she bailed."

"That was a smart move," Barb said. "So, are we all going to stand in the parking lot, or should we go inside?" She pointed toward the main house instead of the cottage.

As they walked toward it, Wren remembered the three siblings walking toward the cemetery after their father's funeral. Perhaps she should have spent more time in the main house to purge her memories. Right now, walking along with Jack and Barb brought the past piercing back.

Wren remembered the day Jack had come home, just one day after he'd been found and flown to the hospital. Ruth and other family and friends said it was a miracle that he didn't have hypothermia or any injuries.

Jack would hardly talk, and friends and relatives spoke in hushed tones about how he was surely traumatized by the event—staying out in the cold for two full nights alone. He might need therapy, and who wouldn't after such an ordeal. He'd been found scrambling along the rocks, terrified but unharmed and surprisingly healthy. Children were so resilient, someone said. Wren heard everything secondhand or from over-hearing conversations. Only Grandma Ruth gave her direct updates, but she was often busy coordinating everyone.

When asked where he'd been, Jack mentioned a tiny cave, but he couldn't remember where it was. The shoreline was craggy with hundreds of tiny indentions where a boy could find shelter. Jack said he was trying to catch a lizard that ran down the sea trail, and then he'd gotten lost.

There were tears of joy as the story was relayed, balloons and toys were brought to welcome Jack's safe return, and the local fire department made another trip to Fern House to give Jack a fireman's hat, stickers, and a ride in the fire truck.

Wren stayed along the edges of everything or else completely secluded in her room. For all the festivities, she knew whenever someone noticed her it was to remember that everything was her fault.

The day after Jack came home, Mom began packing everything that wasn't essential, ordering the girls to help. They packed away summer into their suitcases, and in many ways, Wren realized their childhood was packed up, never to be reopened again.

Dad was released from the hospital soon after, and they left Fern House the next day. Dad had to ride in the car with the seat all the way down. Jack rode in the front middle seat, and neither Barb nor Wren asked to switch with him. Mom sometimes reached over and squeezed his arm or shoulder as if to reassure herself that he was there.

When school started, Wren signed up for choir. Mom shuddered as she held the flyer. "Whenever I hear you sing now, I think of that horrible, horrible day."

From that moment on, Wren stopped singing.

She dropped out of choir without responding to her teacher's probing as to why she'd quit. Mom never asked about it. At Christmas, Ruth called to get the date for her Christmas program, and Wren heard Mom tell Ruth she was happy Wren hadn't joined.

Wren had become invisible to her mother. Dad, too, seemed to blame her; he didn't play with her any longer and was grouchy and impatient with her. Once when she told him about something she'd learned at school, he snapped, "Don't you ever shut up?" He could be loving on occasion, surprising her with a sudden hug or too much emotion, which only frightened her further. Other times he was irritated at the television being too loud or Wren blow drying her hair. Physically, Dad wasn't recovering, and he stayed home from work on disability.

Barb moved on as if the weekend never happened; she was preoccupied with sneaking out of her window and keeping their parents from knowing she smoked cigarettes now.

Looking back, Wren understood that Dad had become addicted to his prescription painkillers. But that was an era when people didn't look at it that way. He just wasn't getting better and needed his pills to minimize the pain. His temper was short with Wren, and maybe it was with all of them, but she guessed Mom had told him whose fault it was, and now he hated her too.

Grandma Ruth came for a visit and made cookies with Wren, gave her a few lessons on the piano. Her grandmother loved her; Wren knew that. Ruth didn't seem to notice the change in her family. She came and smiled and laughed as if everything were normal. In Ruth's world, maybe it was the same, maybe it wasn't as glaringly different as Wren thought it was. Their family had turned a different color in her mind's eye.

At the doorway to the main house, Wren stopped with a knot in her stomach. "I'll go see if Grandma is awake."

She left as they walked inside, wishing she had memorized those verses in Psalm 27; she could use them now. Wren also reminded herself she only had to do this for five more days.

20

They drove into town that night for dinner. It was loud and busy and perfect, in Wren's opinion, for a family with an elephant in the room they were all trying to avoid.

Bradley sat on the other side of Charlie and would lean over from time to time to show things to Charlie on his cell phone. During the drive to the restaurant, Charlie had told Wren that Bradley cussed a lot and liked to tell dirty jokes.

"What are you guys looking at?" Wren asked after the third time.

"Nothing," Bradley said with a sly smile on his face, pulling the phone back to his lap.

Charlie glanced at Wren, then to Bradley, who shrugged his shoulders.

"It was just some funny YouTube videos."

"What were they about?"

Charlie's face turned a hint of pink, and Wren knew he didn't want her to know what they were.

"Charlie, tell me."

Charlie moved his food around on his plate. "Mostly they were just crazy stunts, but in one, a girl's shirt fell down."

"What?"

Charlie looked helplessly at Bradley. Wren leaned around Charlie.

"Bradley, please don't show Charlie things on your phone that you wouldn't want me to see. Remember he's a lot younger than you."

Barb cleared her throat. "You're so protective, Wren. Your son needs to be able to deal with real life."

"He's ten years old."

"I'm just saying."

"Well, I'm just saying that maybe you could pay more attention to what your son is showing or saying to mine."

The table had become instantly silent.

"Whatever, Wren. This isn't the time to be talking about this."

That night Grandma Ruth moved into the main house now that Jack and Megan were there. Wren had her bed back. Wren slept deeply and told herself that she'd never take her bed for granted again.

A soft knock rapped on the front door the next morning.

"I hope I'm not intruding," Megan said when Wren opened the door.

"Of course not, come on in. Do you want some coffee or tea?"

"No, I'm good. This place is adorable." Megan turned around in the small living room.

"Thank you. Is everything okay over there? Everything's working after all these years?"

"It's perfect. I didn't expect to be on such a great vacation. Jack didn't tell me much about all of you or Fern House. It's a topic he avoids."

Wren didn't know what to say, so she asked, "He hasn't told you anything?"

"Well . . . some. He told me he got lost for a few days at a family reunion. That your father was injured, and it changed a lot for your family." Megan's eyes didn't reflect any accusation toward Wren, but still Wren wished to know what he'd said.

"Yes."

"I know Jack wants to talk to you and Barb about that summer though."

310

Wren's back stiffened. "It might be good if he waits until after the party. The last time I tried talking about it with Barb and Jack, we had a major blowout—at our father's funeral. It was not pretty."

"Jack told me about that. I think you'll want to hear what he has to say. But I heard you took today off from work and Charlie's out of school, so I was seeing if the family was doing something together?"

"We didn't have plans yet, but we can definitely do something. I wanted to look for a dress in town later for the party. I think Barb and Logan are taking their RV into town to get the refrigerator looked at."

"The weather said the fog would burn off soon. I haven't touched the Atlantic Ocean yet."

"So a half day at the beach?" Wren said, thinking how excited Charlie would be.

"That's what I was hoping to do. I brought some kites."

"We have plenty of chairs, sand buckets, and castle-making tools. That would be really nice, especially for the kids."

"Great. Ruth said she could cook something for lunch."

"How about sandwiches in town?" Wren said.

"That bad? I did notice that Jack winced when she mentioned it."

Wren sat on the arm of her overstuffed chair.

"She's never been a cook. Grandma Ruth was quite a diva in her younger years—at least, that's how she describes herself. Never the homemaker type, but at home in San Francisco upper society. I'm not sure why she's suddenly trying her hand at cooking now."

"Ruth seems like a woman who will be trying new things until she leaves this world."

"You've pegged her already."

Megan glanced around the cottage again. "Would ten or eleven be a good time?"

"Great. I'll get our stuff together."

Wren watched Megan walk across the road and up the stone path toward the main house. What a strange and pleasant surprise to have a sister-in-law, and one she already liked.

Now if the siblings could continue to get along, this weekend might work after all.

The fog had burned off at Black Cone Beach, revealing a beautiful autumn day. The breeze was cool and salty, touching Wren's face and soothing her as it had on her forest walk. Perhaps it was Megan's presence and Barb's absence, or Charlie and Lucy who immediately took to one another, or perhaps it was the drawing in toward God, but Wren's awkwardness with Jack felt nearly gone as they carried beach bags, chairs, toys, and ice chests to the soft yellow sand.

The sea also helped, as it always did. If only

Wren could capture this moment of peace the sea offered, bottle up the waves, the scent of the sea, the sense of escape from reality when eternity felt within reach and reality was of little importance beneath the grandeur of forever.

The moment they kicked off their shoes and dropped what they carried, the kids ran straight for the waves.

"There you have your Atlantic Ocean," Jack said to Megan.

"I have to touch it." She ran toward the water, light-footed and beautiful, and Wren could understand why Jack stared after her with such emotion in his eyes. Megan was enchanting as she laughed and jumped away from the waves with Charlie and Lucy. She bent down and stuck her fingers at the foamy edge, scooping some up and flinging it toward the kids.

Wren laughed at their screams and laughter, while Jack stood beside her deep in thought as he took in the sight.

Megan returned as they set up their chairs and blankets. Wren called to Charlie to roll up his pants higher. They settled in as the kids raced with their buckets to the wet sand to build a castle.

Wren asked Megan about her background. She'd grown up in California and been a ballet dancer, as Wren suspected, but a knee injury changed her life plans. She was a hospice nurse now.

"Hospice nurse—that's the one who comes in when someone is dying?"

"Yes, exactly. We go into the homes during the final weeks."

"That must be very difficult." Wren couldn't imagine this bright, cheery woman in such a dark, morbid position.

"Jack would like me to do something else."

"I didn't say that," Jack said, leaning over to take a quick glance at Wren. Jack barely looked at her, she'd realized the night before at dinner.

"No, you didn't say that," Megan said, reaching over to touch his face with the open palm of her hand. "But I know he worries. It's a challenging job, but extremely rewarding. I get to be part of the last moments of a person's life before he or she moves on."

"That's amazing, Megan. I hadn't thought of it that way."

"It's the worst time for the family, but I feel called to try bringing comfort and closure—something of beauty to all of them. In a way, that's what I wanted to do with dancing, but this is bringing beauty to the darkest moment of people's lives. Though it also includes changing bedpans and other things I won't mention."

Wren knew she wasn't created for any field of medicine—she nearly fainted every time she had blood drawn. But while she hid away within stories and books, Megan was an integral part of people's lives and their deaths.

Jack leaned around Megan and asked, "Do you mind keeping an eye on Lucy, while Megan and I go for a short walk down the beach?"

Again, it was only a glance at her, and for a second, Wren felt the sting of it and the thought of whether he really trusted her to watch another child after what had happened when they were kids.

"Sure," she said, swallowing back a sense of shame.

Jack stood, brushing off the sand.

"Thanks, Wren," he said, taking Megan's hands and pulling her up as she laughed. He really loved her . . . how very strange to see her brother in love. And she supposed it took someone like Megan to draw out such devotion in her brother.

"We'll be right back," Megan called to the kids.

Wren pulled a book out of her beach bag, mainly to feel it in her hands. Her usual pace of reading had slowed in the past few weeks, and she missed it. But Wren could never go anywhere without a book or two.

She watched the waves, the kids, and the hand-in-hand departure of Jack and Megan. They leaned in together, talking and sometimes pointing at one thing or another. Wren enjoyed watching them, but she also felt acutely alone in a way she hadn't known in years. Not inwardly alone, she realized. She knew God was with her, but how nice it would also be to share life and love with a partner. She remembered Paul saying he wanted to share life with someone. Was he interested in that with her? She pictured Paul pulling her up from the sand to walk hand in hand down the beach.

"Look, Auntie Wren!" Lucy called from within the sand castle.

"It's looking great," Wren called back.

Wren wondered what her mother would think if she could see this—her children and grand-children together. But since childhood, Mom had increasingly distanced herself from each of them. Even her coddling of Jack seemed more overbearing than loving.

This moment at the beach was something Wren hadn't expected to see. Maybe long ago she'd wished for this, especially when Charlie was small. He lacked not only a father but an aunt and uncle, cousins, and grandparents.

The sand castle was growing. Wren watched the waves rise and fall beyond them far out in the sea until they flattened and smoothed into the straight line of the horizon. Their endless motion never failed to capture something deep within her, as if it were a glimpse at eternity. The power and grandeur of the ocean was really just one element of God's creation, one element of who He was. And yet that small piece of God was His artwork, a drawing like something Charlie would tack to his bulletin board. That same ocean could crush rock into sand, take a tree and soften it into drift-wood, toss a ship onto the rocks.

Thinking of God took away the myriad of worries: about the past, what Jack thought of her, what to do about Barb, whether they'd move to Boston or not, her attraction toward Paul, and of course, Derek. God was here, whom should she fear? God was her shelter, of what did she need to be afraid?

God, thank you for this moment, here at the beach with this gift of family that I'd given up on. Thank you for never leaving me as I so often leave you.

"Mom, come see our castle!" Charlie stood and waved her toward them.

Wren rose from her chair as the kids motioned for her to come their way. She slipped off her shoes and rolled up her jeans, then walked toward them.

"This is impressive."

They'd built a deep moat surrounding their castle town. The towers were somewhat lopsided, and Wren could see where they'd patched up different areas of the wall when it crumbled. Inside, they'd made roads and more towers.

"Help us—we want to build a big wall down here to stop the waves."

Behind them, the line of waves was getting closer.

"The tide's coming in," Wren said.

Charlie was as serious as a construction

foreman. "I know. We need to get some driftwood and use sand to build a protection, and fast."

"Okay, tell us what to do." Wren winked at Lucy and pulled up her sleeves. She didn't want to ruin their idea by telling them that no sand wall was going to withstand the waves coming in.

"I wish I lived at the ocean. You guys are so lucky."

"We need to enjoy it more, don't we, Charlie?"

"You bet we do. I haven't built a sand castle since summer vacation."

"Maybe I can come visit on my vacations."

"That would be cool," Charlie said, glancing at Lucy fondly.

They spent the next twenty minutes gathering driftwood and packing it with sand.

"I'll be right back, I think I brought some little flags for the towers."

Wren stood up in the sand, brushing herself off. As she walked toward their picnic area she saw something fluttering in the breeze. She glanced upward but didn't see any birds nearby. A flock of seagulls were down the beach, pecking at something in a pile of seaweed.

The feather landed on Wren's towel.

She picked up the feather, bringing it close to identify it.

A sparrow. It wasn't a kind of sparrow she'd seen in Maine, and certainly not on the beach. Her thought jumped immediately to the song Grandma

Ruth wanted her to sing at the party. The same song Wren had sung at the family reunion of their childhood.

Was this from God, a nudge toward something He wanted of her? Or was it a coincidence?

A line of the song came to mind.

His eye is on the sparrow. And I know he's watching me.

Wren carefully tucked the sparrow feather into her bag. She returned to the sand castle and spent the rest of the afternoon at the beach playing with Charlie and Lucy.

Ruth had cooked a large pot of chili when they returned to the main house, all sun soaked and windblown.

Jack, Charlie, and Wren peered at the chili with some trepidation, until Charlie ventured a bite.

"Yum!" Charlie announced.

Jack took a bite and confirmed it. "When did you become such a great cook, Grandma?"

"I still have some surprises up my sleeve," she said with a grin.

After dinner, Charlie saw the delivery bags from Paul's café stuffed down in the garbage can. He pointed them out, which made Grandma confess.

"I didn't know they deliver," Wren said.

"Yes, your fella did it special, just for me."

"Your fella?" Megan asked, and Charlie watched her with wide eyes.

"My *friend*. So Paul came out?" Wren wished

she'd seen him and felt an ache of missing him. Where did that come from? Probably from seeing Jack and Megan together, she decided, though the feeling wouldn't dissipate.

Barb, Logan, and Bradley showed up and joined in the chili feed. The family sat around the large living room eating and telling stories about the day at the beach and memories from their own lives. Bradley sat in a corner chair plugged into his iPod. Wren hadn't seen him smile since the fishing day.

By bedtime Charlie's cheeks were bright pink from their day at the beach. His eyes looked heavy, but he was doing everything to stay awake.

"I like our family," he said as she tucked him into bed.

"I like our family too." Wren kissed his forehead and the tip of his nose. "Night-night."

21

Wren carried a pan of cinnamon rolls over to the main house. It was silent inside, but a fire crackled in the fireplace. Jack was pouring a cup of coffee when she walked into the kitchen.

"Those smell good," he said when Wren set the pan on the old cutting board in the center of the kitchen.

"They're definitely not health food, though."

"I think we can splurge for the weekend. Want a cup?" Jack pulled a coffee cup off a hook over the stove before she said yes. He inspected the inside, then poured her coffee.

"Do you like living in Williamsburg?"

Jack nodded, handing Wren her coffee and glancing at her. "I like it a lot. We'll be there awhile with Lucy's school, and her father lives there as well. Luce spends one week a month at her dad's house."

"You get along with him?"

Jack shrugged as he set two plates on the cutting board. "Well enough."

Wren wanted to ask more questions about Lucy's father. She wondered how they all worked together, did they have conflicts, and if it was hard for Lucy to bounce from one house to another. When did it get hard, and when was it easiest? How did they spend the holidays? Divorced and blended families were a topic she often wanted to hear about. She hoped it might help in how she raised Charlie. At times it reaffirmed the life they were living with Derek completely out of the picture; other times she wished for the broken but working dual families like what Lucy had. It wasn't the ideal mother-father arrangement, but that wasn't always the best situation either, as Wren knew from her own childhood. And there might be special gifts in having four parents who could work together for the good of one child.

"This is one good cinnamon roll." Jack took a second huge bite.

Wren dipped her finger into the cream cheese topping on the cinnamon roll Jack set in front of her.

She glanced up at Jack, then said, "Derek e-mailed me a few weeks ago. He wants to see Charlie. He said he's coming back to the States in a few months, and he wants to have a relationship with his son. He also wants Charlie to apply for a summer music program in Malta. Barb thinks I should have Charlie try out for it."

Jack was silent a moment as he chewed his cinnamon roll and took a sip of coffee. "And you believe him?"

"What do you mean?"

"I mean, if he's been absent all of these years, what makes you think he'll do what he says now?"

Wren thought a moment. "I guess there's no reason for me to believe him. I hadn't thought of that."

"Lucy's dad makes her a lot of promises. Megan and I don't believe anything until it happens. It's hard on Luce, and Megan gets pretty upset about it. So if I were you, I'd wait to see if Derek comes back to the States and follows through with staying in contact with you in the first place."

"He implied that he'd like us to give it another try."

Jack laughed. "Typical deadbeat. Well, unless you're interested in that, which I hope you aren't, Derek will most likely disappear as he did before."

Wren realized Jack was probably correct. She'd been worrying about this. Yet it had never occurred to her that Derek wouldn't follow through with the plans he expressed in the e-mail.

"But, if he doesn't, it'll be okay. You've raised a great kid and that won't change, whether Derek is in his life or not. You won't lose your son."

Wren nodded and a weight lifted from her chest. "Thanks, Jack."

"Sure thing." He looked at her, really looked right at her, and their eyes connected.

Wren picked up her cinnamon roll and took a bite.

"Good morning," Megan said cheerily as she walked into the room, pulling a sweatshirt over her head.

Wren caught the way Jack's face softened and lit up at the sight of her. He didn't move from the chair, but the glance between them said more than words could express.

"How did you sleep?" Wren asked as Megan pulled up a bar stool and sat beside Jack, putting her arm around him and kissing his cheek.

"I slept great. It was surprisingly cold, which felt good under the covers. Your brother is like a heater, which isn't so great in the summer, but wonderful in the winter."

Jack slid his coffee mug over to Megan.

"Wren made cinnamon rolls to die for," Jack said matter-of-factly, but the compliment made Wren smile.

"Yum, and they're still warm," Megan said.

"Would you like your own cup of coffee?" Wren asked.

"I'll share with Jack. I don't need much coffee in the morning, just a few sips are good for me."

Megan was so comfortable with Jack, and he with her. Wren had never seen this before with her brother. Even in his friendships while growing up, there appeared a rigid boundary with everyone.

"This place is amazing. I can't imagine getting to come here every summer as a kid."

"Yeah, we have a lot of memories here," Wren said, and she noticed how Jack's eyes bounced toward her when she said it.

"Jack said your mom is thinking of selling it."

"She is. I think she's going to decide when she and Howard return from their world travels next summer."

"Where would you go if that happens?"

"Not sure, but Charlie and I might move to Boston whether or not Mom sells the property."

"Why?" Jack asked, taking his cup back from Megan.

"Charlie's being considered for admission to a music school there."

"That's amazing," Megan said. "Jack told me that he's a little virtuoso."

"He did?" Wren didn't know Jack knew anything about her or Charlie.

"Ruth sent me a link to one of his recitals."

"She did? I guess there's a lot that I don't know about."

"There always was," Jack said with a smile, and Wren realized this was the first time he'd teased her in over a decade.

Back at the cottage, Wren checked in on Charlie, but he was sleeping soundly. She found a text on her phone from Paul.

PAUL: Hope time with your family is going well.

WREN: Going surprisingly well, thanks.

WREN: Talked to my brother about that e-mail from Charlie's dad. He doesn't think Derek will follow through.

PAUL: Good chance of that actually.

Wren sat for a moment, looking at her phone. It was nice having a male to discuss such things. Another text came through.

PAUL: I didn't try giving advice. Hope that was the right thing. I'm in a conflicted position.

Wren read his text over several times, then wrote him back.

WREN: Confused.
PAUL: I don't want to give advice about your
  ex-husband in case I'm not being objective.
  My motives might be clouded.

His motives were clouded . . . was he saying what she thought he was?

PAUL: This isn't best said over text. Let's get
  together soon. If you want, that is.

Wren didn't know how to respond. Her own feelings were growing toward Paul, and it both thrilled and terrified her. She typed several responses, saying too much, then immediately deleted them.

WREN: Okay.
PAUL: Okay is all I need to hear. See you
  tomorrow at the party. I'll be the guy in the
  apron.

Wren's face flushed and the fluttering inside of her chest felt very seventh grade—but she was enjoying it immensely.

She opened her computer and worked on an e-mail to Derek while she had the courage, making several attempts that were too long or too rude or too informative. Did she use "Dear Derek" or just his name? Should she sign it "From" or "Sincerely" or what? Finally, she reread her e-mail and was satisfied.

Derek,
  I received your e-mail. Right now I have family visiting and would appreciate more time to process this. When you know for certain if you are coming to the States or not, let me know and we can discuss Charlie further.
Wren

It was formal enough to cut the familiarity, but it also didn't stop Charlie from potentially meeting his father. Wren felt it was the best she could do. Her phone had beeped several times while she was working on the e-mail, and she hoped it was Paul again. The first one was from Missy—she'd be arriving with the centerpieces for the party soon. Wren went down the hall to wake Charlie.

"Hey, sleepyhead. Franklin will be here in just a bit."

Charlie popped his head up. "Great. Oh, but I better hide a few of my things."

Wren grimaced, but it was probably the best way to avoid another scene like that last one. She heard a knock on the door.

"That must be them," Wren said as Charlie jumped out of bed.

Bradley stood at the door, his hood pulled over his head. He popped an ear bud from his ear, and Wren saw the hole where he'd previously had a piercing.

"We're out of milk, do you have any for cereal?"

"Sure, come on in."

In the kitchen, Wren pulled out two bowls, the milk, and cereal.

"Oh, hey," Charlie said when he saw Bradley. His hair was sticking up in the back. Wren frowned at her son's "hey" that sounded nothing like his usual greeting, and she hoped Bradley would hurry back to his video games before Franklin arrived.

Wren's phone beeped a reminder that she had an unopened text. Not Paul, but Barb.

Family meeting ASAP, main house. We have a problem.

22

"It took you long enough," Barb said when Wren came through the front door.

"I was getting our sons some breakfast," Wren said. Barb's sour mood wouldn't spoil her own. Barb, Logan, Megan, and Jack sat around the living room, looking none too happy.

Missy came up the porch stairs behind Wren.

"This is Missy." Wren made introductions as Lucy came skipping into the room.

"Where's Charlie?" Lucy asked.

"He's in the cottage with Bradley, and his friend Franklin should be there now too. Will you tell them to play outside or over here?" Wren didn't like leaving Bradley with the younger kids even for a short time.

"Sure," she said, racing out the door.

"Where's Grandma?"

"She's on the phone with some guy from her retirement home."

"It's probably Lonnie," Megan said with a mischievous smile and a glance at Jack.

Barb cleared her throat. "Excuse me, we need to figure some things out."

"Oh yes, the problem. I assumed it wasn't an emergency since you didn't walk across the yard to tell me. Let me show Missy where the side entrance is and the downstairs bedroom so we can unload the rest of the centerpieces."

"I'll help with unloading. Then you all can talk," Logan said, jumping up from the chair. Megan rose to help too, but Logan told her he could take care of it.

Wren returned from the bedroom after showing Missy the side door. She sat on the sofa and looked at Barb.

"Okay, what's the problem?"

"Logan heard the weather report. An unexpected storm is coming in, just in time for the party."

Wren glanced out the front windows. The sky was covered with thin clouds resting high in the sky and looking as menacing as a kitten. But Wren knew the power of a Maine storm and how quickly it could show up.

"This could change everything," she said, looking at the green lawn where the party was set to take place.

"You didn't make a plan B?" Barb stared at Wren with her arms crossed.

Wren wanted to snap back at her sister's comment, but she'd had a beautiful morning— coffee with her brother, texts with Paul, and the e-mail to Derek.

"No plan B. I guess that's what we'll do now."

"It's tomorrow," Barb said dramatically.

"Let's get to work, then," Jack said, hopping up. "What first?"

Wren wondered if they should get Ruth and her binder of ideas. "Well, we have a violin quartet coming, and with all of us, some friends from town, Ruth's new friends, and her old friends from town, we'll have about thirty to forty people. We could call a few restaurants and see if there's availability. Or we could squeeze inside here if we need to."

Barb sighed. "Let's make a few calls first and

see what we come up with. Unless things are different from what I remember, the electricity isn't all that dependable in a storm."

"I have a small generator, but I'm not sure how much help it would be for a party."

As they were making calls and writing down information, Franklin, Lucy, and Charlie burst through the door with Bradley walking in behind them.

"Can we play outside?" Charlie's cheeks were pink from playing hard.

"Is that okay with you?" Wren asked Megan.

"Sure, just stick together," she said.

"And stay close. If you guys go into the RV or back to the cottage, let us know, okay?"

The children agreed and took off back outside. Bradley hadn't spoken and Wren hoped he'd remain with them, but he shuffled out the door a few minutes later.

Missy and Logan came in from the back room.

"Logan told me about the storm. I know someone with a large canopy tent," Missy said.

Barb stared at Missy as if she were from a lower class. "Let's find out how bad the storm is supposed to be. A tent might be useless in the wind. Logan, go get an update on your weather radio."

"What's wrong with you, Barb? Is it somebody's fault that a storm is coming?" Jack asked.

"She's just frustrated, honey," Megan said, putting her hand on Jack's arm.

"Meg, don't defend her. She's always like this." Jack stared at Barb.

"You shouldn't talk to your wife like that."

"Like how nicely you talk to your spouse?"

Wren glanced from one to the other. Neither were going to back down, she knew that from experience.

"What's that supposed to mean?" Barb asked.

"It means, you should worry about your own marriage instead of giving me advice about mine."

Wren interrupted, "I think we need to get along instead of arguing. We've made it this far, and the party is tomorrow."

Barb and Jack turned toward her. Barb huffed as if mocking Wren.

"Oh really? This from the *relationship* pro?" Barb asked.

Wren set her cell phone and pen onto a pad of paper. One part of her warned her to back down, another part wanted to unleash harsh words upon her sister. She tried to control what she said. "Yes, that's right. I went through a divorce, as if that's news to everyone. So if you end up divorced, do you want me to drop lines like that to you? Do you want to be discredited from every discussion?"

"So you think I'm going to get a divorce? Been talking to my husband, have you? Was that before or after you almost kissed him?"

Everyone in the room halted, and Wren's breath left her.

"We did not—no one almost kissed, and don't try to make it sound like that."

"Whatever. As if I care."

"You should care. Your husband does, yet you're the one who told me you didn't expect your marriage to last your lifetime. How sad is that."

"She told you that?" Logan stood in the doorway between the living room and kitchen. Wren had thought he had already left.

"Nice. Classic Wren. Thank you very much."

"Why did you say that, Barb?" Logan asked.

"This is getting us nowhere. Let's give Ruth a good birthday and talk about all this later." Barb was nearly shouting by now.

"Barb, calm down," Jack said. Megan looked as if she wished to disappear.

"Me calm down? Who are you to say anything? You're barely in this family anymore. You checked out long ago, and what now, you want to try being involved. You want to make a few phone calls and feel like you're back with the family."

"I don't blame him from checking out of this family," Wren said. "We've all checked out in one way or another. Mom might be the worst of all, but we've all done it."

"Everyone is to blame, so no one is to blame. Is that how it works, Wren? You want to keep the peace so badly, you never get to any truth."

Wren felt a growing panic of where this was going. If Barb mentioned the funeral or that weekend here as children, Wren knew every-thing would unravel.

"That's enough from all of you." Ruth walked step by slow step down the stairs. "Everybody needs to sit down and close your mouths."

"But—" Barb began, but Ruth interrupted her.

"I want all 'butts' in their seats and none on your lips—got it?" Her voice was stern, at least for Ruth. "Now I've been praying for this family since 1935, before any of you were born. I've prayed continually that this family would find healing and be what God wants. It might appear that God hasn't heard my prayer. Now it's my birthday, so I get what I want. When you've lived ninety years, you can get what you want."

"What do you want, Grandma?" Wren asked.

"I want us to talk about what's really going on with this family. It's time for the truth to come out."

23

"What truth?"

Barb asked the question that hung in the room. But Wren didn't want to talk about this. She didn't want a family meeting rehashing the events of that long-ago day.

What was truth? The truth was that Wren was

blamed for something that a child shouldn't have been blamed for. She shouldn't have been asked to be responsible for her brother in the first place. She knew these things now, but only now —after years of a mother's scorn that tainted every one of her relationships, after decades of living with the blame for Jack's disappearance and her father's injury.

Wren didn't need her grandmother or the entire family to acknowledge this. It didn't change anything.

"The truth is not what any of you think," Ruth said.

"What are you talking about?"

Jack cleared his throat and leaned forward. "I need to tell all of you. I already told Grandma. I'm in AA."

"AA?" Wren muttered, staring at her brother.

"You're in AA? You're an alcoholic? Since when?" Barb's voice scoffed as if not believing him.

"Since college, or probably high school."

Despite what she knew, Wren felt that old jolt of guilt again that made everything seem her fault. She'd failed her brother, and he'd become an alcoholic.

Jack leaned forward with his arms resting on his knees. "As you may or may not know, part of AA is seeking forgiveness. That's what I need to do—ask you all for forgiveness."

"For what?" Barb said, still in her sarcastic tone.

"For the condition of this family."

Wren's head pounded. "Jack, please. You don't need to ask for forgiveness. Could we just not do this?" She stood and moved toward the doorway. She had to get away, get away from all of them.

"Wait, Wren, I need to say this."

Wren turned and leaned against the doorframe.

"It really was my fault."

"You were eight years old," Barbara said.

"But you see, I ran away on purpose." He looked at Wren. "I ran away and hid from you. I thought it would be funny."

"You ran away and hid?"

"Yes. So all of these years, when Wren was blamed, it's my fault that our family is the way it is, and it's my fault that Dad got hurt, which is why he's dead now. I was never in any danger."

Barb stood and walked to the window. "You spent two nights outside in a storm."

"No." He shook his head. "I lied about that too. I was okay. It scared me when I saw all the emergency crews searching for me. I was just going to hide for a while, then all these people were calling for me, then the search-and-rescue people came. Mom was so frantic, and everyone was crying. There were people risking their lives to save me. But I was totally fine."

"You were a little kid who stayed two nights in a cave. How could you have been totally fine?" Barb said with her arms hugged together.

"I wasn't in a cave."

"Where were you?"

"When it got dark, I snuck down to old lady Mary's cabin."

"The senile old woman down the coast?" Barb asked.

"Yes. She thought I was her son visiting, so when the search and rescue came, she went along with everything. She hadn't seen little Jack Evans, she'd been busy with her son's visit."

Wren's mind was whirling. She couldn't quite get a grasp on what Jack was saying. Was this really true?

"How come you never told us this? Our entire lives were changed because of that night."

"I didn't know how."

"None of this matters anymore," Barb said, looking down at her hands.

"Of course it matters." Wren stood up then. Her entire body shook. The years of shame, feeling humiliated around family as if everyone looked at her like the girl who lost her brother. Her relationship with her parents that was never the same.

"You lied? You were safe? I can't believe this. Our family fell apart that day."

"It was falling apart before that," Barb said. "You two were just too young to see it. Mom and Dad were going to get a divorce—I bet neither of you knew that."

Wren remembered Ima Carter's words about her parents. So that's what she was talking about.

"So what, we're just supposed to forgive and forget now? Do you know what this did to us, to me?"

Jack nodded his head solemnly. "Yes, I know. And I've been a coward allowing you to be the scapegoat. Wren, I truly am sorry."

"Well, sorry isn't good enough." Angry tears boiled down her cheeks. Jack didn't fully know how the event had changed her.

"Wren. This isn't like you," Ruth spoke softly.

"This isn't like me—why? Because I'm also complacent and allow everyone to push me around? None of you realize what this did to my life! It's affected every relationship I've ever had. Maybe it's part of why Derek left me and Charlie, or why no one really thinks I share myself with them. And what about our parents? Mom can't stand me. Dad died hating me."

"He didn't hate you," Barb said, sitting on the edge of the couch.

"How do you know? He blamed me. He didn't want to, but I could see it in how he looked at me. And Mom, she was quite vocal about whose fault all of our problems were."

Jack nodded. "Mom did blame you. I talked to her about it."

"You talked to her, when?"

"A few months ago."

"Nice. And she hasn't called me and she couldn't show up here."

"Mom is . . . well, she's Mom. She said it would be too hard." Jack squeezed his eyes shut, and Megan was leaning against him. Nice, Jack had support even now.

"Isn't that great? Mom is Mom. I wish I could just be Wren and do whatever I want to people without care for the consequences."

"This family is so screwed up," Barb whispered.

"So this party was really about your confession. You wanting to ask us for forgiveness." Wren couldn't believe it.

"No," Ruth interjected. "I wanted a party. A time for us to come together and to hopefully heal."

"Unbelievable."

"I'm sorry, Wren." Jack was so sincere.

" 'I'm sorry'? It's so empty. So worthless to me."

The room was silent as Ruth took a seat in one of the overstuffed chairs.

Footsteps up the porch interrupted the awkward silence. Missy burst through the door.

"Where are the kids?" she asked Wren with a tone of forced calm.

"They're playing in the yard." Wren wiped beneath her eyes and realized she hadn't heard them in a while.

"They're probably playing in the RV or at your house," Barb said, annoyed.

Wren glanced out the small windows of the

front door, scanning the lawn and driveway over toward the cottage.

"I'll go check on them," Jack said, jumping up from the couch.

Wren looked at Ruth. "We'll be right back. Then we'll talk about this, I promise."

She followed Missy outside; Jack was ahead, already at the RV.

"I checked your house already, and kept knock-ing on the RV, but no one answered."

"They're probably in there. Let's check the cottage again."

Wren picked up the pace and jogged toward her house. She called out the kids' names as she burst through the front door. Missy went to check the garage. The house was quiet, but still Wren checked each room.

Jack was coming inside the house as she hurried toward the door.

"They're not in the RV," he said, his brows crunched together.

"Not in the house."

Missy looked panicked. "Are you sure they aren't in here?"

"They said they'd stay outside. Maybe they're building a fort or something."

Jack studied her face. "We'll find them."

"Yeah, I know," Wren said, but her heart was pounding. She took Missy's arm. "You go check back in the main house, maybe they came in through the back and are upstairs. I'll check the front. They're all together. I'm sure they're fine."

"I'm heading toward the woods," Jack said.

Wren was turning around in the yard one more time when she spotted the open back gate. Charlie wouldn't go there, he knew better. She'd warned him further about going out to the back garden and sea trail since their company had arrived. She'd told Bradley as well. Still Wren ran through the gate and scanned the garden.

She stopped short when she spotted Lucy with her back turned away, standing near the edge of the embankment at the top of the sea trail. Wren ran toward her.

"Lucy, where're Charlie and the other kids?"

She looked at Wren with both worry and fear on her face.

"Um, he and the other two boys are playing."

"Where? You won't get in trouble, just please tell me if you know where they went."

"Down there," she said, pointing down the trail—the very trail they'd searched when Jack had been lost those many years ago.

Wren's hand and voice shook. "Run as fast as you can and tell your dad where they went, okay?"

"Okay," she said with her eyes large and full of tears.

Wren wouldn't let her mind think, she just ran. Her shoes, without much tread, caused her to slip several times going down. One elbow started

341

bleeding after she scraped it on some sharp rock shale.

At the bottom of the trail there was no one in sight, not on the small pebbly beach, the old dock, or along the other paths that went high over craggy, gray rocks or up toward one of the neighboring properties.

The waves were rough though. High tide and the coming storm churned up and flung the waves hard against the rocks. But it wasn't like they all could be swept into the water, could they?

"Charlie!" Wren called out.

"Wren!"

She whirled around and saw Jack running down the trail. Logan was following behind.

"I can't find them," she told Jack.

"We've got to call 911."

"No! It's too soon for that," she cried. "They're down here somewhere."

"We need help finding them."

Wren was shaking her head. Jack grabbed her by the shoulders. "We need help now."

Movement caught Wren's eye. Bradley was climbing over the top of a huge rock that towered over them.

"See, there they are," she said, pointing. Relief flooded her as she rushed to the bottom of the rock, waiting to see Charlie's head rise over the top.

Bradley didn't turn around to help Franklin or Charlie. No one came behind him. But they'd be slower, Wren told herself as Jack climbed up toward Bradley. Her feet slipped on the rock, so she waited at the bottom.

Jack reached Bradley. The roar of the waves drowned out their voices. Bradley pointed toward the dock, then back behind where he'd come. Wren remembered that there was usually a boat tied there. One of the neighbors kept it there during the summer.

Jack sped down toward her, instead of over the rock where the boys should be coming. His jaw was clenched and his face serious, Wren felt the fear mount larger than ever.

"They're in a boat. Bradley tried to get them back, and he followed the boat as long as he could. But Charlie and that other boy are out there."

Wren thought her legs would collapse beneath her.

"Call for help."

24

As Jack gave the details to the 911 operator, Wren raced up the trail for her own phone without stopping to tell Logan what had happened.

"Ask Bradley," she shouted back as she zipped up the trail. Her lungs tightened as she reached the cottage. Wren found her cell phone beside the laptop, and it felt like days since she'd written the letter to Derek.

Wren found Paul's number and tried to regain her breath.

"Please answer," she muttered to herself, carrying the phone with her toward the front door.

"Hey, nice surprise," Paul said when he picked up the line.

"Charlie is missing! He's in a boat, out in the ocean!"

"What? Wait. Calm down."

"Charlie and his friend Franklin are missing. They went out in the neighbor's boat, just the two of them."

"Okay, it's okay. I'll get my boat. I'll be there in thirty minutes, but I'll call you once I'm on the water."

"Thank you. Please hurry." Wren could tell he was already on the move. He shouted to someone, "There's been an emergency. I'll be back later."

"Wren. It's going to be okay."

She didn't respond. He didn't know if it would be okay or not.

"Did you hear me?" he asked, and she heard the beeping of his car door.

"Yes."

"Pray, start praying now."

"I don't know if I can."

"You can. Do it, and I'll be there soon."

• • •

"Can you give me a description?" The first responder stood before Wren writing everything down.

"He's ten years old. Sandy hair and blue eyes." Wren didn't know how she was speaking with the numbness and sense of being out-of-body. But she heard her voice in her own ears, somewhat calm and giving the details for the fourth time.

"What was your son wearing?"

Wren shook her head and wrapped her arms together at her chest. "I don't know. He'd just gotten up and I didn't pay attention, and we were planning the party . . ."

"It's okay."

How could she not know what Charlie was wearing? She couldn't give a description to the search-and-rescue teams. All she remembered was that his hair was messy. She hadn't given him a kiss that morning, hugged him, or told him that she loved him.

This couldn't really be happening. It was a nightmare she'd wake from. If she could just go back, just an hour or so. If she had paid more attention.

She'd not once expected something like this. Bradley had been her concern, and for good reason, but she was worried about him being a bad influence, not endangering her son's life.

Charlie.

She thought of Franklin too. Little Franklin, so innocent and hard to control. Were they both terrified? Where could they be? What if it was already too late? They might be smashed against the rocks or adrift far out on the ocean by now.

Why hadn't the coming storm been a warning to her? Everything was so like the other time. It could have been a redeeming weekend, and just as she'd failed to protect her brother, now she'd failed to protect her son. She'd become distracted instead of paying attention. Now it was too late. Maybe too late forever.

Missy was on the verge of hysteria. Wren couldn't be near her, though she wished to be strong for her friend who had always been strong for her. Missy had already lost a son, but Wren felt crippled with fear and the nearness of Missy only made it worse. Finally someone led Missy upstairs and gave her something to help her calm down.

Paul was out on the water with other local boats, the Coast Guard, and search-and-rescue crews. He called her periodically, but he couldn't hear well on the water, and she had little to say once she knew they hadn't found any sign of the boys.

News of their crisis raced through the community. People started showing up, offering to help, bringing food.

Ramon from the Mexican restaurant brought chips and salsa and joined the search party that included grouchy Jenks Bledshoe. They scoured the coastline in case the boat had crashed along one of the rocky inlets. Bands of people from the community set off along the trails. Wren recognized faces and some came to hug her tightly. Margaret from the bakery, Sue and Dr. James, the minister from her church, numerous women from her women's Bible study, and several baristas from the Village Brew who brought pastries and set up a coffee machine in the kitchen. There were others; Wren could take them in, see the faces, and feel a sense of gratitude, but she could barely respond to them.

Ruth started a prayer group. They met in the downstairs bedroom, and her grandmother assured her that several people would be praying continuously until the boys were found. Wren stared at Ruth, but had no response. She tried to pray, muttered a few lines from Psalm 27, but she hadn't fully accepted that this was happening.

What Wren really wished was for everyone to go away, and she could return to the cottage with Charlie and their life before that early-morning knock on the door that brought Ruth and all of this into their lives.

It whirled around her. While she couldn't accept what was happening, the horrible truth gripped her like a vice, threatening to tear apart her sanity.

Wren changed into boots and a coat and joined a search party for an hour, but she went back to the house where she could hear from all of the boats and rescue crews at the command center.

As the afternoon wore on, Wren sometimes couldn't distinguish between the now and the past. They had cheated Death once, but he was back for one of them. What possibility was there that they'd escape again?

Nightfall brought a rescue captain to the house. The family gathered around her, and Wren held the railing of the porch to keep from falling.

"Did you find them?" Barb asked, her voice strained and face pale.

"Not yet. We have our guys out there, and they'll be looking through the night. But without lights on the boat, it's almost impossible for us to find them."

"Jesus, be with them," Ruth whispered.

"We're going to keep looking, and the storm will lessen after midnight. We'll do everything we can, I promise."

The captain left them on the front porch where the men had set up a command center. Wren's knees felt weak, and she ran to the downstairs bathroom to throw up. She coughed and cried, her eyes stung from the salty tears.

How could this have happened? Charlie would have never dared such a feat, though he had just gone out on Paul's boat. They'd taught him to drive the boat, and he might actually believe he could captain a boat. Why had Paul done that?

Or it might have been Franklin's idea. Maybe he hopped in the boat first. She wanted to ask Bradley, but Bradley wasn't talking. Wren suspected why—Bradley had probably dared the younger boys to get in the boat. Then it had gotten away from them.

Wren could hear Barb's voice loud and complaining about the emergency-response crews. They were doing something wrong in her opinion, and the sound assaulted Wren's brain.

"They're doing the best they can," she muttered as she returned to the living room.

"Well, it's not enough. These small-town emergency-service people are always understaffed and lacking the best equipment."

Wren stared at her sister and wanted to scream at her to shut up. But Barb didn't stop talking, she criticized everything.

"What are you complaining about? This is your son's fault. Or yours. If you paid attention to him, he might actually listen to you."

"Oh, that's nice, Wren."

"You have a husband and son who love you, and you're throwing them away."

"I'm glad you have it all together and can tell me this."

"I don't have it all together, but your son is at fault here, I know it."

Wren opened her mouth to say more, much more. She wanted to hurl blame and accusations around at all of them. Grandma Ruth should have never forced them into having this party. Barb and Logan were so lost in their own discord they neglected their son, who was becoming a future felon. Jack should have done something, she didn't know what, but Lucy could have run and told them what was happening. Everyone had had a part.

Wren opened her mouth to speak again when movement at the top of the stairs caught her attention. Bradley was sitting there with his face leaned against the rails, his eyes filled with tears. Wren knew that view, knew that sense of outcast shame, and had felt the bite of words from adult blame.

Sudden sobs overwhelmed her, bursting from her uncontrollably. She flew out the front door. Someone called after her, but Wren kept going without direction. The rain and cold engulfed her, slapping her face and chilling her down to the bone.

At the edge of the sea trail she stared out into the blackness.

"Charlie!" she yelled over and over again. She fell to her knees and with her face up toward the pouring rain, she cried.

"God, God help us! Save my son. I beg you to save my son."

Wren's cell phone rang from her pocket. She was still in the rain and cold, shivering violently. But her son was in this too.

The phone woke her up. What if there was news?

"I'm coming into your dock. I'll be there in ten minutes," Paul yelled.

"Did you find him?" she shouted into the phone.

"No."

"Keep looking. Please, Paul."

"I am, and every boat that I had in is out there as well as half the town. But I'm stopping by. Can you meet me at the dock?"

"Yes, I'll get down there."

Jack was beside her, and Wren wondered how long he'd been sitting out in the rain near her. He flipped on a flashlight.

"I'll help you down there," Jack said, and Wren didn't argue as he took her arm.

The wind whipped around them, but Wren and Jack hiked down the sea trail with only a few slips down to the rocky shoreline. The lights of Paul's boat swept the small cove as it came in toward the dock.

Wren could see numerous men on the boat, then Paul jumped over the railing and tied the boat off as it rocked on the waves.

She hurried to him.

"Tell me the truth. What are the chances that he's okay? Is there any hope?"

Paul took her by the shoulders, practically holding her up.

"Yes, definitely. There's always hope. It's not good, but there's hope."

"He's out there, Paul," Wren said, pointing to the dark, cold sea. The waves rocked the dock though the rain had mellowed to a sprinkle.

Paul hugged her tightly.

"I picture him out there, or lost in those waves, or scared and trapped somewhere, or . . ." She sobbed against Paul's chest.

He held the back of her head against him and another arm pressed her strongly to his chest. "Listen to me. You must stop creating all these things in your head. Let the worries and scenarios go."

"How do I do that?"

"Don't let your mind go there. You can stop it. Just pray, have faith, and believe he'll be all right."

She squeezed her eyes shut a moment and wondered why he was saying something as ridiculous as that.

Wren wanted to scream and cry. There was a madness threatening to take her in and sweep her away. If something happened to him . . . if she lost Charlie . . . Wren didn't see how she would survive if Charlie was gone.

"I'm falling apart, Paul. I can't do this. I can't live without my son."

"God can take care of Charlie. God can care for him better than even you can. No matter what happens, God is with him and caring for him."

Wren hated the "no matter what happens" part.

"Rest now. Rest in those promises," Paul said.

"How can I rest with my son in this? He might not even be alive."

"Can God take care of him?"

She nodded meekly.

"Can you do anything right now to help him?"

The panic rose with those words, and she again wanted to race into the storm and search for Charlie.

"You can't, Wren. You can't do anything right now."

"I know that," she yelled in frustration. "You aren't making me feel better."

"I'm not trying to make you feel better. I'm trying to help you find real peace. Not some fake assurance. But real peace. Now, I'm going back out there."

"I want to go with you."

"You can't come with me, you'll get too sick. Go back to the house, get warm, get strong for your son. Cling to hope."

"I said terrible things."

"It's okay. Put your energy into something productive. Pray, believe, trust. Whatever happens next, I'm here and God is with us. But don't start thinking of what's next, only rest in God's promises now."

Wren wanted him to stay with her, but she

wanted him out searching for Charlie even more.

"Stop imagining what you don't know has occurred. I know you can do it."

Wren nodded. Her legs felt stronger. She would be strong for Charlie. Until she knew something, she would try to do what Paul said. She thought of some verses, possibly from Psalm 27, she couldn't remember for sure.

Wait for the LORD;
be strong and take heart
and wait for the LORD.

Jack and Wren walked toward the house, drenched and exhausted. Wren lifted her hand to take her brother's as they reached the door. The effort to grasp his hand was enormous, and Wren wished to simply crumble and be held like a child in her daddy's lap.

Wren met her brother's eyes. His haggard face had aged in a day and was lined with stubble from not shaving.

"I forgive you," Wren said, squeezing his hand.

"Thank you," Jack said, and Wren opened the front door.

She pushed her wet hair away from her face and looked around the room at her family. Megan jumped up and ran to her aid, pulling off her coat and wrapping a blanket around her shoulders.

Barb sat on the sofa with her face in her hands.

Logan rubbed her back as he stared at the fire. Lucy had fallen asleep in a chair. Ruth held her Bible and stood beside the fireplace. They were all there, except for Charlie.

"Where is Bradley?" Wren asked, her voice cracking. She saw him, sitting on the floor between the sofa and the wall.

Wren kneeled on the floor in front of him. He wouldn't look at her, but his eyes were swollen and he reminded her of a wounded animal hunched down, waiting another beating.

"Bradley. I'm very sorry for what I said. It was wrong of me." Wren's spirit felt crushed and broken. Yet deep in her soul she knew this was right. Her life might end if she lost Charlie; she couldn't imagine her heart surviving such a thing. But this boy was just a boy, and he shouldn't carry the blame as she had all of those years.

"When we were all children, Jack was lost, and I was supposed to be watching him. Everyone blamed me, including myself, but things like that just happen. We make mistakes. There are accidents. I don't want you carrying the blame. It wasn't your fault."

The room was quiet, and Bradley sniffed as a tear went down his face. He cleared his throat and muttered, "I shouldn't have let them get in the boat. They were showing off and I knew it. The other boy said he could sail. I thought it was funny, but then they just got away so fast."

Wren struggled to hear this; she didn't want any images right now, for they quickly rolled out of control.

"It's okay, Bradley. Charlie knows he's not supposed to go down the sea trail. He . . . he . . ." She closed her eyes.

"Let's get you some dry clothing." Barb led Wren up the stairs. She helped her out of her wet clothes and into warm sweats that came from somewhere, Wren didn't care where or who was in the room as she changed. Then she remembered Franklin's mother.

"Where's Missy?"

"Still sleeping in Grandma's room."

Wren walked down the hall.

Missy's eyes were swollen, but at the moment, she slept. Wren brushed back Missy's hair. The woman had lost one child already. Wren hummed softly, praying to God for help, for peace, for salvation.

She knew that God gave and He took away. It felt nearly impossible to accept His taking away when she received His giving without a second thought. Wren prayed that she might trust Him, no matter what happened.

Footsteps raced up the stairs and Jack burst into the room, drenched and pale.

"Wren. They found them. They're all right. They're going to be all right."

25

Charlie sat in the emergency room bed with Franklin in the curtained-off bed beside him. Wren and Missy ran to their boys.

Charlie's face had a long razed scrape along one side.

"Are you all right? Is he all right?" she asked the nurse looking him over.

"Just a few scrapes, but nothing else that we can find so far."

Wren pulled Charlie tightly into her arms, savoring the feel of his small body and smelling his damp, weathered hair. He was here, really here, safe. She might have lost this forever, but he was here. Wren didn't want to ever let him go as she sobbed with him nestled against her.

Finally, Wren pulled back and felt the top of his head. "I've gotten your entire head all wet again."

"Yep, you rained on me," he said, looking so small and pale—but alive, so very alive. It made her cry once again.

"I'm sorry, Mom. I'm really sorry."

"It's okay. As long as you're safe now."

"I was showing off for Bradley and Franklin." He lowered his voice. Wren and Charlie could hear Franklin loudly relating the story to Missy beyond the vinyl curtain. "Then Franklin untied the rope because I said that I could sail it and he said that he could sail too. It happened so fast. We were in the water for a long time, it felt like. Then the boat came toward this huge rock, and I thought it was going to smash us. Then a wave swept us around the rock and up beside it enough that we jumped off before the boat disappeared. It was really cold, but we hid like the birds do."

"What do you mean?"

"Remember we read about what birds do during the storm. They look for a safe shelter near the ground under a rock or strong tree. That's what Franklin and I did. We found this place in the rocks that was out of the rain and wind. Then finally, we saw the boat shining its light, and me and Franklin jumped out and started waving."

"Who found you?"

"Captain Harvey!"

One of Paul's boats.

"He yelled for us to stay there, and then a helicopter came and got us. We rode in a helicopter, which was pretty cool except I knew you would be really scared."

"I was really scared, but I knew God was with us. I'm really happy now."

They stayed several hours at the hospital with family popping in and out of the ER. Franklin opened the curtain between him and Charlie, and Wren and Missy periodically switched beds to hug each other's son. Franklin's dad was on his last flight home and kept making in-flight phone calls to get updates. Wren hadn't thought to call Derek during the crisis. His absence in their life might be coming to an end, but for now he played no part in their family, in their immediate thoughts, or in the role that a father should hold. Wren felt no guilt or remorse, only peace that her son was safe, and that God was truly taking care of them in the little and big details of their lives.

The hospital rules were relaxed with the rescue of the boys, and the waiting room was packed with family, friends, and people from the community. Charlie had to be wheeled from the hospital in a wheelchair due to hospital policy, then he could get up at their car. Jack brought his car to the door as Wren waved and thanked the gathering in the waiting room. She was ready to get her son home.

Paul stood by the exit door, looking tired yet smiling broadly.

Wren grabbed his arm and paused in pushing Charlie's wheelchair.

"Thank you, for so much," Wren said, falling against his chest with his arms taking her in. She lifted her face and pushed up on her tiptoes to kiss his cheek, then leaned back to look at him. Paul pulled her into a firm kiss on her mouth and she felt lost in him for a moment. Whistles and cheers surrounded them, bringing Wren back to herself. She couldn't tear herself away from Paul's eyes. Then Wren glanced down to see Charlie with his hand covering a wide smile as he watched them.

"That's gross," he said, trying to turn his smile into an expression of disgust as his shoulders shook with laughter.

As Wren tucked Charlie into her bed and snuggled down beside him, she brushed his hair softly away from his face as she'd done when he was a child.

"You know, Mom, even if I get accepted to that school, I don't think we're supposed to move to Boston. This town is our home now."

Wren stared at her son and nodded. "I feel the same way. And I promise we'll figure out how to get you the musical training you need."

"Then that settles it. And you know what else?"

"What?"

"God heard my prayer."

"He always seems to hear yours."

"He heard all of ours. But I mean the prayer from a long time ago, when school started."

Wren remembered the prayer. "God, help my mom be happy."

"He brought our family together, and new friends too. And now you can be happy."

26

The sound of movement progressively tugged Wren from sleep to consciousness. At first she couldn't remember what the day was about, what had happened, or where she was. Her room. Charlie was asleep on his side, facing away from her.

Charlie.

Wren rose up on an elbow to look at him. The scrape on his face now held light-yellow and purplish hues rimming the edges. She wished to wrap him up and squeeze him, and she thanked God over and over again for keeping him and Franklin safe.

The noise outside was a light rain and wind. The clock read 11:25 a.m.; they'd arrived home at five that morning. Wren sat up completely. Today was her grandmother's birthday.

Through her bedroom window, Wren could see a white van backed up near the main house. Jack, Logan, Bradley, and another guy carried chairs and tables from the van and up toward the main house.

Wren walked down the hall and smelled coffee and food. A pile of pastries and fruit were heaped on platters on her counter. Megan, Ruth, and

Barb sat in the living room with steaming cups in their hands and pastries on plates that littered the coffee table.

"Good morning," Wren said, stretching her arms.

"We hope you don't mind, but we wanted to be closer to you and Charlie," Megan said, rising from the couch.

"I'm glad you're all here. So what's going on? I saw the boys outside. Is the party still on?" Wren hoped not; the idea of a party sounded overwhelming after the night they'd had.

"We revised the plan. No fancy schmancy party after all," Barb said with a smile.

"What then?"

"Just an easy leftover feast for family, friends, and people who keep coming around. You sure have a lot of friends here. And it's going to rain again."

"Grandma, are you okay with all of this? We could still have the party we planned. Why don't we just move it until next weekend?"

Ruth sipped her tea. "I got what I wanted for my birthday. Our family is back together."

Wren and Barb glanced at one another, and she knew they weren't quite sure how accurate that was, but Wren was willing to suspend her doubts—especially after the night before—and simply enjoy it.

That afternoon the main house busted with

people. Margaret delivered the cakes and included a special decorated brownie just for Charlie. Paul brought in large kettles of soup and chili and stacks of sourdough bread. Wren wondered if she'd feel any embarrassment around Paul after their very public display of affection the night before, but the moment she saw him, she felt an inner sense that all was right with the world. His presence calmed and exhilarated her at the same time, though she didn't understand how the combination was possible.

"I'm just going to tell you," Paul said, taking her arm as she passed him. He'd been so busy during the meal, serving food and keeping the food flowing, that Wren had barely spoken to him.

"Tell me what?"

He bent and whispered near her ear, his breath sending a tingle down her neck, "*The Little Engine that Could.*"

Wren realized he was talking about his favorite book. "You aren't serious."

"I am. Over coffee—that you'll be buying—we'll talk more about how the book symbolizes the American dream. My favorite version is by Watty Piper—that was actually the pen name for a publisher of many children's books."

"I concede. I'd never have guessed that one. I'm still not sure I believe you."

"Understandable, and don't you dare tell a soul. It might hurt my manly image. But if you don't believe me, ask my nieces and nephew. I've read it to them so often they started hiding the book from me. Imagine that."

Wren laughed and wove her fingers through his. "My admiration continues to grow."

Wren pulled away only as someone announced it was time for the cake. Family and friends sang happy birthday to Ruth, and Charlie and Lucy helped Ruth blow out the candles. Then Ruth stood and put her hands up to get the crowd's attention.

"Where are my grandchildren? Barb, Wren, and Jack? Gather around, I have a confession to make." They made their way through the group and sat on the hearth before a glowing fire.

Ruth turned toward them. "I lied to all of you, and I hope that you'll forgive me."

Wren looked at her sister, then to Jack, who both carried confused expressions.

"The truth is, I'm not actually ninety years old today."

Wren knew that today was Ruth's birthdate; what was her grandmother talking about?

"How old are you, Nana?" Charlie asked.

"I'm actually ninety-one." There was a murmur of chuckles around the room. Ruth shrugged innocently. "But how could I get all of you to gather for my big birthday if I said it was already a year behind us?"

Wren shook her head and laughed.

"You gotta be kidding me," Barb muttered with a smirk on her face.

Jack leaned over and muttered, "Grandma's more wily than all of us combined."

"Do you forgive me?" Ruth asked.

Jack stood up with his wine glass in hand. "Of course we do. Here's to Grandma Ruth's ninetieth and ninety-first birthdays."

Ruth laughed as the glasses clinked together in the toast. Then her gasp caught Wren's attention.

"Are you all right, Grandma?" Wren asked. Ruth didn't move but stood with her hand over her mouth.

"Why are you here?" Ruth said, looking toward the doorway.

An elderly man stood among the group with a bouquet of flowers in his hand. The room quieted as more and more people stared between Ruth and the man.

"That's Lonnie," Barb whispered to Wren.

"I'm here for you, Ruth Elizabeth. You need to give me an answer."

"An answer to what?" someone asked loudly, and the entire room settled into a complete hush.

"She needs to give me an answer to my proposal. I asked her to marry me, and she ran off saying she had a party to plan. Every time we talk on the phone, she gives me some excuse or avoids the subject."

Ruth's hands covered her mouth.

"Grandma?" Wren asked. "You have quite a few secrets you haven't told us about."

Ruth's eyes remained on Lonnie. "I can't believe you came all the way here."

"Didn't I say I'd go to the ends of the earth for you? Maine was nothing compared to that." He chuckled, and Wren saw her grandmother blush.

"I'm an old woman."

"She's ninety-one," Charlie said to the man.

"And I'm eighty-seven. So we may not have a lot of years ahead of us, but it will make us cherish every single day, won't it? Come on, Ruth, won't you do me the honor of becoming my wife?"

Several giggles and murmurs rippled through the room.

"Let's talk about this after cake," she said, looking down at the cake and then back up at Lonnie. She suddenly slapped her hands together. "Oh, all right. Why not live a little while I still can?"

The roar in the room of cheers and excitement made Wren laugh and Charlie hugged Wren tightly.

Someone carried in plates and knife, and Barb went to work cutting and handing out cake as Lonnie and Ruth stood among the well-wishers.

Wren glanced around the room at Paul, her friends, and her family—a family that had been fractured for so long that she'd forgotten who they were. The bond of childhood and blood had knit them together. No one else could understand certain aspects of who they were, or what they had been. They had been a family of secrets.

How could one day change them all forever? First one day harmed them deeply, but now one day redeemed each one of them and bound them back together.

What if their childhood had been different? Who would they be now? What if she'd never met Derek? What if she'd never moved to Cottage Cove?

So many what-ifs, but here they were with all their fractured memories and broken pieces joined together. How miraculous it was to see their brokenness bound into something beautiful.

Wren thought of Jane Austen, Scarlett, and Anne Shirley—her literary female icons. Their stories were no more dramatic than her own now. She knew a camaraderie with them and smiled, thinking of the women being here with her.

What the future held, Wren couldn't guess. Derek might return to their lives, disrupting everything, and possibly hurting Charlie in the process. Or Derek might disappear from their lives as quickly as he'd popped in. She and Paul might have a falling out. Her siblings might again as well. Their mother might never be close to them—she hadn't surprised Ruth at the party as Wren suspected she might, or even called since they'd been all together. Someday Ruth would pass away, and they would all experience grief.

But they were together now, and this day would shape them just as surely as the tragic ones had. Even more than that, Wren knew God wasn't distant and cold and far away. He was there among them, woven within the love and laughter, the tears and pain, and filling their lives with as much of Himself as they opened up to Him.

Her breath tightened and fingers shook with emotion for this moment. Her heart raced as she tapped her glass lightly and stood as the group again settled down.

"I want to thank all of you for last night and for sharing in this day to celebrate our grandmother's life. In honor of my grandmother's birthday and what appears to be her upcoming nuptials, I would like . . ." Wren turned to Ruth, took a breath, and continued, ". . . to sing a song for you."

"Oh, Wren, thank you, thank you," Ruth said, clapping her hands together.

"Please, and I really mean it, please . . . join in and sing with me if any of you know the song."

Wren closed her eyes as she began. Then she opened them and, instead of casting a bubble of safety around her as she'd done when singing as a child, she felt herself connected and joined with the many people in the room. Charlie slid his hand into hers and sang with her as more people joined in with the song.

I sing because I'm happy, I sing because I'm
free,
For His eye is on the sparrow, and I know He
watches me.
"Let not your heart be troubled," His tender
word I hear,
And resting on His goodness, I lose my
doubts and fears;
Though by the path He leadeth, but one step I
may see;
His eye is on the sparrow, and I know He
watches me;
His eye is on the sparrow, and I know He
watches me.

Paul slid his arm around her shoulders as the song finished, and Charlie looked up at them with a wide grin.

The future stretched before them, unseen, and full of both wonder and grace.

Acknowledgments

Sheila would like to thank the following people:

Allen Arnold and the wonderful team at Thomas Nelson Fiction: I continue to be amazed at your commitment to bring the best you have and are to everything you do. I know it honors God and it amazes and encourages me.

Ami McConnell: Ami, you are one of a kind, passionate, intentional, brilliant, and so much fun to work with.

Eric Mullett, Natalie Hanemann, and Katie Bond: thank you for all you tirelessly do every day to take written words to wounded hearts.

Cindy Coloma: I loved your writing before we worked together. Now I'm also crazy about you! You have such heart, Cindy, and it shows in every word you put to paper. Thank you for the joy of this project.

Cindy would like to thank the following people:

First of all, I have to thank God for this collaboration with Sheila Walsh. I felt Him asking me to trust Him about what to write next, and this was the gift He gave. Sheila's kind of a superstar, but let me tell you, her heart, honesty, grace, deep wisdom and great humor are genuine, rare and both down-to-earth and filled with a heavenly aura. She has this inspiration that's a little like pixie dust—you feel you can fly being around Sheila Walsh.

Gratitude to our incredible Thomas Nelson editors Ami McConnell and Natalie Hanemann for making this book come to life. Your guidance and skills never fail to amaze me. And you both are such fun to be around!

The fiction team at Thomas Nelson with Allen Arnold at the helm—I greatly appreciate you and all you do (Becky Monds, Katie Bond, Ashley Schneider, Andrea Lucado . . . et al).

Rachelle Gardner, it was really nice working with you, and your final edit was excellent.

Janet Kobobel Grant—my super agent. Thanks for always being so!

Julie Marsh, thank you for your insights about sensory integration disorder, and for friendship as well.

Four generations of women are a stronghold in my daily life: my grandmother Ruby Duvall, my mom Gail McCormick, my sister Jennifer Harman, and my daughter Madelyn Martinusen.

Prayers and/or friendship and family: Katie Martinusen, Amanda Darrah, Kimberly Carlson, to name just a few. Rev. Jim and Diana Wilson, the way you've reached out to pray for our family has been amazing. And to my Coloma family—

thank you for such unfailing support, prayer and love.

Jenna Jane Benton—our "most-every-morning" prayer time on your way to work started several years ago when you kind of forced me into it—I must admit that I didn't exactly love praying aloud over the phone at first. But it's shaped our lives in such amazing ways. Thank you for the push and the gift that it's been and will continue to be. We may live hours apart, but we are certainly joined in a realm beyond this one.

My children: Cody, Madelyn and Weston Martinusen, you'll never know how much you impact my life or how much I love you. And my husband Nieldon Coloma—I cherish our life, laughter, friendship, belief, discussions, and love. Words cannot express.

I'm blessed by incredible people in my life. You're in my writer's group, my book club, old and new friends, readers, my family and friends. You are too many to list, but I hope you know who you are and how sincerely I appreciate you.

Reading Group Guide

1. A child's prayer and then a knock on the door start an avalanche of change for Wren. What surprises have shaped your life and forced you to grow?

2. When Charlie's father contacts Wren, she feels an immediate panic and begins imagining all kinds of scenarios. Do your imagination and worries ever roll out of control? What do you do to combat them?

3. Charlie's friendship with Franklin brings parenting challenges to Wren that also strain her friendship with Franklin's mother. Have you dealt with any similar situations? What lessons have your learned from them?

4. Wren struggles to bring her spiritual life, prayer, and relationship with God into her day-to-day living. Have you experienced such a challenge? When have you felt God being the most evident in your "normal" life?

5. When contemplating the direction of her and Charlie's future and going back and forth

about the pros and cons, Wren wishes she'd get all the right answers delivered in a letter to her. Have you felt like this, and how has God guided you through it? When has God's guidance been clear?

6. Ruth tells Wren to "Seek and seek some more. Seek and you will find. It's a promise." She also says that God sometimes allows our lives to be messy, but that He's with us in the mess. Have you felt God in the mess of your life? Do you seek God and seek Him some more during these times? When have you been sure that you've "found God" or His promises?

7. Have you experienced a shift in perspective as an adult that let you see a childhood situation with new eyes? Did that shift help you to heal, forgive, or move beyond something in your past?

8. Through the story, Wren's life is changed by the past and all its painful and healing truths. Have you experienced anything similar to Wren's journey?

9. What does it mean to really find shelter in the promises of God? Do you feel there are any situations where you couldn't find

shelter in God and what His Word promises?

10. Not all areas of our lives have happy or resolved endings. Where is God in the midst of our tragedies and in the areas that will never be resolved? Do you believe that as "his eye is on the sparrow" that He is also there in the intricacies of life for you? How do your beliefs shape how you live?

Dear Friend,

I have always been deeply drawn to a good story. When it is told just right, you often forget that it is a story at all. It's as if you know the characters so well that they have become familiar friends. In those stories, you laugh and cry and feel a little less alone. A good story will do that for you as will a circle of friends. I would love to introduce you to my circle.

Over the past fifteen years I have had the privilege of being a part of a team called "Women of Faith." As we have travelled from coast to coast, sharing our stories with over four million women one thing had become crystal clear; each one of us has a story to tell. Every weekend I watch something take place, which is still a mystery to me. As each of my friends gets up on stage to sing or speak or perform a piece of drama I feel the audience lean in and listen. At times you could hear a pin drop, at times the laughter is so intense it fills the arena. Sometimes as tears flow you know that because of God's redemptive plan healing is taking place.

I'd love to invite you to join us one weekend and experience this for yourself. The most common response from women coming for the first time is, "I had no idea!" I understand that sentiment, as that's how I felt after my first weekend in 1997. So check your schedule and gather up some of your circle and join us. I think I'm fairly safe saying, it will be life changing . . . and when you come, find me and let me know what you thought of *Sweet Sanctuary*, I'd love to know!

Your friend, Sheila

About the Authors

SHEILA WALSH is a powerful communicator, Bible teacher, and best-selling author with more than 4 million books sold. A featured speaker with Women of Faith®, Sheila has reached more than 3.5 million women by artistically combining honesty, vulnerability, and humor with God's Word.

Author of the best-selling memoir *Honestly* and the Gold Medallion nominee for *The Heartache No One Sees*, Sheila's most recent release, *The Shelter of God's Promises*, has also been turned into a DVD curriculum and in-depth Bible study. The *Gigi, God's Little Princess* book and video series has won the National Retailer's Choice Award twice and is the most popular Christian brand for young girls in the United States.

Sheila co-hosted *The 700 Club* and her own show *Heart to Heart with Sheila Walsh*. She is currently completing her master's in theology.

Visit www.SheilaWalsh.com to learn more about Sheila.

CINDY MARTINUSEN-COLOMA is the best-selling author of several novels including *Caleb + Kate*,

Ruby Unscripted, *Beautiful*, *Eventide*, and *Orchid House*. *The Salt Garden* was chosen by *Library Journal* as one of the five best Christian fiction books of 2004.

Visit www.CindyColoma.com to learn more about Cindy.

Center Point Publishing

600 Brooks Road ● PO Box 1
Thorndike ME 04986-0001 USA

(207) 568-3717

US & Canada:
1 800 929-9108
www.centerpointlargeprint.com